THE
McGRAW-HILL
36-Hour Course

REAL ESTATE
INVESTING

SECOND EDITION

Other books in The McGraw-Hill 36-Hour Course series:

THE
McGRAW-HILL
36-Hour Course

REAL ESTATE
INVESTING

SECOND EDITION

Jack Cummings

New York   Chicago   San Francisco   Lisbon   London   Madrid   Mexico City
Milan   New Delhi   San Juan   Seoul   Singapore   Sydney   Toronto

8 9 10 11 12 13 14 15   QFR   21 20 19 18 17

ISBN   978-0-07-174082-1
MHID   0-07-174082-1

This publication is designed to provide accurate and authoritative information in regard to the subject matter covered. It is sold with the understanding that neither the author nor the publisher is engaged in rendering legal, accounting, securities trading, or other professional services. If legal advice or other expert assistance is required, the services of a competent professional person should be sought.
        —From a Declaration of Principles Jointly Adopted by a Committee of the
        American Bar Association and a Committee of Publishers and Associations

Library of Congress Cataloging-in-Publication Data

Cummings, Jack, 1940–   .
        The McGraw-Hill 36-hour real estate investing course / by Jack Cummings. —
2nd ed.
        p.   cm.
        Includes index.
        ISBN 978-0-07-174082-1 (alk. paper)
        1. Real estate investment—United States.   2. Real estate investment—United
States—Examinations, qusestions, etc.   I. Title.   II. Title: McGraw-Hill thirty-
six hour real estate investing course.   III. Title: 36-hour real estate investing
course.   IV. Title: The McGraw-Hill 36-hour course: real estate investing.

HD255.C858   2010
332.63'24—dc22   2010028044

McGraw-Hill books are available at special quantity discounts to use as premiums and sales promotions or for use in corporate training programs. To contact a representative, please e-mail us at bulksales@mcgraw-hill.com.

This book is printed on acid-free paper.

CONTENTS

ACKNOWLEDGMENTS

When a writer sits down to write a book, there is an anticipation that a love affair is about to start, and no matter how tedious the work may be, the affection for the manuscript is steady, virtuous, and faithful. That love affair occasionally is renewed when the audience—and therefore the publisher—demands a new edition. Like all love affairs, the second time around can be far more demanding than the first. So it has been with this edition. Demanding because of the need to improve, to be fresh and up-to-date, and to deliver more information that is helpful and informative to the book's readers.

When the work to attain those goals is completed, there is a period of mixed emotion—an elation that the newly revised child is born, yet a sadness that the love affair has ended, and worst of all, despair that until the next book is begun, the writer is out of work, a feeling that many writers and actors understand very well.

When finally asked to "dedicate" the book to someone, there is a moment when all writers scramble to find the person they should acknowledge as a primary driving force for the book, while at the same time not prematurely ending offers for new books, and certainly not stepping on toes, hurting feelings, or cutting off possible loan sources when times might get tough.

Fortunately, for this book at least, this dedication is made with a clear conscience and sincere thanks. Many years ago, my first editor for the first book I was to sell was a young editor at Prentice Hall who called me on the phone one day to ask me if I would be interested in writing a book. That book turned out to be *The Real Estate Financing Manual*, and that man was to teach me a great deal about the writing profession, and about myself. That book is as of 2008 in its ninth edition, and my sincere hope is that there will be many more to come.

It is because of his continued faith in me that I dedicate this book to my good friend and first editor, Ted Nardin.

INTRODUCTION

We are in a historic time of financial upheaval. This is the time of chaos and opportunity. Each of these produces the other, and here we are: the start of the decade is well behind us, and both chaos and opportunity still exist. At the time of this writing the real estate marketplace has undergone the greatest drop in prices you may ever see. Yet I and all my investor "insider" friends are excited about this—though the excitement is not without mixed emotions. Opportunities are popping up all around us, while at the same time many people are losing their jobs and their homes and are frustrated with what is happening to their lives. And who is to blame? Or is that really important now? The important thing for all of us is to realize the market does rise, fall, and rise again. Lessons of what we should *not* have done hopefully will protect us from making similar mistakes in the future. What we need to do is to realize that we can now prosper in this chaos.

All of this sadness, as does all the darkness of sadness, has a silver dawn. For us who consider real estate the gold mine of our future, all of this is good news. Now is the time to move into this market. But now is also the time to be cautious and mindful that whenever there is chaos there are charlatans ready to take your money. So this revised book, which has survived the years since it was first written, is dedicated to the survivors of this chaos and to those who need not have experienced the drama of its impact to learn the lessons it has taught. This book will pillow you through the darkness and show you how to apply proven methods and techniques so that you can take advantage, not of those who have lost their fortune but of the moment your opportunities present themselves to you. This is the ripe time of real estate investing. Do not let the season slip past you.

Today, sellers are the most motivated I have ever seen them be, and buyers who are prudent, patient, and persistent will be able to make the best investments they may ever see.

Are you new at the real estate game, or have you been investing in real estate for years? Either way, the time is right, and this book has been updated to provide you with the hottest tips and advice possible. Not only is this book for you, it is the best place for any real estate investor to begin because it is designed to deal with the modern problems that real estate investors will likely encounter. This book will show you how to best attain your desired goals, whether they are modest, such as to get out of renting and own your own home, or more lofty, such as to become wealthy and financially independent through real estate investing.

The simple but wealth-building techniques in this book are designed to stimulate your creativity and build your confidence. In fact, by the time you complete the book and have begun to implement its outline for your comfort zone plan, you will be on your way to becoming an expert in your area and a true "insider" in the real estate investment club.

Not only will you grasp the concepts of investment, but you will also realize that with the right plan, you can double your investment even if you have to sell your property for less than you paid for it. Does this sound like a paradox? Not so, and its secret is so easy to understand you will wonder why you didn't think of it yourself.

This book will get all would-be real estate investors moving in the right direction and help all investors, no matter how knowledgeable, to maximize their efforts to reduce risk and to produce more profitable results from their investments.

Are you concerned or confused about timing? Do you wonder, *Is now the right time to get into real estate?* The simple answer is yes. Now may be the very best time in your entire life—because the real estate market is about to end its spiral to rock-bottom prices and bust wide open. The mortgage interest rates indicate it, the mood of the market is in favor of the buyer, and "now" is here. All you need to do is to learn how to invest successfully in real estate—not just learn some tricks that worked for someone else, but *learn the solid foundation that the "insiders" use to build fortunes.*

But don't be surprised, and don't be misled. To learn this art properly is not as simple as some TV promotions and late-night lecturers would like you to believe. Let's face it: learning how to become wealthy requires effort, study, and determination. *The McGraw-Hill 36-Hour Course: Real Estate Investing* will be your college education in real estate investing, and it will lead you to the self-confidence you need to be successful in real estate investing.

Real estate investing is, as you will discover, a study of history. The history of why the real estate market goes up and down will give you the inside track on where your local market is headed. Successful real estate investing is nothing more than seeing opportunities, realizing they are the right ones for you to grasp, and knowing what to do next. These opportunities, by the way, are easy to spot when you understand the marketplace and how and why you can turn a property into a cash cow or an item you can resell for a substantial gain on your investment.

You will find that the factors that govern the rise and fall of real estate values are relatively simple. Most of the forces that affect the real estate market and control this rise and fall of values are evident for everyone to see and follow. The key is to know where to look, how to read the signals, and what to do to take advantage of the situations and opportunities as they present themselves to you. The idea of becoming an expert in the real estate market is not a complex task of knowing 100 techniques or being able to calculate mortgage interest rates in your head. The ultimate key is to know what your goal is and to become the *local* expert on the kind of real estate that can help you attain that goal.

All real estate fluctuates in value, and this fluctuation is governed most dramatically by local situations such as the local economy, population growth, and so on. Wider-based secondary forces such as nationwide building starts or national unemployment figures can often be more misleading than helpful unless you know and understand the local picture of things. It is quite possible that your local area defies the national trends.

This book is a unique approach to the idea of "learning how to become a real estate investor." It is an easy read, and it provides an easy-to-follow course of study that will establish a sound platform for you to launch your real estate investment career.

HOW TO USE THIS BOOK

In writing this book, the author has drawn on more than 30 years of solid and very successful real estate investing experience. The material provided within this book is based on varied experience as an investor, developer, financial adviser, Realtor, and a widely published author of many real estate investment and finance books.

The book is divided into four main parts. Each of the four parts contains chapters that relate to the main topic of that section. These divisions are as follows:

Part 1: How to Begin Your Successful Real Estate Investment Career
Part 2: How to Maximize Property Value
Part 3: Finding the Best Property for You and How to Purchase It Right
Part 4: How You Buy Establishes How You Profit in Real Estate Investing

A final exam is available online in addition to helpful tabular materials.

How the Book Is Designed to Work with You

Each of the chapters has an introduction that describes chapter goals and segments that define key terms and discuss the chapter concepts. In addition, some chapters include examples, case studies, practice exercises, and useful forms.

As you examine the book you will discover that these segments provide the basis for this 36-hour course. They are the primary elements of this text, which, within an average of 36 hours, will give you the fundamentals you need to approach real estate investing as a knowledgeable insider. In a unique way, once they are introduced, some of the trends, techniques, and concepts mentioned reappear in future chapters. This is purposefully designed to show you these items from a different perspective. When this happens the text reinforces the importance of these elements in the concepts that are being discussed in each chapter.

Below you will see the breakdown of each segment of the chapters you will encounter.

• **Chapter goals.** The introduction to each chapter lists the goals of the chapter and what you should expect to learn. Review the chapter introduction both at the start of the chapter and after you have read it thoroughly. If, when rereading the chapter goals, you are not sure you have a good understanding of them, you need to review the chapter material prior to moving on.

• **Key terms.** Each chapter contains a number of key terms that aid you in understanding and making use of the concepts of the chapter. These key terms will build on one another as you progress through the book so that you expand your knowledge in a systematic and useful way.

• **Chapter concepts.** These are the basic concepts or steps that you will discover are essential to attain the goals established for each chapter. They are presented in the building-block method, which allows you to broaden your base of information and knowledge continuously. At the same time, you will develop a solid understanding of what makes real estate "tick," how you can reduce risk in investing, and how you can determine which of the opportunities you discover will best help you attain your goals.

• **Examples, case studies, exercises, and forms.** Many chapters contain these added elements to enhance your understanding of key concepts, direct your attention to potential problem areas for real estate investors, and allow you to practice the concepts you are learning.

The Real Estate Investor's VIP List

As you read, and especially in Chapter 15, you can begin to compile your own Real Estate Investor's VIP List of important sources of the information on your local real estate market that you will need to be a successful investor. This list, which follows Chapter 21, should be filled out faithfully. When you finish the book, there will still be some blank areas, which you can complete at your leisure. The investor who has a fully completed list will have the edge over any other potential investor in the same community. This list is to be *used*. It will help you build personal confidence in the real estate arena. Its success depends on you to obtain the data called for. Do not skip this important part of the book—your future may depend on it.

As you move into Part 1 of this book, you will be building your real estate investment foundation while at the same time enhancing your confidence in your ability to make the move to become a property owner. You will discover the simple elements of finance as they are applied to real estate. Best of all, you will discover how easy it is to learn so much about a neighborhood so quickly. This knowledge will provide you with "insider's information" that in reality has been there for your picking all the while. Take advantage of that knowledge, and this book.

HOW TO BEGIN YOUR SUCCESSFUL REAL ESTATE INVESTMENT CAREER

1

A SOUND INVESTMENT STRATEGY BEGINS WITH A GOAL-ORIENTED PLAN

This chapter is the foundation for all that follows, and its first purpose is to help you establish a positive outlook on the task of real estate investing. It will do this by illustrating that there are seven important personal characteristics that, depending on how you direct them, will shape whatever you do in life.

The seven personal characteristics are determination, attitude, sound goals, a plan to attain those goals, patience, due diligence, and perseverance. Each of these seven is easily attained. All you have to do is to apply your best efforts toward each of these tasks.

This chapter also tackles the problem of **risk** in real estate investing and shows the keys to reducing that element in the investment portfolio. The ultimate aim of this chapter is to show the reader the importance of establishing sound and meaningful goals and how they are applied to an investment plan.

This chapter and those that follow are directed to the **goal-oriented investor**. The problem is that most novice investors are not properly and effectively goal oriented. The consequence of this is that most investors have difficulty staying focused on their task and achieving success. Good goals are essential for sustained success in any venture, so real estate investing should not be an exception. The connection between a firm focus (a goal clearly in sight) and a winning attitude is very important, because it will shape your self-confidence and provide a road map for the future. The result will enable you to overcome needless frustration and to dispel the idea of fruitless effort.

Take everything one step at a time.

KEY TERMS

In this section, the following terms related to establishing a goal-oriented plan are defined and explained:

- Success-oriented attitude
- Apparent opportunity
- Attainable opportunity
- Positive failure alignment
- Successful elasticity
- Comfort zone
- A goal-oriented plan

Knowing and understanding these terms and issues related to them will help you to learn and apply the concepts presented in this and future chapters.

Success-Oriented Attitude

The *little engine that could* is the basis of this concept. Knowing that you can succeed is the driving force that results in effective and worthwhile effort. When virtually every task begun is completed, strong **self-confidence** is generated. This self-confidence is the inner reflection of the right kind of success-oriented attitude. In person-to-person contact, this self-confidence must be so positively charged within you that it shows in everything about you. In sports, this kind of self-confidence is what gives one player the edge over another. In essence, the adversary is "psyched out." The positive attitude keeps the winner charged with the vision of success right from the beginning. It pays off in sports and also in real estate investing.

In the business world, this simple element is often the only thing that separates a closed contract, a signed order, or a profitable venture from failure. It is a natural course of events. People *want* to do business with people who exude success and who have the confidence to prove it.

The idea is to look and think the part. It takes both aspects to work. Just thinking success is not enough. You must look the part as well.

- **Know that you can and will learn the tools needed to be a success in real estate investing.** Just as a novice pilot learns to fly, you will learn the keys and the insider techniques in real estate investing and you will be a success—if you want it to happen.
- **Don't rush anything.** Take this book step-by-step and become comfortable with the concepts and your ability to apply them as they relate to your goals. Building your own self-confidence is an essential part to building a success-oriented attitude.

Apparent Opportunity

The moment you begin to learn anything new you will have the urge to grasp what jumps out at you as an **apparent opportunity**. It is like the budding psychiatrist who first learns of a mental disorder and begins to see it in everyone. Learning about real estate investing is *learning how to take advantage of opportunities that may have been around all the time*; the only difference is that you did not have the ability to see them, so they went unnoticed. Apparent opportunities may be both *dangerous* and *worthy*.

Novice investors often jump at a deal that looks good for the wrong reason. For example, dealing with highly motivated sellers is a very good source for making excellent deals. However, to acquire property from a seller simply because he or she will sell it for nothing down may not be an opportunity at all because that property may not serve to move you closer to your desired goals.

Every purchase or acquisition should be part of an investment plan. If the property can fit into that plan and can be purchased or acquired in such a way that the obligation does not overburden you or sidetrack you from your goals, then you have examined the apparent opportunity and determined that it is an **attainable opportunity**.

Attainable Opportunity

Not every worthy opportunity will be attainable. The reason for this is that not every seller will be willing to meet your acquisition requirements. One of the elements of being successful as a real estate investor is to convert *obstinate sellers* into *willing sellers*. This book is designed to help you concentrate on attainable opportunities rather than waste your time trying to acquire properties that are owned by people who are not motivated or who are unrealistic about property values. You need to make an early decision about whether the property is right for you and, equally important, whether the owners will work *with* you. If not, move on.

Positive Failure Alignment

Failure is not your enemy. Failure is not the opposite of success. Failure is an essential part of the attainment process of every goal. Without failure along the way, you will not have that sweet taste of success at the end of the path.

Successful Elasticity

A football running back knows the advantage of being able to make sudden changes in direction and speed. In real estate investing, the ability to make sudden adjustments to your goals and your plans will enable you to move with the changing trends. In this way, you can avoid economic disaster when outside factors have a negative influence. Fixed and unbending goals and plans must be avoided. However, do not be too quick to make changes until you have thought out the new plan or the adjusted goal. Change for the sake of change is not always wise.

It is prudent to write the following sentence on a small card that you look at anytime you are about to make a goal-oriented decision: "Does this property that I am about to buy or sell take me closer to my goals?"

If you are not sure of your answer, then you have not laid the proper foundation to make the decision.

Comfort Zone

An investment **comfort zone** for real estate is the combination of a geographic area and a specific type of property in which an investor decides to specialize. This concept is unique, and later chapters are devoted to providing details on how to establish and maintain your investment comfort zone.

A Goal-Oriented Plan

Investing in real estate, or for that matter in any other commodity, should be approached as one might plan a military operation. There will be objectives to attain both during the planning stage and in the plan's implementation. These objectives should be reached prior to moving on to the rest of the plan. They are interim steps that build your knowledge of the area and subject properties you may consider acquiring.

Because goals have their own criteria and will be different for you than for someone else, do not be persuaded to act on a plan that fits another person's needs and goals unless you are certain that your objectives can also be reached by implementation of that plan.

HOW TO BUILD SELF-CONFIDENCE AND A SUCCESS-ORIENTED ATTITUDE

The key to a success-oriented attitude in real estate investing is to build your self-confidence to the level where you can deal with the total involvement of buying and selling real property. It is logical, then, that the first part of your plan to become a successful real estate investor should be to outline all the steps needed to obtain the necessary knowledge and tools of the trade.

Five Steps to Building Self-Confidence

1. Accept the fact that by the time you complete this 36-hour course you will have the basic foundation on which to select objectives that will move you closer to your desired goals.
2. Anticipate that you will have strong points from which you can build as well as weak points that you will have to strengthen or circumvent.
3. Set down clear and attainable long-range goals and work to refine them.
4. Establish intermediate goals and timetables. These mini-goals are steps you need to take to attain, increase, or fine-tune your knowledge and abilities so you can succeed at longer-range goals. Your list of mini-goals or steps should never have more than three or four items at any given time. Keep your timetable short. No item should be on the list if you cannot complete it within six months. You can

begin your mini-goal list with item 1: complete *The McGraw-Hill 36-Hour Course: Real Estate Investing.*

5. Celebrate each intermediate step you attain. Pat yourself on your own back and be proud of your accomplishments. By continuing to set intermediate mini-goals that can be reached in short time periods, you are setting a pattern for success. Continual achievement creates a strong success-oriented attitude and helps build your self-confidence quickly.

HOW MUCH TIME IS NEEDED TO GET STARTED IN REAL ESTATE INVESTING?

The amount of time needed to become a real estate investor is divided into three segments: preparation, implementation, and action.

Preparation: Build Your Knowledge

This is a combination of active study, such as reading this book, and development of investment habits that will become a natural part of your everyday life. Much of this "awareness building" will not take additional time from your current activities, but can become a part of them. For example, instead of merely driving to work, change your route to get to know the neighborhood where you plan or hope to invest. Look at properties on the market, jot down phone numbers from "for sale" or "for rent" signs, and so on. Then follow up by calling the numbers and getting the details.

Implementation: Start Your Comfort Zone Plan

Following completion of *The McGraw-Hill 36-Hour Real Estate Investing Course*, this book can become your guide to investing. It is designed to take the investor through a systematic process and is an ideal reference guide.

One morning each week plus one full day during the weekend is a reasonable amount of time to devote to fieldwork. Fieldwork is the time spent driving around the community, getting to know the geographic area of your comfort zone better than any taxi driver ever could. This means not only knowing the streets, but also knowing the zoning, neighborhood boundaries, school districts, churches, public transportation, proximity to shopping, employment, and so on.

Action: Put Your Plan to Work

By the time, you have completed this book you will already be spotting opportunities within your comfort zone that had slipped right past you earlier. Remind yourself that because you have gone through this course you are miles ahead of others who are still clueless as to those same opportunities. Spring into action and demonstrate that you have become a member of the true "real estate insiders" fraternity.

HOW TO REDUCE RISK IN REAL ESTATE INVESTING

If there were a way to eliminate risk entirely, that secret would carry a very high price tag. However, the prudent investor who follows simple and proven rules can greatly reduce the element of risk to acceptable levels. To understand how this is accomplished, one must first realize that risk is a relative term that does not apply equally to everyone for the same situation or circumstance. It should be obvious that a trained pilot with a 1,000 hours of flight time in a Boeing 747 jet has much less risk in landing that giant of an aircraft than would a part-time single-engine student pilot. Likewise, the real estate investor who knows his or her comfort zone like the back (and front) of his or her hand and has astutely followed the market for several months or more is better equipped to deal with investments in that area.

As your knowledge of the local area increases, opportunities that you would never have seen before start to stand out, almost as though they had a neon sign blinking "buy me." At first, you will have to be cautious and fight the urge to take advantage of every apparent opportunity that comes along. Soon, however, you will gain confidence in your own knowledge and information. Once this begins to happen, you will feel your success-oriented attitude take over, and then all your effort will be directed toward your long-range goals. The apparent opportunities will give way to attainable opportunities, and you can begin to build a real estate investment portfolio.

THE IMPORTANCE OF MEANINGFUL GOALS

Goals are not essential for life, as many people never grasp the advantage of setting meaningful goals or never set any kind of goal at all. Not having any goals or setting the wrong kind of goals does not mean you will not arrive at a destination. However, it leaves the choice of that destination and the timetable you will follow to others or to indecision.

A goal that is more distant in time than one year should be divided into intermediate mini-goals. As each step is completed, within a defined timetable that you set for yourself, another mini-goal can be added. Frequent attainment of these mini-goals will strengthen your self-confidence and promote a healthy outlook and success-oriented attitude.

For a goal to work for you it must have four qualities. It must be attainable, measurable, tied to a timetable, and clearly defined.

Goals Should Be Challenging Yet Attainable

The fastest route to frustration is to set goals that are not attainable at all or not within the timetable you have set. The goal "I want to be a millionaire by the end of this year," for example, while an interesting approach to financial independence, may not be attainable.

Goals Must Be Measurable

All goals must have a scale that allows for readjustment and fine-tuning. This means that there should be a way to tell how close a goal is to being attained. Esoteric or vague goals can create chaos as you go about setting your interim or mini-goals, and frustration is bound to occur. These kinds of goals are often not easily spotted at first, as they seem to have measure at the time they are set. "Financial independence" as a goal, for example, becomes immeasurable later on because financial needs and obligations change.

Goals Should Be Tied to a Timetable

The timetable serves several functions. First, it requires time management and the prioritization of effort. Most people work better if they know they must complete something by a deadline. The key to setting a timetable is to allow a reasonable time for each item placed on the list.

Avoid putting things off. This is a self-established timetable, and if the deadlines are constantly pushed ahead, the whole concept of setting goals and attaining them will be defeated. Frequent measures must be taken to judge your progress in accomplishing the task and if adjustment is needed. If any part of the goal is changed, there must be a very good reason.

Goals Must Be Clearly Defined

A vague goal can cause more problems than it is worth. Consider a stated goal to own 100 apartment units within three years. Is that a clearly defined goal? I think not. It needs further definition so that the investor is not lulled into thinking that the end goal has been attained when in reality it is even farther away. A more precise definition could be to own at least 100 rental apartments free and clear of any debt. One element of a goal being clearly defined is essential—the goal or goals must be written down and placed where they can be seen. In this way, they become an important force in setting daily priorities.

FINE-TUNE YOUR GOALS

A vague understanding of exactly what it is that you want to attain will tend to move you in an unsure course to a destination. Therefore, as you set goals you will need to fine-tune your ultimate goals as well as the interim steps necessary to reach those goals.

Start with the Principal Goals

Principal goals are the rungs of the ladder that reach from now to a future date at which there is a plateau. These goals are rewards that come from fulfillment of your interim goals. To be specific, say your main goal in real estate investing is to replace your job with income-producing investments that exceed your present annual income by 20 percent. If your current income is $80,000 a year, this means you have targeted the monetary measure of $96,000 a year. As you will discover when it comes time to pay your income tax, the real estate you have acquired may provide an additional bonus to your income in the way of reducing your actual income tax.

Work on Your Interim Goals

To attain your principal goals you must first go through a series of steps, or interim goals, to reach the stages defined by each principal goal. Level by level you move toward the end goal. The speed at which you progress will be governed by the following:

- Your initial capital available to invest
- The time you can devote to this process
- Your talents and abilities to improve the properties you acquire
- Team members you have to help out
- Partners to help with the capital needs

BEGIN TO DEVELOP YOUR COMFORT ZONE

As you go from now to a future date, your investment process will take you through the development of a comfort zone. This will be your proving ground, so to speak. It will let you become an expert in that geographic area and become acquainted with building and zoning rules, regulations, and ordinances that control the *use* of real estate As you journey up this ladder, you will inspect dozens of properties and "crunch" the data on income and expenses of real properties in your comfort zone. This process teaches you about the real estate in your zone and gives you the information you need to assess future investments by comparison with properties you have already seen. Remember, real estate is local and visual. You can never effectively analyze real estate you have not carefully inspected to gain a clear vision of how it relates to other properties of the same category.

Assume that you have a principal goal to obtain an effective comfort zone that will feed your investment needs. Look at how this plan can develop. Groups of steps on this ladder lead you from goal to goal. One segment of that might look like the following.

Goal: Begin to Build Your Comfort Zone

To begin to build your real estate investment comfort zone, first drive around town looking for areas where you would like to own property. Select an area and get city maps for it. It is very helpful to have a digital camera and make sure you are familiar with how to use it so you can take pictures of the general area as well as the individual properties you investigate.

As you explore the area you have chosen as a possible comfort zone, try to meet people in the area. Make notes of properties that are for sale or for rent. Call the phone numbers on signs or check out the websites listed. Make appointments to inspect both properties for sale and for rent, and get detailed information on those properties. Keep record of what you have learned about each property on cards or computerized records, and take pictures of each property. Be sure to check with the local property tax assessor to find out what aids they can provide to help you. Most communities provide a great deal of information about the real estate in their jurisdiction. Once you discover how to navigate their Web pages, there will be few secrets about what is going on in your local real estate market and why. A visit to their offices will give you access to one of the staff there who will generally be available to show you what you can obtain and how to do it. Make sure that the area you have selected has sufficient properties for you to analyze. If you feel you made a mistake about the area, stick with it a little longer, but if after a couple of weeks longer, it does not look promising, add to the territory, or move your comfort zone to another part of town.

Through these steps you have now begun to accomplish your goal to begin to build a real estate investment comfort zone.

Become Acquainted with Building and Zoning Rules

Once you have begun to accomplish the goal of becoming familiar with your chosen comfort zone area, you can map out the interim steps for further goals as well. In the comfort zone process, you can really be working on the frosting as you think of what kind of cake you will bake.

Make sure you know the jurisdiction of the building and zoning rules for the area you have chosen. Do not begin with a geographic area that consists of more than one building and zoning department and other city services.

Pay a visit to the building and zoning department and get copies (in person or by Internet) of the building and zoning codes. Read the codes, and if you do not understand something, go to the building and zoning department and ask someone to explain it to you.

Become an Expert in Your Comfort Zone Area

Following are further steps you can take to find and gather information from valuable sources of "insider" information on the comfort zone area you have chosen.

- Go to the county tax assessor's office and ask staff members to show you how to use the computers there as well as the Internet to look through their files to get information about real estate in the area.
- Drive around the area that you plan to make your comfort zone (a bike is a good way during the day) and get a feel for what is there and what makes this the area where you want to own property. Check the area

on weekdays and nights as well as weekend days and nights to get the full picture of what goes on there.

- Take digital photos of everything that is for sale or for rent whether you plan to buy, rent, or just find out what is what.
- Make a card or a computerized record for each property and date all the data you put there, including the file name for the photo you took.
- Call the phone numbers on the "for rent" or "for sale" signs. Get the data and make an appointment to inspect the property.
- If a property is income producing, go over the income and expense figures.
- Check out the tax assessor's files on the properties (this is easy on the Internet) and look for anything critical. Find the assessed value, annual tax bill, and whether it is homesteaded property (which may show a lower tax bill).
- Ascertain when the present owner bought the property and what he or she paid for it.
- See if improvements have been made (if they were permitted improvements, this would show in the building and zoning office files), and so on.

Begin to Analyze the Information You Have Gathered

Make mental comparisons between properties you inspect and make notes on the card or computer file that corresponds to each property. If you are using a laptop computer you can store everything in a simple file as you go. Use the owner's name and the street address of the property as the identification of the file to make it easy to sort through things.

After you have inspected a dozen properties, think about what you have seen. Ask yourself if you see something here that is interesting. Did you notice anything about the rental properties that would tell you *why* one rents for much more than another? Is there a scarcity of nice rentals available (because all are rented)? Have you seen some properties for sale that could use TLC? If you have no answer to these questions, inspect another dozen properties. When you start to see a void, which I will talk about throughout this book, you are ready to start making offers.

YOU ARE ON YOUR WAY TO SUCCESS

This is the process that you go through to make your map to success. Whenever you are at a loss for what to do next, you simply back up and go through the same process again. As you look at properties, you will begin to add more knowledge-building interim steps to your process. What bus routes serve the area? What public and private schools would the children go to (or your future tenants work at)? Are any of the properties in the area zoned for possible uses other than what they are currently being used for? This is important because some areas of town may have a wide range of uses that can be approved, which is important to you in increasing your revenue potential.

Look at your targeted goals and fine-tune their description. Know your target and build the interim steps between targets, then ascertain your position in your timetable. If you feel confused, then review what you have accomplished. If you are frustrated that nothing positive seems to be happening, decide which of the critical elements is off-kilter and adjust your goals accordingly.

C H A P T E R

2

FUNDAMENTAL REAL ESTATE TERMINOLOGY MADE EASY

The primary goal of this chapter is to acquaint the reader with basic terms so that you will be able to move easily through this book. The terms contained within this chapter are by no means a full glossary of real estate terminology; however, they are the most basic elements dealing with real estate investing. After introducing a few key terms, the chapter divides the terminology into five segments important to real estate investing: getting started, property values, finding the best property to buy, buying and selling techniques, and pitfalls in real estate investing.

KEY TERMS

In this section, the following terms related to fundamental real estate terminology are defined and explained:

- KISS
- Not universal
- Due diligence

Knowing and understanding these terms and issues related to them will help you to learn and apply the concepts presented in this chapter.

KISS

Keep it simple, silly (KISS) is a good rule of thumb in any kind of business activity. Every investor should get into the habit of using plain English and not fancy or legal-sounding terms. While all real estate investors should be able to understand the technical and legal terminology as it applies to real estate, it is not essential that investors actually use the same language themselves.

Not Universal

Not every term is used universally. Terms used in city and county ordinances are especially vulnerable to misinterpretation when they apply to property uses. As the allowed use of land is critical to its value, any misunderstanding in what can and cannot be placed on the vacant lot you are thinking of purchasing can be catastrophic. A lot that is zoned with a classification of R-25, for example, may mean that a builder could build up to 25 multifamily units (condos, houses, townhouses per acre) per acre. That might suggest that if the land consisted of two acres, 50 units could be built there. Notice I said "might suggest," because there could easily be some limiting factor, such as setbacks or parking or, well, there are many things that could come into play in this scenario. Never be ashamed to ask the officials or individual using the term to explain exactly what it means and how it is applied. You may discover that they do not really know.

Due Diligence

The single most important aspect in real estate investing is due diligence. The best description of this term or concept is that **due diligence** is the focused attention given to research and study about a specific property being considered for acquisition or sale. The focus given by the investor must be from the point of view of that person's goals, and the research and study should answer these questions: Does the original information given to me check out? And, are there any roadblocks I have overlooked that may hinder the attainment of my objectives and goals?

Because effective due diligence is important, many potential investors assume that every question must be asked and all questions reviewed and verified before moving forward to acquire a property. This can, however, be very counterproductive. Misdirected due diligence often causes investors to make a decision that directs them away from their goals rather than closer to them. Effort extended in research and study without having a lock on the property can result in many hours, days, or even weeks of wasted time. Good investments may not go unnoticed by other investors, so while the student of due diligence is spending those days or weeks of investigation into every nook and cranny of a property, other investors may have already gone to contract and a good opportunity may be lost.

The key to effective due diligence is to have a certain knowledge of the area, the nature of the property, and basic elements that are important to you and your goal and how that property relates to the objectives you want to attain. This information is intrinsic and unique to you and is more about you than about the property. If your basic intuition says "go forward," take the process to the next level by entering into negotiations to "tie up the property." This process may center on price and terms, all of which would be tied to your completion of your more thorough investigation. At the end of that period you may discover you offered too much, in which case a renegotiation may be necessary for you to want to purchase the property. The more complicated the deal, the more time you may need to complete this process. Because of the time and level of due diligence you may need, much of this book is dedicated to showing investors how to maximize this due diligence effort.

GETTING STARTED

This section defines terms you will encounter as you begin to investigate the real estate market.

Acre The standard land term. An acre consists of 43,560 square feet (sq ft) of land area. Farmland, commercial sites, and other real estate are often referenced by acre. Prices are also given in this format. For example, a tract of land that consists of 100 acres may be priced at $500 per acre, giving a total price of $50,000.

Homesites are often shown as a quarter of an acre, half an acre, and so on. Developmental land may have a density allowed by the local government, often seen as 5 units per acre, 25 units per acre, and so on. If a developer were to acquire a tract of 100 acres with a density of 10 units per acre, he or she could, without any modification and after obtaining appropriate approvals, build up to 1,000 dwelling units on that tract.

A square lot consisting of 1 acre is equivalent to 208.71 feet by 208.71 feet (the square root of 43,560 square feet), which we can round off to 209 feet. No investor will ever find a lot of this exact size, but every investor should have a mental image of it. It is a good idea to find a parking lot or other open area that has two sides against a structure (walls, buildings, even hedges will do). Mark off a square whose sides are 209 feet long and walk around it. Have a friend walk opposite you so you can get the feel and vision of what an acre looks like.

Building Codes The rules and regulations that govern the methods, materials, and designs used in construction. Each community may vary the overall standards from neighboring communities. If the area in which you plan to invest is made up of several different municipalities, make sure you have copies of the building codes that are specifically unique to each of these areas.

Building Permits When construction has been approved according to the local building codes, the local authorities, which are the building and zoning officials of that municipality, usually require that a building permit be obtained (and paid for). This permit may require the contractor to have inspections made at various stages of the work. These periodic inspections ensure that work is being done according to the building codes. We live in a world of "do-it-yourself," and it is very common to find that "ideal property" whose owner was a wiz at doing things himself or herself. And all of that nice construction may have been accomplished without a permit. Some if not all of the work may not even meet code, which can be a major problem and expense to you after you have closed on the deal. Work done in advance of your purchasing the property may fall into that category of "having been done without a permit." The local officials may have passed over it (sometimes with a blind eye) or simply out of ignorance of the work having been done. Yet, when a prospective tenant applies for an occupational license and gets turned down, you are potentially in for a nightmare of problems. Make sure you are clear of this potential problem by requiring the seller to verify that there are no code violation problems.

Most cities have a process where they will do a building code inspection to ascertain if there are such problems. The building and zoning department normally has detailed records of all building permits taken out for work at any specific location or site. If an investor discovers that construction has been done without a permit, a flag of caution should be raised, and the matter should be cleared through the building and zoning department prior to buying the property.

Contingency Clause Any clause or condition put into an agreement or contract that allows one or both of the parties to the agreement to modify or withdraw from the agreement. One such clause that can be used to deal with possible building and zoning problems could be the following:

> This agreement is conditioned on there being no building code or zoning violations on the property being purchased. The buyer, therefore, has a period of 10 working days to obtain assurances in writing from the governing building and zoning office that there are no existing code violations. Should any violations exist, the seller has a period of no more than 30 days from the date the violations are revealed, and notice thereof given to the seller, to remedy those violations. Without such remedy the buyer has the option to withdraw from this agreement any time prior to closing, which if elected, will cause this agreement to become null and void.

Demised Premises The term that describes leased property.

Duplex This word has two distinct meanings:

1. A duplex may be a building that has two residences under one roof. This two-family building is a good starter home for many investors who live in one part and rent out the other.
2. A duplex is often a home or apartment with two or more levels. In this meaning the home consists of only one residence. In the case of a duplex apartment, the unit has two levels but the building could contain any number of residences.

Federal Housing Administration The FHA is an agency within the U.S. Department of Housing and Urban Development that administers many different loan and loan guarantee programs.

Federal National Mortgage Association The FNMA, which is often called Fannie Mae, is a corporation that buys mortgages from banks, savings and loan institutions, and other loan sources.

GI Loan (Also VA Loan) Loans that are insured by the Veterans Administration and are available for qualified and eligible veterans (usually 120 days of active duty in the armed forces qualifies). This loan program can provide up to 100 percent of the acquisition funds for a home loan.

Lien The name for any obligation that must be discharged that is against a property or person. A lien that is recorded against a property must generally be paid to obtain a clear title.

Market Analysis A detailed study of an area showing the condition of the market. In the case of real estate, a study should include the following data:

> **Selling information:** A list of all similar properties within the area that have been sold over the past 12 to 24 months. Helpful statistics would indicate how long the property was on the market and the spread between the asking price and the actual selling price.
> **Available on the market:** A list of all similar properties within the area that are currently on the market, their price, and how long they have remained unsold.
> **Rental data:** A list showing available rental and rented properties that are similar to the subject property. Helpful information would be the square footage under roof and the rent prices. A strong rental market with high rent prices indicates a good sales market. Declining rental prices and/or many vacancies of similar properties show a soft sales market.

Metes and Bounds This is the original legal description method used in the original 13 colonies of the United States as well as earlier in other parts of the world. It uses several different methods of identifying the size and location of a property by locating the boundaries of that property. The different means are often combined into one narrative of the property. These include the following: **Survey lines** that are generally compass directions in degrees, and distances using feet, or other dimension terms. If there is a natural geographical element such as a river, creek, lake, or other such item as a boundary, that may be used as the direction and line of the boundary. **Descriptions** such as the large boulder, two oak trees, and other such outstanding features. **Names of property owners**, which would lead to other descriptions for that property that may need to be verified. The following are two examples of this process:

> From a point of beginning at the NW corner of the Adams property go N300W 900 yards, thence S210W 450 yards and meander to point of beginning along a northerly flowing river.

From the South West Monument of Section 7, Township 49 South Range 42 East, Broward County, Florida, go 1200 feet due North to a point of Beginning, thence westerly along the right-of-way of McNab Road 300 feet, thence due South 600 feet, thence due East 300 feet, thence due North 600 feet back to the point of beginning.

Offer and Counteroffer The process by which most real estate is acquired. The art of making an offer and negotiating to a satisfactory conclusion is learned through practice. Each party in a contract needs to keep its own goals clearly in focus and look for the benefits in the transaction rather than be ruled by emotions.

PITI The principal, interest, taxes, and insurance portion of a mortgage payment. Most institutional lenders collect all four of these items as part of the mortgage payment, escrowing the taxes and insurance to ensure that those two items will be paid when they come due.

Planned Unit Development (PUD) A zoning classification that allows flexibility of design within a subdivision, usually set to a maximum density for the overall property, but which allows the developer to cluster or concentrate the residential buildings to specific parts of the overall site.

Plat The actual drawing of a subdivision or part of a subdivision. Most areas of the country require a developer to record a plat of any subdivided land showing the divisions or lots within that property.

Plot Plan (or Site Plan) A drawing showing the footprint of the buildings on a specific property. Excluded in this drawing are any details of the building itself or elevations of buildings. The plot or site plan shows all boundaries and should therefore indicate if there is any foreign encroachment into the property. This foreign element might be a driveway, a building, or some other element that should not be there without your notice and approval prior to your purchase of the property, any encroachment of construction from or to the specific property in question.

Prime Rate The lowest commercial interest rate charged by banks on short-term loans to their best customers. Many loans are based on a level over the prime rate; for example, a bank may make a commercial loan at 2 points (percentage points) above the prime, which might be stated as 200 base points. If the prime is, at that moment, 6 percent, then the loan would carry an interest rate of 8 percent until the prime went either up or down, requiring an adjustment in the loan rate. LIBOR, which stands for "London Interbank Offered Rate," is often a benchmark for a loan that is quoted at, for example, "LIBOR plus 2 percentage points."

Square Foot A size that is equal to a square with four sides of one foot (12 inches). Square footage is a standard measurement and pricing term for anything from land to rental area within a building. It is critical as a measurement of acreage, as 43,560 square feet equal one acre. A tract of 10 acres contains 435,600 square feet (10 × 43,560 sq ft). If the price of the 10-acre property is $2 per square foot, the total price is $2.00 × 435,600 sq ft = $871,200. Rental prices for commercial buildings are usually quoted in either a monthly or annual price per square foot of the area rented.

Square Yard An area that is equal to a square with four sides one yard (3 feet) long. A square yard is equal to 9 square feet (3 feet × 3 feet = 9 sq ft). Both square yards and cubic yards (a cubic yard if a cube with sides 1 yard or 3 feet of length, width, and height) are used in construction. Concrete, sand, and other similar material are sold by the *yard*, which is a cubic yard of material. Carpets are sold in rolls but are priced by the square yard or sometimes by square feet.

Subdivision An area of a community that has been platted independently of adjoining areas. Investors should learn everything about one subdivision prior to expanding to an adjoining one as the best way to become an expert on property in their area. *Subdivision* is also used in the more modern version of a legal description by naming the lot and block of a specific subdivision that has been recorded with the local authorities. An example would be "The Bradshaw property as determined to be Lots 2, 3, 4 of Block 28 of the Oak Park Subdivision located in Thousand Oaks, California."

Ordinances Each community has laws that govern everything from the size of signs to the setbacks from streets. These laws will vary according to many different reasons and are critical, as they govern many aspects of property use. Investors are warned that logic does not always apply in the administration of these rules and regulations. For example, what is being done across the street may not be allowed anymore, but it may have been "grandfathered in" to that specific location and nowhere else. Violations of these laws (which include building and zoning rules and regulations) must be cleared before buying any property.

PROPERTY VALUES

The following terms are important to know in relation to property values.

Ad Valorem Tax The real estate tax on any specific property. This tax differs from other assessments or charges that may occur. The amount of the tax for any given year is found by multiplying the tax assessment (after any deductions for homestead exemption) by the tax millage rate. This rate is a function of a percentage of the taxable value of the property. Check with your county tax assessor as to what their rate is and how it is applied.

Appraised Value The value established by an appraiser. Appraisals are subject to differing opinions by appraisers, depending to some degree on the intent of the appraiser. If the appraisal is being accomplished by the local real estate tax authority, the resulting value may take into account only the property size, building square footage, and age of the construction, whereas an appraisal ordered by a property owner to show maximum value possible usually shows comparable properties that are on the market or that have been sold that support a higher value. Investors should not trust any appraisal offered by the seller as justification of value; while such an appraisal may be accurate, investors need to examine other information as well.

Basis The term that describes the "book value" of any asset. In real estate, basis is the price you paid for a property *plus* any capital improvements made to it, *less* any depreciation (or asset write-off) taken for tax purposes. Basis is important because it is the amount that establishes your capital gain. If you buy a building for $100,000 and add a second floor at a cost of $30,000, you have an adjusted basis of $130,000. Subtract the depreciation you took of $20,000, and your final basis is now $110,000. If you sell the building for $200,000, your gain is $90,000 ($200,000 − $110,000 = $90,000).

Buyer's Market The market condition that is favorable to the buyer.

Cash Flow The amount of cash from an income-producing property left at the end of any period (monthly or annually) after all expenses and debt service have been deducted. This is one of the major benefits obtained from investing in income-producing property. Investors need to think of this "flow of cash" as return prior to income tax calculations. Because real estate often provides a tax buffer between regular income (such as income from your job) and your real estate investment income due to depreciation, it is likely that some if not all of the cash flow from real estate investments will be "tax free."

Economic Conversion The act of converting one property use to another. This is one of the best ways to increase rental income for a property and is measured against the cost to effect the conversion. For example, after a study of the rental market, an investor realizes that the income from an apartment building can be tripled by a conversion to offices. If the cost to convert allows a greater yield after the conversion, then this economic conversion could be worthwhile.

Loan-to-Value Ratio A term used by lenders that shows the ratio of the debt to the actual value of a property. If a home is worth $150,000 and there is a total debt of $75,000 outstanding, the loan-to-value ratio is $75,000 to $150,000, or half loan and half equity. This term may be quoted as a percentage, the above example being 50 percent loan to value (calculated as loan amount ÷ property value, or in this case $75,000 ÷ $150,000 = .5, or 50 percent).

Seller's Market The market condition that is favorable to the seller.

Tax Assessment The actual annual ad valorem tax that the local taxing authority levies on any given property. It is worthwhile to compare this assessment and the corresponding tax appraisal value to those of surrounding properties of similar nature to see if these values are in line with each other. If the tax assessment is higher than the general average, it is possible that the tax assessment can be reduced through negotiations with the taxing authority. In any event, any shift from the average should be examined to determine the reason for the shift. Perhaps the taxing authority has information that could be important to any prospective investor.

Title Insurance Every property has a legal trail of paperwork associated with it that will show recorded liens, mortgages, transfers, and sometimes even leases that may be in effect. It is important that as an investor you are sure that the reported seller or owner is indeed the individual or individuals you are negotiating with. It is essential that prior to closing on any real estate your closing agent (lawyer or title company) has checked the title. I recommend that buyers always obtain title insurance to protect the title in the event of some unknown issue, such as the improper transfer of a title, death of a previous co-owner, or other similar matter that can cause a new owner problems, if not immediately, then in the distant future when the buyer attempts to pass on good title to a new investor.

Upside Down This term refers to the imbalance in a ratio of debt to value. When the amount of debt on a property, as represented by one or a combination of several mortgages on the property, exceeds the market value of that property, then its owner is upside down. This occurs in any market when property value has been reduced either by conditions that the owner could not control or simply by excessive leverage, which created excessive debt and less than anticipated rental revenue. This situation became prevalent because of the overleverage of debt in the early 2000s that, in turn, prompted the term *short sale*, whereby buyers would request the lenders to "eat" the debt (reduce the amount of debt owed) so that the buyer could acquire the property at a realistic value, often to fail in that attempt.

FINDING THE BEST PROPERTY TO BUY

You will encounter the following terms as you seek to decide which property is the best purchase to help you meet your goals.

Broker Versus Realtor Registered real estate brokers and salespeople are licensed by the state and are not necessarily Realtors. Realtors are brokers or salespeople who also belong to a local board of Realtors. Realtors agree among themselves to abide by rules that can offer some additional protection to their clients and prospects over and above state regulations. Other in-house services that the local boards of Realtors provide to their members can also be an aid to investors in buying or selling their property. In terms of effectiveness, dealing with a broker, whether a Realtor or not, becomes a personal relationship, the success of which depends on the qualifications of the salesperson more than anything else. Realtors are licensed brokers who belong to a national association that agrees to follow a higher standard of qualifications than the general state requirements for the profession.

Builder-Developer Often the best source for property in a buyer's market. These people are in the business of selling their own real estate, and if they have an inventory of unsold property that is eating a hole in their pockets because of high interest payments and carrying costs, they can become highly motivated sellers capable of working out a good deal for any buyer.

Code Violations A violation on a current city building code can occur when the building was constructed to conform to an older code—or the builder "cut corners" and an inspector found the violation. Many such violations must be corrected. This is a problem for the owner but perhaps an opportunity for the buyer. For example, when a property has a building code violation that can cause hardship for the current owner, he or she may suddenly become a motivated seller. Because codes change from time to time, this kind of situation can catch a property owner at a difficult time. For example, consider if the state changes the building code for fire protection and now requires buildings of a certain category to have fire sprinklers installed. A sudden added investment of $20,000 to accomplish that work may be more than an owner wants or has to spend. The property may then be put on the market at a reduced price—or, to raise the $20,000, the owner may decide to sell off another property at a bargain price.

Foreclosure When the borrower had not met his or her repayment requirements, the lender may follow a procedure that places the loan in default. At that point, the lender may seek to foreclose on the delinquent loan and the property may ultimately be "sold" at a foreclosure sale. This sale is a form of auction, usually advertised in the local newspaper's legal announcement section or in legal publications available to the public. All institutional lenders, including VA and FHA, end up with "real estate owned" (REO), or foreclosure properties, and these are a prime source for good buys.

FSBO (For Sale by Owner) This is often the first sign that a property is for sale. Many owners prefer to sell their own property rather than listing it with a real estate agent (broker or Realtor) to avoid paying a commission. Many buyers feel that they can make a better deal working directly with the seller because there is no commission to be paid. The reality is usually different, however, as direct confrontation between buyer and seller can create problems when emotion gets in the way of a successfully negotiated deal. Nonetheless, when properly handled, FSBOs can be a good source for good buys.

Management Problems One of the prime reasons people sell income property. It is not uncommon for professionals to invest in income property only to discover later that they do not have the time to manage the property themselves and that the cost of management is too high to maintain the desired return on their cash invested. The proper development of a comfort zone will enable investors to discover who owns the property within that zone. The investor can find and approach such owners before the property is actually placed on the market and exposed to every possible buyer in the area.

Short Sale When a lender agrees to reduce the amount of debt at the time of sale of a property that secures that debt.

Zoning Ordinances Zoning is the law that establishes the parameters of use for any property. Zoning is not absolute, however, as it can be changed under some circumstances. Zoning varies among communities, and the classifications used to describe zoning use are not universal. No property should be acquired unless the investor knows the full extent of the zoning ordinances as they apply to that specific property.

BUYING AND SELLING TECHNIQUES

You will encounter the following terms as you learn about real estate buying and selling techniques.

Addendum An attachment to any offer or counteroffer, often containing additional terms and conditions to the deal. In a series of counteroffers, care must be taken to ensure that each contract is complete and that each party has all the addenda that may become attached during the back-and-forth negotiating process.

Adjustable Rate Mortgage (ARM) Any mortgage with an interest rate that is adjusted during the loan term. Usually the adjustment is tied to a periodic (quarterly, annual, etc.) change in the prime or another commonly accepted interest rate.

Annual Cap In adjustable rate mortgages, it is important to the borrower that the loan have an annual or even a maximum cap to the amount by which the rate can be adjusted upward. This protects the borrower from excessive interest rates.

Balloon Mortgage A mortgage that becomes due and payable in advance of the payment schedule set. For example, Able borrows $400,000 from Brown and sets up a 20-year repayment plan as though he were going to pay back the money over that length of time. However, the mortgage note requires all unpaid principal to **balloon**, that is, become due and payable at the end of a shorter period of time, say, 5 years. Able must then either pay Brown the remaining principal at the end of the shorter period or refinance the loan with Brown or another lending source.

Blanket Mortgage A mortgage secured by more than one property. Often lenders want additional security when an investor borrows against a new acquisition. The lender wants to lower the loan-to-value ratio, and to do that it may insist that other property be added as security on the mortgage loan.

Closing In real estate terms, this is the moment when the contract is transacted and each person fulfills his or her role under the terms and conditions of the agreement. In a sale, it is the moment when the title is deeded to the buyer and the seller gets the proceeds of the sale.

Escrow Deposit The amount of deposit held by another party. In buying or leasing, the owner or his or her lawyer or agent generally holds a deposit in escrow from the buyer or tenant. Realtors are required to provide a separate bank account to hold such deposits; they are responsible for these accounts and must keep careful records. In the event of a dispute over the disposition of an escrow deposit, some third party—a court or arbitration board—may be called upon to intervene prior to either party to the agreement being able to use or recover the escrow deposit.

First Mortgage The mortgage that is recorded first or that has a previously recorded mortgage subordinated to it. The bold banner that says *First Mortgage* may not actually describe the document itself. The law provides that mortgage liens be ranked in the order they are recorded, unless there is an agreement that allows a subsequently recorded mortgage to have priority over a previously recorded mortgage (subordination occurs when a lien holder allows a subsequent lien holder to have a superior claim on the security). This aspect is important because an unscrupulous person may actually have more than one "first mortgage" on a property with each mortgagee (lender) thinking it is first in order of priority when in reality it may not be.

Fixed Rate Mortgage A mortgage that has a fixed interest rate for the whole term of the mortgage.

Graduated Payment Mortgage (GPM) This is a mortgage in which the payment changes over the term of the mortgage. Often the payment starts out lower than it ends up, giving an investor time to get situated in the property. If the payment is less than would be sufficient to pay interest, the unpaid interest is added to the principal due, and the mortgage amount owed can actually grow over a period of time until the payment increases sufficiently to start to reverse that trend.

Installment Sale This is a method of a sale allowed by the Internal Revenue Service that allows the seller to spread the tax due on a gain over the period of time from which the seller receives that gain because he holds a purchase money mortgage. If Brown holds a $400,000 mortgage from Able that provides for $40,000 per year of principal payments, then Brown will pay tax on the percentage of that $40,000 that is gain. The installment sale is a good tool for a seller to use when there might be a large tax to pay on a gain and the interest rate the seller can get from the buyer is more attractive than taking cash and reinvesting it into the market.

Institutional Lender Any lender that is a public entity licensed to lend money, such as savings and loan institutions, commercial banks, thrift institutions, mortgage bankers, insurance companies, credit unions, and so on.

Kicker Something a party to a contract wants over and above the terms offered, often in the form of extra security or benefits. Lenders may want a percentage of income over and above a set or flexible amount. Sellers may want to stay on in the property for a period of time rent free, and so on. There are numerous forms of kickers, and any benefit that can be given to a lender or seller over and above the actual price and payback of debt can be seen as a kicker.

Lease and Lease-Option It is not unusual for a lease to be used instead of a direct purchase. This can result from a circumstance where there is existing debt on a property that, while providing excellent terms and interest rate, is not assumable. The prospective buyer may find that a lease, with terms to meet the "seller's" needs, can be an effective way to allow the buyer to have access to the property. This lease may contain a provision that allows the "tenant" to have an option to purchase the property at some future date when financing is available, or options to continue the lease can be used to avoid having to deal with outside financing. Both of these techniques can have positive benefits to the buyer/tenant and/ or the seller/lessor.

Loan Assumption When an investor assumes a loan, he or she relieves the mortgagor (original borrower) of the obligations he or she has on that loan. When property owners go to banks to get loans, they give the banks (or other lenders) mortgages. The mortgage is evidence of the security given and is accompanied by a mortgage note, which is the document that details the repayment of the loan. The lender (the mortgagee) looks to the original borrower (the mortgagor) as the responsible and liable party to that loan. With the sale of that property, the mortgagor may want the new buyer to assume the loan rather than paying it off with the proceeds of the sale. Some lenders restrict or prohibit assumption, so each loan must be reviewed to ascertain what, if any, restrictions the lender can or will impose. Frequently lenders require a fee and extensive documentation to allow loan assumption. Sometimes this is not so elaborate, but simply a "due on sale" provision that prohibits an assumption unless the lender relents and grants an assumption under its imposed conditions. Those conditions generally require a change in some or all terms of the loan repayment.

Investors should never rely on verbal assurances from any source on loan assumption or any other loan information and should review the actual mortgage document and note as well as obtain an **estoppel letter** (legal assurance of the status), showing the circumstances of the loan.

Purchase Money Mortgage (PMM) Any mortgage the seller takes back in a transaction. If Able sells his home and there is both a first and second mortgage already in place that the buyer is to assume, and Able holds a third mortgage, then Able has taken back a third PMM. It is important that the buyer clarify whether or not the existing mortgages will allow this additional debt to occur. If not, then no additional seller-held debt can occur.

Second Mortgage The mortgage that is in second place in the recording of mortgage liens. Unless there are other provisions that subordinate this mortgage to future debt, the second mortgage will automatically become the first on the satisfaction (payoff) of existing first mortgage liens.

Subject To A phrase used in contracts that is of great importance. A buyer who takes a property "subject to" the existing debt does not assume that debt but merely acknowledges that he or she is aware of the debt and the rights of the mortgagee. Because the buyer has not legally assumed the obligations of the seller (or existing mortgagor), if the buyer were to default on the payments and the lender had to foreclose, the buyer could lose the property but would not be liable for any deficiency if a foreclosure sale did not produce sufficient funds to cover the debt and cost. The last mortgagor to assume the obligation could be held liable for this deficiency. Some buyers attempt to purchase a property that has a "due on sale" provision in the existing mortgage, which would ordinarily force the buyer to attempt to assume the loan or the buyer or seller to pay it off, using a contract with a "subject to" clause rather than complying with the "due on sale" provision of the seller's mortgage. If such a transaction were to take place (whether or not the buyer knew of the "due on sale" provision) and the lender were to discover that this had occurred, the lender could potentially bring legal action against the seller as well as the buyer.

PITFALLS IN REAL ESTATE INVESTING

Understanding the following terms will help you avoid the pitfalls in real estate investing.

Accrued Interest Outstanding interest that has not been paid, either by agreement or in default. When buying any property, obtain an **estoppel letter** from the lender. This letter will indicate the status of the mortgage and show the outstanding principal and any unpaid interest or other charges.

Adverse Possession A function of law that varies from state to state. Because a title can ultimately be transferred to another person by adverse possession, investors should be aware of the possible danger of not receiving proper title to the property. Because **adverse possession** must be *actual, hostile, notorious, exclusive, continuous, and under claim of right,* the claim is very hard to impose, but it can be raised against an absentee owner who may not be aware of what is going on. With an inspection of the site and a recent survey or plot plan showing locations of buildings and possible encroachments from neighbors, most adverse possession problems are quickly spotted. If any problems are evident they should be rectified prior to closing on a sale *even if there is no claim being made by the adverse party at that time.*

Cloud on Title or Title Defect When the chain of title (history of ownership) of a specific property is examined by the buyer's closing agent (lawyer or title company), it is possible to discover an unsatisfied lien or an improperly executed document from a prior sale, mortgage satisfaction, or other legal action. These items represent a cloud or title defect that should be remedied prior to the buyer's taking title. In some cases the defect is so minor that the buyer may close and take title, aware of the problem.

Closing Costs The cost of preparation of all the documents between the buyer and seller to effect a transfer between the two parties. There may be a "normal" division of these costs between the two parties, but in reality whatever is mutually agreed to in the contract is what is followed.

Cost of Living (COL) Found in many leases and in some mortgage interest calculations; also called COLA for *cost of living adjustments*. Its purpose is to make periodic adjustments in payments to adjust for increases (or less likely decreases) in the annual cost of living. The U.S. Bureau of Labor Statistics publishes a monthly Consumer Price Index that tracks the changes in the cost of living. This index is rather comprehensive and is divided by regions of the United States as well as by specific services and commodities. The usual index to be used in COL adjustments is the *All Item Index*.

A lease that called for annual COL adjustments in rent to begin at the end of the 10th year of a 30-year lease could have a massive increase in rent for the 11th year on if the adjustment went back to day one of the lease. On the other hand, if the adjustment at the end of the 10th year only took into account the increase between the start of the 10th year and the start of the 11th year, a modest and likely acceptable increase would occur. The key in understanding COL adjustments is to know which index and what base year (the start of calculations) is being used.

Emotion Emotion is the human factor that can get into the way of making a sound decision. Salespeople love to "push the buttons" that turn buyers on, and smart buyers know their own weaknesses and try (often unsuccessfully) to keep emotion out of their decision making.

Government Controls Regulatory controls in the real estate business abound, from the federal level down to local subdivisions. Every real estate investor must be aware that governmental controls and bureaucracy can greatly affect the use of and cost to use real property.

Grandfather Clause When changes in local rules and regulations are enacted, it is not uncommon that a prior use that is now nonconforming (not permitted under the changed rule or regulation) is allowed as a "grandfather right." For example, a building being used for auto repair may be in an area rezoned to allow only clean business activities, but as long as the "grandfather right" is in effect, the auto repair shop can continue to operate. But the owner may not be allowed to alter the building in any way, including replacement in the event of a fire or other casualty, without then conforming to the current laws.

Land Lease The land lease is a financing technique that is frequently used by both buyers and sellers to good effect. However, when using this technique or acquiring a property that has a land lease in effect, it is important to understand all the terms and their ramifications contained in the lease.

Seven Critical Aspects of Land Leases
1. Cost of living adjustments. Method and formula to adjust for future increases in the cost of living.
2. Subordination of lien rights by lessor to lessee or a lender. If subordination is a provision in the lease, what are the limits, if any, and how is it dealt with in the advent of new financing?
3. Default remedy. What exactly defines a default, and what are the ramifications of its consequences?
4. Options to buy or extend the lease
5. Exact dates and methods of required notices. The dates of notices can be critical, especially if they occur in the distant future. Make sure they are clear and precise.
6. Renewal options
7. Termination provisions

Management Most real estate requires some form of management, and real estate investors of income properties will quickly discover that management problems can be the number one reason why that category of property is offered for sale. Investors who own income-producing real estate are most successful when they have solved management problems.

Percolation or Perk Refers to the drainage of water into the ground. Some areas of the country have very poor percolation. If a property under consideration has to have a septic tank (because sanitary sewers are not available) or "green" areas to absorb rain water within the property, problems could occur or greater than anticipated expenses could be incurred due to poor percolation. This term is often used in a short version, *perk*.

Rising Interest Rates Adjustable mortgages can look very attractive when the rates are low, but they can rise suddenly when economic conditions change. Investors should know and fully understand the maximum that any rate can reach. Most adjustable mortgages have a cap that the rate cannot exceed over any period or for the life of the loan.

Subordination A provision that allows a lien to supersede a prior one. For example, Lucy Baker sells a vacant lot to Allen and holds back a $100,000 mortgage. Allen plans to build an office building on the lot and needs to get a first mortgage to finance the construction. Baker agrees to subordinate the $100,000 mortgage she is holding to another first mortgage to finance the building. If Allen later defaults on the new first mortgage and the property goes into foreclosure, Baker may not be able to collect anything on the $100,000 she is owed. Other examples of subordinated rights can occur in land leases, which may have subordination provisions that allow the lessee to finance over the land lease by pledging the land as security for the desired financing. A default on that mortgage could cause the landowner to lose the land in foreclosure if he or she were unable to assume or pay off the defaulting mortgage.

Tax Liens Evidence that there is unpaid tax owing as a result of IRS or another taxing authority's actions against the property owner.

C H A P T E R

3

SIMPLIFYING REAL ESTATE MATHEMATICS

T
he primary goal of this chapter is to acquaint the reader with the different kinds of mathematic calculations used by investors, to illustrate why these are so important, and to show how to arrive at simple solutions.

A simple battery-operated calculator can be used for any of the problems contained in this chapter, or for that matter, in this book. However, it is recommended that a calculator capable of printing be used. It is very easy to enter the wrong amount on any calculator, and without a printed record of all entries, checking for errors requires the calculation to be repeated.

Prior to continuing with this chapter, the reader should be comfortable with the operation of the calculator to be used. Take special care to ensure that the decimal is being inserted in the proper location to show dollars and cents.

KEY TERMS

In this section, the following terms related to real estate mathematics are defined and explained:

- Gross revenue
- Net operating income (NOI)
- Cash flow
- Debt service

Knowing and understanding these terms and issues related to them will help you to learn and apply the concepts presented in this chapter.

Gross Revenue

This is the total sum of all revenue produced by any income property. Some property owners divide the gross revenue into departmental income. For example, for a hotel the income could be segmented as room revenue, food and beverage revenue, telephone revenue, sundry income, and so on. Rental apartments may divide income between rents collected and miscellaneous income (laundry, shops, and so on).

When reviewing income and expense documentation, it is important to know the difference between actual gross revenue and gross revenue possible. Actual gross revenue reflects the collections for the period, whereas gross revenue possible assumes that the maximum income possible occurred. Neither of these amounts may reflect normal vacancy factors.

Because most rental apartments have occasional vacancies as leases expire, it is rare for the actual gross rent collected for the year to equal the gross revenue possible for the year. When these sums are equal it indicates a **zero vacancy factor**, which is either the sign of very good management or a **unit rental price** that is below the market. The unit rental price can reflect any given factor depending on what is being rented. In the example of rental apartments, the unit rental price would be the price asked per apartment (either monthly or annually). Commercial rentals for office space are usually quoted by the square foot (either monthly or annually), whereas the unit rental price for land is usually given by the square foot or by the acre.

There are only two methods to increase gross revenue from a fixed number of rental units: first, increase the amount of rent; second, reduce the vacancy factor. A combination of these two methods is the usual way to achieve maximum results.

When an investor sees a high vacancy factor or a great spread between the potential gross revenue and the actual gross revenue collected, it is likely that some or all of the following problems exist.

Possible Problems with Rental Properties
1. Mismanagement
2. Deferred or needed maintenance
3. Problems in the area that cause high vacancy rates
4. Overstated potential gross revenue
5. Current unit rental prices are too high

An investor would apply due diligence to ascertain which of the five problems existed. Clearly, problems 3, 4, and 5 would suggest an overstated value in the property being reviewed. The first two problems, on the other hand, are exactly the problems that investors often like to see because they are indications that there is potential for the investor to increase the revenue.

Net Operating Income (NOI)

The net operating income, or NOI, of any income property is the resulting sum of money left after the operating expenses have been deducted from the actual gross revenue collected. Once an investor has satisfied himself or herself that the actual income collected is reported properly, the review then shifts to the expenses to be deducted.

To increase the net operating income once the annual income is fixed, decrease operational expenses.

The problem with decreasing expenses is that it is easy to cut down on expenses by forgoing a needed new roof for less expensive, yet temporary roof repairs, or to let other normal maintenance chores fall behind. Savvy investors look closely at several years' expenses of any income property to see if there has been a trend of poor or neglected maintenance. In most cases sellers either understate their expenses or fail to account for their own time and effort, which does not represent a *real* cost of operations. The result is a misrepresented NOI.

Potential investors usually need to determine the amount of increase of the actual expenses when they acquire the property rather than ways in which expenses can be reduced. The best way for an investor to approach the deferred maintenance aspect of the property is to ascertain the cost to put the property into good shape and then add that cost to the intended capital investment. If the investor estimates that repairs and deferred maintenance will cost $50,000, the investor should add that $50,000 to the cost of the investment. Once a property has been upgraded, the annual expense to maintain the property in good repair can more easily be estimated.

Cash Flow

Cash flow is another real estate term that is often misunderstood or incorrectly used. When a seller discusses "cash flow," make sure you know which "cash flow" is being discussed. Here are the different terms expanded to clear up how this phrase can be misleading.

Total cash flow is often used to describe the gross rent a property produces. Ten apartments that rent for $1,000 a month would have a gross rent of $10,000 a month or a total cash flow before any expenses or debt service of $120,000 a year.

Net cash flow generally means gross or total cash flow less operating expenses. But take notice that debt service is often not calculated here because in reality, the return on an investment is generally calculated on the total cost of a property as if there were no debt at all. This is where things tend to be misunderstood, so let me illustrate this more clearly in the next section.

EFFECT OF DEBT SERVICE ON
RETURN ON INVESTMENT

A 10-unit apartment building is for sale at a price of $750,000. Using the example outlined earlier, we have a gross revenue potential of $120,000 a year if all the units are indeed rented at $1,000 a month. Assume that after complete due diligence the investor determines that all operational costs total $55,000 a year. Included in these costs would be every dime that is spent on the operation, maintenance, upkeep, insurance, taxes, cleaning, legal, accounting, and anything else that becomes an expense to keep the property in operation. Thus far we have a building that has a net cash flow, before debt service and capital expenses, of $120,000 less $55,000, or a total of $65,000. If the investment cost $750,000 and was paid for in cash, the investor would have a return on invested cash of 8.667 percent on his investment. This is found by dividing the net cash before debt service and capital expense by the total price.

$$\$65,000 \div \$750,000 = .086666$$

The resulting decimal is changed to an interest rate by moving the decimal two places to the right so that it becomes 8.667 percent (rounded off).

However, we have not taken into account those two other sums, debt service and capital expenses. To show a true pretax yield on an investment, all cash outlays must be taken into consideration, including total debt service plus other capital expenses.

Assume that the investor was able to obtain an **interest-only loan** of $600,000 at LIBOR (London Interbank Offered Rate), which was presently at 4.5 percent per annum. This would represent an annual interest cost of $27,000 ($600,000 × .045 = $27,000). It would also reduce the investor's out-of-pocket cost to acquire the property (the price of the property less the debt amount) to $150,000.

Contract price:	$750,000
Loan amount:	−600,000
Buyer's cash:	$150,000

However, there is now an additional deduction from the previous net operating income of that $27,000 in interest. This reduces the net cash before capital expenses from $65,000 to $38,000 ($65,000 − $27,000 = $38,000). If there were no capital expenses such as additional buildings constructed or principal payments on the debt, the return of $38,000 would represent a pretax return on the invested capital of $150,000.

In this scenario, what is the yield or return on the $150,000 invested? To calculate yield you would divide the cash return of $38,000 by the amount invested, $150,000.

$$\$38,000 \div \$150,000 = .25333$$

Now convert to a percentage by moving the decimal two places to the right to get 25.333 percent. The cash yield is no longer 8.667 percent, but 25.333 percent. This is a greatly improved return that is attributed solely to the effect of leveraging the investment by using cheap debt.

The debt service (see next section) is the actual cost of the repayment of borrowed funds, including the principal portions of any mortgage. Cash flow is strictly the accounting for actual money taken in less money paid out. It does not show the true yield on the invested funds because other factors, such as income tax and equity buildup, are not taken into account. However, cash flow is an important factor for all investors when making comparisons between various properties in consideration. Because no impetus is made to the investment by virtue of its ability to be financed, the true potential of a yield based on the total purchase price and not the investor's financed equity is still an important mark to obtain. In essence, true yields in real estate investments will vary depending on the borrower's ability to obtain favorable loans. The investor must examine how effectively a property can be leveraged and at what level he or she wishes to add risk to the investment before making final decisions about if and how to acquire the property.

To increase net cash flow with a fixed NOI, the total cost of debt service must be reduced.

This approach generally uses **creative financing** as the primary technique to reduce the actual cost of debt service. Clearly, if a $100,000 mortgage with an annual debt service of $17,000 can be reduced (or refinanced) to a total annual cost of only $12,000, the resulting cash flow would be increased by $5,000. This modest increase in the cash flow could increase the total value of that same property by $50,000 to an investor intent on earning 10 percent on his or her invested capital (because $5,000 is 10 percent of $50,000).

Debt Service

Debt service is the total amount of principal and interest that is paid to all lenders in a combined total of all mortgage payments. Many investors look wrongly at this amount and believe the debt service is only the interest on the debt.

Interest may be a substantial part of debt service, but as both interest and principal are part of the periodic check written to the lender, both must be seen as debt service, and both are out-of-pocket expenses that reduce the **net cash flow**.

In review of this key word, it is important to remember that repayment of the debt for which the subject property is pledged as security is often greater than the income that is produced by the property. In other words, more money may be required to cover the loan payments than is brought in as income from the property during a particular period of time. Other expenses necessary to hold on to the investment include a multitude of costs that will vary in category and amount depending on the type and size of the property. A vacant tract of land, for example, that is purchased as a location for a future office building may have a $1,000,000 mortgage, which even with an interest-only loan at 6 percent interest annually would be an expense of $60,000 per year. Add insurance to protect the owners and real estate taxes, and the total costs to "feed" this property could easily exceed $100,000 a year. Unless there is some way to get temporary rent from this property to offset this cost, there will be no expected revenue, or at best, a substantial negative impact on this investment.

Fortunately, all the interest on the debt is a deduction against the property's revenue to arrive at taxable income. The payment of principal (repayment of the outstanding loan amount), however, while a direct deduction from revenue to arrive at net cash flow, will not be a tax-deductible cost.

PROPERTY SIZE AND PRICE

This section introduces the units used to measure property size and to calculate land prices.

Units Used in Lot Size and Price Calculation

Land has value primarily because of its location and the use allowed on it. The value of land is usually given in one of three basic terms: square footage, front footage, or usable area.

Square Footage Price

Remember that an acre consists of 43,560 square feet. Commercial lots and building rental prices are usually quoted per square foot.

To find the square footage of lot A (Figure 3-1), multiply the length of the lot by its width:

$$193.6 \text{ ft} \times 225 \text{ ft} = 43,560 \text{ sq ft}$$

Say the price is $5.00 per square foot. To find the total price of lot A, you would multiply the number of square feet by the price per square foot:

$$43,560 \text{ sq ft} \times \$5.00 \text{ per sq ft} = \$217,800$$

Figure 3-1   Sample of square footage.

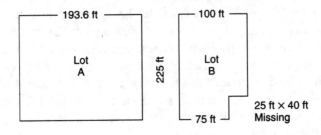

If the total price was quoted as $200,000 and the price per square foot needed to be determined, you would divide the price by the number of square feet:

$$\$200,000 \div 43,560 = \$4.59 \text{ per sq ft}$$

To find the square footage of lot B, you would multiply the length by the width:

$$100 \text{ ft} \times 250 \text{ ft} = 25,000 \text{ sq ft}$$

Then you need to deduct the area of the missing corner, which is a rectangle 25 feet wide and 40 feet long. To do this you must first find the size of the "missing" piece:

$$25 \text{ ft} \times 40 \text{ ft} = 1,000 \text{ sq ft}$$

And then you subtract the size of the "missing" piece from the square footage of the larger rectangle that contains the lot:

$$25,000 \text{ sq ft} - 1,000 \text{ sq ft} = 24,000 \text{ sq ft}$$

This gives you the square footage of the odd-sized lot, 24,000 square feet. If the price quoted is $5.00 per square foot, you would multiply the number of square feet by this to get the total cost for the lot:

$$24,000 \text{ sq ft} \times \$5.00 \text{ per sq ft} = \$120,000$$

Thus the total price for the lot would be $120,000.

If the price for lot B was quoted as $100,000 and the price per square foot needed to be determined, you would divide the price by the number of square feet in the lot:

$$\$100{,}000 \div 24{,}000 \text{ sq ft} = \$4.17 \text{ per sq ft}$$

Front Footage Price

In an area where all the property is more or less the same depth, prices are often quoted per front foot, or the length of the front of the property.

If lots A and B have road frontage of 193.6 feet and 100 feet, respectively (see Figure 3-1), these tracts, each having more or less the same depth, could be priced per front foot.

If lot A is priced at $217,800, you would find the front footage price by dividing the total price by the front footage:

$$\$217{,}800 \div 193.6 \text{ front feet} = \$1{,}125.00 \text{ per front foot}$$

If lot B is priced at $120,000, the front footage price would be:

$$\$120{,}000 \div 100 \text{ front feet} = \$1{,}200.00 \text{ per front foot}$$

Usable Area

The ultimate value of any vacant tract of land may depend on the investor obtaining maximum utilization of the site. The total square footage of the property generally cannot be used in its totality. Investors should be aware that setbacks (from the property line) are not the only element that can restrict the amount of usable land that a property owner ends up with. Other factors that affect the usable area of a property can include the following:

- **Utility easements:** These areas are reserved for public utilities, usually within front or side setbacks, but they can run through a property as well.
- **Density allowed:** Often a property that fronts along one street or avenue has a different set of requirements than its adjoining neighbor that fronts along another street or avenue.

Converting Between Different Units of Lot Size

Often it is necessary to convert between the various measures of lot size and the different methods of stating and calculating land prices.

Converting Acreage to Square Footage

One acre contains 43,560 square feet. Therefore the number of square feet in any acreage size can be determined by multiplying the number or fraction of acres by 43,560.

A tract of land consisting of 0.624 acres, for example, would contain 27,181.44 square feet:

$$0.624 \times 43,560 = 27,181.44 \text{ sq ft}$$

Sections and Townships

A section is a tract of land approximately one mile square. A quarter of a section contains *approximately* 160 acres:

Use of the word *approximately* will be clarified shortly. The United States is divided into **townships**. Each township contains 36 sections and is a square six miles (more or less) on each side. Because of the curvature of the earth, adjustments are made to some of the sections within a township that cause a slight variation in their size. However, every property in the United States is defined within a specific section or sections located in a specific township.

Converting Square Footage to Acreage

There are times when the square footage is known and the number of acres is desired. To convert square footage to acreage, divide the number of square feet by 43,560. For example, to find the number of acres in a tract of land that is 4,000 feet by 1,360 feet, you would do two calculations. First, find the square footage:

$$4,000 \text{ ft} \times 1,360 \text{ ft} = 5,440,000 \text{ sq ft}$$

Next convert the square feet to acreage:

$$5,440,000 \div 43,560 = 124.88 \text{ acres}$$

To find the number of acres in a lot that is 250 feet by 300 feet, you would first find the square footage:

$$250 \times 300 = 75{,}000 \text{ sq ft}$$

Then convert the square feet to acreage:

$$75{,}000 \div 43{,}560 = 1.72 \text{ acres}$$

Calculating the Size and Price of Odd-Shaped Lots

Sometimes the odd-shaped lot is really a rectangle with one or more pieces missing. Such was the case of lot B shown earlier that had a 25 foot by 40 foot corner missing. In this example the square footage for what would be the whole lot (if the piece were not missing) is found and the missing area is subtracted from the whole. However, many odd-shaped lots are not as simple and follow property lines that are on unusual angles or curves. Signing up for a course in geometry is not necessary for these calculations, because in almost every situation you will be able to rely on one of three simple solutions.

1. Look at county deed records.
2. Tie the price to verifiable square footage.
3. Tie the price to usable area.

County Deed Records

In most areas of the United States, the local county property records contain information that is very helpful to real estate investors. One such bit of information that, when available, is usually accurate is the gross size of the property. This information may be stated in square footage or in acreage. In the case of lots that are smaller than 1 acre, the acreage shown will be in a decimal fraction, such as 0.624 acres.

When the area is shown in acreage you may want to convert to square feet, and conversely when it is shown in square feet you may wish to covert to acreage.

Tie the Price to Verifiable Square Footage

Assume that an investor has done his or her due diligence and is satisfied that if a property can be bought for no more than $4.00 per square foot, the investment will be very attractive. The problem is that due to the shape of the property, no one, including the county property record keeper of really odd-shaped property, may provide the exact square footage of the property. In these situations the investor may draw up an offer based on the seller's estimation of the square footage but limit the offer so that it does not exceed a set price per square foot.

For example, Charlie wants to buy the north end of a block to build a medical office building. The property fronts three meandering streets and contains two wide arcs at each of two corners. The seller states that the site is approximately 4.5 acres.

First, find the total number of square feet in the stated size of this tract.

$$4.5 \text{ acres} \times 43,560 \text{ sq ft} = 196,020 \text{ sq ft}$$

Charlie knows he cannot pay more than $4.00 per square foot and have the project succeed, so he calculates the total price of the property at the estimated size:

$$196,020 \times \$4.00 = \$784,080$$

Charlie then offers $784,000 for the property ($80.00 less than the calculated price). He puts the following condition in the agreement:

> Said price to be adjusted at closing to be the lesser of $784,000 or $4.00 per square foot of the actual square footage of the property being purchased. Said square footage to be calculated by a certified property surveyor.

In this provision, Charlie has set the maximum he will pay as $784,000 even if the property turns out to be slightly larger than the 4.5 acres the seller believes it to be.

Tie the Price to Usable Area

In situations when the property must be *platted* or when *site plans* must be approved, the investor may not know in advance what the end usable area will be. This uncertainty occurs because in each of these two situations local governing authorities, such as the department of transportation, school boards, environmental groups, utility corporations, etc., may require easements or dedications or additional setbacks. As this process can be long and expensive, the investor may want to have a provision that would tie the price of the land to the final **usable product**.

If Charlie knew that in this approximately 4.5-acre commercial site for his medical office building he needed an absolute minimum area of 4.1 acres of usable land, then he would tie the offered price to that smaller number.

First, he would find the square footage of 4.1 acres:

4.1 acres × 43,500 sq ft = 178,596 sq ft

Then he would calculate the square footage price at a gross price of $784,000 by dividing this price by the square footage of the 4.1 acres:

$784,000 ÷ 178,596 sq ft = $4.38 per square foot

This indicates an increase to the per-square-foot price, but in the original contract Charlie had tied the final price to the usable land area that was allowed as a result of platting. Naturally, Charlie would show the price as "not to exceed $784,000."

BUILDING SIZE

The square footage of a building is found in the same way as that of vacant land. However, many buildings are not simple rectangles but in essence a combination of rectangles. To find the square footage of a typical home may require dividing the home into its rectangular parts and adding them once each box or rectangle has been measured.

Gross Versus Net Area

With most commercial rental property, there are two areas that are important to know. The **gross area** is the total floor space of any building. This area can be found by taking the outside measurements of the building, finding each floor's gross area, and multiplying that area by the number of floors.

For example, the outside measurements of a building 100 feet by 150 feet would give a gross floor area of 15,000 square feet.

100 ft × 150 ft = 15,000 sq ft

If the building had five stories and each floor was the same size, then multiplying the square footage of the one floor by the number of floors would give the total gross area of the entire building:

15,000 sq ft × 5 = 75,000 sq ft

This shows that the building has a total gross area of 75,000 square feet.

If this was a rental building, note that not all the area in a building is rentable. There are corridors, stairwells, elevator shafts, equipment rooms, maintenance areas, and the like. The size of each of these nonrentable areas needs to be calculated and deducted from the gross area to arrive at the **net rental area**.

In a simple, single-story building, such as a strip shopping area or **freestanding building**, the gross area and the net rental area can actually be equal. In comparing the values of different properties, knowing the spread between the gross area and the net rental area can be important. Two buildings that appear identical, with the same gross area, may vary substantially in the net rental areas. Because rents are usually based on the net rental area, a price comparison based just on gross area could be misleading. Everything else being equal, a greater net rental area would be worth more.

FINANCING

Begin with the concept of borrowing money. If Patrick borrows $100,000, someone (the lender or mortgagee) lends him the money. This person or institution expects to get a return in the form of interest earned. In addition to interest, the lender usually insists on a principal payment against the amount of the loan outstanding, either monthly or at some other set time. In the case of institutional lenders (banks, thrift organizations, savings and loan institutions, and so on) there may also be a monthly escrow payment that the lender saves to pay the annual real estate tax and often property insurance as well as other charges such as loan insurance.

If Patrick has a $100,000 interest-only loan at an annual interest rate of 9 percent and nothing more, Patrick would pay $9,000 of annual interest each year with the outstanding principal balance of $100,000 still due at some future date. Some mortgages are stated in those terms, as in the following:

> Said $100,000 loan (or mortgage) shall accrue interest at the rate of 9% per annum payable on the anniversary of the closing of said loan for a period of years shown on the note. At the end of said term the total outstanding principal shall be due and payable.

The amount of annual interest on a mortgage such as this is found by multiplying the amount of principal ($100,000) by the mathematical equivalent of the interest rate, which is the percent interest (9 percent) with the decimal point moved two spaces to the left (0.09):

$$\$100,000 \times 0.09 = \$9,000$$

A more conventional mortgage requires a payment that is a combination of principal and interest. Under the common method used within the United States, investors can use tables of computed values to determine the principal and interest (P&I) mortgage payment for most interest rates used for nearly any period of years, from 1 to 40, divided into six-month increments. The **Constant Annual Percentage Table** is available online (36hourbooks.com).

Review the following mortgage example: $100,000 is lent for a period of 5 years at 9 percent annual interest with 60 equal monthly installments of principal and interest. According to the table, the annual payment is $24,910, which equals $2,075.83 per month. The constant rate of 24,910 found in the constant rates table is a combination of interest at 9 percent and the amount of principal needed to create an amortization schedule whereby all the payments are the same for the term of the loan.

Table 3-1 is an example of an annual mortgage with equal annual payments. However, not all mortgages are computed this way. The same amount borrowed could be paid back using an interest-only annual payment with no principal repayment until the end of the loan term, or the payment schedule could have equal annual principal reduction, which will greatly change the debt service payments. Watch how this simple change from **equal annual payment** to **equal annual principal reduction** changes the amount of each year's payment.

Table 3-1 Amortization table equal annual payment at 9% interest.

Principal at start of year	Amount of payment	Interest due at end of year	Principal payment	Principal due at end of year
$100,000.00	$25,709	$9,000.00	$16,709.00	$83,291.00
83,291.00	25,709	7,496.19	18,212.81	65,078.19
65,078.19	25,709	5,857.04	19,851.96	45,226.23
45,226.23	25,709	4,070.36	21,638.64	23,587.59
23,587.59	25,709	2,122.88	23,586.12	1.47

Using Constant Rate Tables

Interest, %	24.5 yr	25 yr	25.5 yr	26 yr	26.5 yr
9	10.126	10.070	10.018	9.969	9.922

The numbers under the years are the annual constant rates for any loan of the interest rate shown for the years illustrated. In the example, a $100,000 loan with equal monthly payments at 9 percent for 25 years would have total annual payment made up of 12 monthly installments with an annual constant rate of 10.07 percent (expressed as its mathematical equivalent .1007 in the equation below). This means that the total annual debt service, each year for 25 years, would equal the constant rate times the amount of the loan at day 1.

$$\$100,000 \times 0.1007 = \$10,070 \text{ annual total}$$

But remember, the table provides the total for 12 monthly installments per year. The annual amount must be divided by 12 months to find the monthly payment. For example, for the above mortgage the monthly payment is calculated as follows:

$$\$10,070 \div 12 = \$839.17 \text{ per month}$$

Also remember that when using a percentage in a math problem, you must convert the percent to its mathematical equivalent by moving the decimal two places to the left. For example, if the interest rate was 9 percent for 26 years, the constant, as shown in the table, would be 9.969. To find the monthly payment would be a similar two-step process.

First multiply the mortgage amount by 0.9969 (the mathematical equivalent of 9.969 percent) to find the annual payment:

$$\$100,000 \times 0.9969 = \$9,969$$

Second, divide the result by 12 to find the monthly payment:

$$\$9,969 \div 12 = \$830.75 \text{ per month}$$

Using Constant Rates

Smart investors and many mortgage lenders think in terms of constant rates. These are the actual payments that include interest and principal. Because the

rate is a combination of principal and interest, it will cover the total debt service cost except for taxes and insurance when a lender generates an escrow
to collect for these as a part of the loan payment. The total debt service is
important in arriving at the final **cash flow**, which was discussed earlier in
this chapter, so learning several of the more common **constant rates** that will
reference the interest rate and term that is currently being offered in the marketplace will help to give a mental picture of the cost of the total debt service.
Readers should remember that the table available at 36hourbooks.com is not
the same as a mortgage amortization table, which does not reflect these true
costs to the investor. When using this table remember that this is a special
"insider table" that is not generally available to other investors.

YIELD

Of all the terms used in real estate investing, the term **yield** is one of the most
misunderstood and so is often used improperly. It is therefore important that
the reader understand that yield is relative to the point of view or focus.

In general terms, *yield* is a stockbroker term that references the annual
dividend or interest an investment will pay back to the investor. If you invest
$10,000 and expect a 10 percent yield at the end of the year, then you should
get back a bonus, dividend, or interest of $1,000.

As with any investment, if some of the cash you invest is received from
someone else (you borrow the money) and the cost of that borrowed money
is less than the yield you get from the investment, you have created what is
called **positive leverage**.

For example, if the property has cash on cash yield of 10 percent (if
you invest $1,000 and receive $100 return for the year, that is a 10 percent
cash on cash return) and part of the invested capital is borrowed at 8 percent,
review the comparison below:

Purchase price of income property:	$400,000
Net operating income:	$40,000
Yield on the $400,000 ($40,000 ÷ $400,000):	10 %

But if you obtained a first mortgage of $350,000 with interest-only payments
of 6 percent per year, your debt cost would be $21,000:

$$\$350,000 \times .06 = \$21,000$$

Thus the effect of positive leverage is as follows:

Net operating income:	$40,000
Less cost of debt (6% interest only):	−$21,000
Cash flow:	$19,000

Out-of-pocket invested cash:	$50,000
Yield ($19,000 ÷ $50,000):	38%

To be specific, we will discuss two kinds of yield:

- Cash on cash yield
- After tax yield

Examine each in the following example.

Calculating Yield

Bradford buys a seven-unit apartment building at a total price of $300,000. He borrows $225,000 from a local savings and loan institution at 9.75 percent interest for 30 years with equal monthly payments. He invests $75,000 of his cash plus another $5,000 for the closing cost. His cash out of pocket is $80,000. The apartment complex gives off a solid $33,000 net operating income at the end of his first year. Bradford, due to other investments and income, expects to be in the 25 percent income tax bracket.

Assume that $50,000 of the total price was for land and $250,000 was for buildings plus FF&E (furniture, fixtures, and equipment). Costs not allocated to the land and closing costs are available for depreciation calculations. Assume for the first year this depreciation amount is $11,500. How did he do on his investment? Remember, depreciation expense is based on the loss of value of the acquired asset, which was already purchased. Bradford did not actually pay out of pocket for the entire asset at closing as he used leverage with financing to pay the majority of the purchase price. However, the IRS still allows him to take depreciation during his ownership period even though the asset, if properly maintained, will likely grow in value. The IRS will take a chunk of that growth in value if and when Bradford sells the property and has to report a capital gain at a future date. (*Note:* An IRS-approved technique called "tax-free exchanges" would allow Bradford to skip having to pay a gain on a future transfer of the property. See Chapter 19.)

1. Determine the Debt Service
Use the following formula to find the total annual payment on the debt.

$$\text{Mortgage amount} \times \text{constant rate} = \text{total annual payment}$$

Access the Constant Rate Table and download the entire section, including instructions. You will use this table frequently in many real estate situations. Look at the table under the 30 year column for 9.75 percent interest. This shows a constant rate of 10.31 percent. This means that the total annual debt can be found by multiplying the mortgage amount of $225,000 by 0.1031 (the mathematical equivalent of 10.31 percent) and dividing the result by 12 to get the monthly payment.

$$\$225,000 \times .0.1031 = \$23,197.50 \text{ per year}$$
$$\$23,197.50 \div 12 = \$1,933.12 \text{ per month}$$

2. Find the Cash Flow

Net operating income:	$33,000.00
Less debt service:	−23,197.50
Cash flow:	$9,802.50

3. Find the Cash on Cash Yield
Bradford invested a total of $80,000 out of pocket. What interest rate would pay a dividend equal to the cash flow, which is $9,802.50? Use the following formula:

$$\text{Cash flow} \div \text{cash invested} = \text{cash on cash yield}$$
$$\$9,802.50 \div \$80,000 = .122531$$

Moving the decimal point shows that the cash on cash yield equals 12.2531 percent.

4. Find the After-Tax Yield
To find the after-tax yield, it is necessary to find the taxable income from this property. To do this, three other factors must first be found:

a. The mortgage interest paid
b. The principal portion of the mortgage
c. The tax that is applicable to the income from the property (taxable income)

To find the mortgage interest and principal, look at the Constant Annual Rate under the column for one year less than the years remaining in the mortgage term, in this case, under year 29. The constant rate shown for the 9.75 percent interest is 10.371. Bradford needs to find the actual principal outstanding of a mortgage that has 29 years remaining. Use the following formula:

Annual total payment ÷ annual constant rate = principal outstanding

Because the actual payment is known ($23,197.50 per year), divide by the constant, which is 10.371 percent (using the mathematical equivalent .10371).

$23,197.50 ÷ 0.10371 = $223,676.60

Original loan:	$225,000.00
Less principal at end of year 1:	−223,676.60
Principal paid:	$1,323.40

How much of the payment was interest?

Total payment:	$23,197.50
Less principal paid:	−1,323.40
Total interest paid:	$21,874.10

Now to find the taxable income, deduct the total interest paid from NOI:

NOI:	$33,000.00
Less interest on debt:	−21,874.10
Profit:	$11,125.90 (before depreciation)
Less depreciation:	−11,500.00
Profit:	(375.90) this is a tax loss
Tax bracket (25 percent):	× 0.25
Tax benefit from shelter:	$93.97
Add cash flow:	+$9,802.50
Cash benefit after tax:	$9,896.47

5. Find the After-Tax Yield

Cash benefit after tax ÷ amount invested = after-tax yield
$9,896.47 ÷ $80,000 = .1237

Moving the decimal point shows an after-tax yield of 12.37 percent. (*Note:* The actual mathematical result is 0.123705875, which is rounded off and converted to a percentage by moving the decimal two places to the right.)

The difference between the two yield calculations in the example simply points out how the debt service is taken into account as well as the introduction of **depreciation**, which is a legal deduction for the economic decline of the value of an asset. To be accurate and true to themselves, all investors should consider the fact that the replacement of assets is a real part of real estate investment. Air conditioners, appliances, roofs, windows, and so on someday will need to be replaced. While the IRS allows investors to deduct a percentage of this ultimate replacement cost every year, many investors do not take the ultimate capital cost to make those replacements into consideration. Why? Because most investors bank on appreciation of value to exceed the actual depreciation. Appreciation is *not* guaranteed, however, and when the economy slows down or real estate goes through a slump, property values can decline dramatically.

OTHER BENEFITS THAT COME WITH REAL ESTATE

In certain economic conditions investors may look to different benefits that result from real estate investments and attempt to structure their investments to maximize those benefits over others. Each of these benefits will affect the yield as well as the concept of that yield. Examine the different benefits that an investment in real estate can generate.

Twenty Benefits That Can Come with Real Estate Investments
1. Income stream
2. Financial security
3. Pride of ownership
4. Equity buildup
5. Image desired
6. Payment for staff
7. Shelter other income
8. Something for you to do
9. Being your own boss
10. Roots are established
11. Perks from investment
12. "Free living"
13. Family jobs

14. Great way of life
15. Retirement dream
16. "Free travel"
17. Security
18. Appreciation of value
19. Responsibility
20. Increase self-confidence

While many novice real estate investors do not think beyond the cash flow aspect of real estate or the "roof over their head" concept, the benefits listed, as well as others that may relate individually to a given investor, can become a primary reason why a property will appeal to any specific investor. Each person is, after all, different, and each person's goals are unique.

Equity Buildup

One of the best benefits that come from some real estate investments is the buildup of equity through the systematic reduction of debt by collection of other people's money in the form of **rent**.

Consider Bradford's apartment complex that cost $305,000 ($300,000 price and $5,000 closing costs, described earlier in this chapter). He invested $80,000 of his own cash and borrowed the remainder of $225,000. As long as there is sufficient income from the apartment rentals to pay the expenses of the property as well as make the mortgage payment, Charlie can antici-pate that when the mortgage has been paid off (in 30 years in this example) he will have an equity buildup of $225,000. That is an average principal reduction of $7,500 per year for 30 years. ($225,000 ÷ 30 years = $7,500 per year). Considering that Charlie's investment was $80,000, the equity buildup results in an average of 9.375 percent return (return of $7,500 ÷ investment of $80,000).

Appreciation

Appreciation is the increase in value that occurs when the market value of a property increases. This happens for several reasons, which will be discussed in detail in Chapter 7, but the end result of appreciation is that wealth is cre-ated that did not exist before.

If the value of a property goes up 6 percent per year, for example, for each year there is a compounding effect to the extent that in approximately 12 years, the value would double.

At 6 percent annual appreciation, a $300,000 property would be worth $600,000 in 12 years. This appreciation averages $25,000 per year over the 12-year term.

The yield that any investment will generate should not be the sole criterion in selection of which property to acquire, nor should a drop of yield signal the time to sell or otherwise dispose of that investment. In the final analysis, each investor should buy or sell based on whether or not the investment moves the investor closer to his or her desired goals.

CASE STUDY

Roberta has decided she will buy a small apartment building that fits the category of being a "fixer-upper." Roberta plans to fix and remodel the building to increase the number of rental units it contains so that she can increase the income from the property and build its value. At the same time, Roberta believes that the improved property will command a higher per-unit rental rate, adding to her income.

She has narrowed the property selection to a building owned by Jake that has four beat-up units consisting of two 600-square-foot one-bedroom apartments and two 900-square-foot two-bedroom apartments. Because the complex is in a nice part of town, rental rates are usually much higher than what Jake is getting. Each of the one-bedroom apartments is rented for $500 per month, and the two-bedroom units are rented for $700 per month.

There is a two-car garage in the back of the building with an attached utility room; this building has a total of 700 square feet. Roberta has reviewed the owner's operating expenses and believes them to be accurately stated at $14,800.

All buildings in the complex have flat roofs. The property is on a lot that is a 75-foot-by-140 foot inside lot with the front 75 feet on the street and an alley in the rear, serving the garage. Building setbacks are as follows: front 25 feet, and parking is allowed within this setback; sides 15 feet; and rear 20 feet. Figure 3-2 shows how the property fits on the lot.

The price of the property is $120,000. There is a first mortgage of $75,000, payable in equal monthly installments over 20 years at 8 percent interest. The seller has indicated he would take back a seller-held second mortgage for as much as $25,000, payable over 8 years at 6 percent interest only, with a balloon of the full $25,000 at the end of the 8 years. Interest will be paid in equal monthly installments of $125.

Complete the following:

1. What is the gross income possible for the seller?
2. With a 5 percent vacancy (5 percent of the gross potential income is lost because of potential vacancy), what is the NOI?

Gross income possible: _____

Less vacancy factor: _____

Collectable income: _____

Less operating expenses: _____

Net operating income: _____

Figure 3-2   Sample of how property fits on the lot.

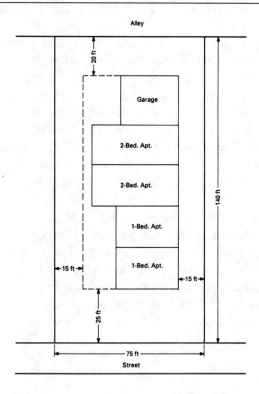

3. With the seller's current debt service and the NOI with 5 percent vacancy, what is the cash flow?

Net operating income: _____

Less debt service: _____

Cash flow: _____

4. Assume Roberta pays cash to the existing mortgage and is able to convert the garage and utility room into two studio apartments that would rent for $400 per month each and there is an additional $3,000 per year of operating expenses due to the added units. Calculate the new cash flow using the debt service offered by the seller.

Gross income possible: _____

Less vacancy factor: _____

Collectable income: _____

Less operating expenses: _____

Net operating income: _____

Existing debt service: _____

Seller-held mortgage: _____

Less total debt service: _____

Cash flow: _____

5. If Roberta buys the property for $120,000 by putting $20,000 down and assumes the existing debt, with the seller holding the balance with interest-only payments each year, for 10 years at 6 percent, at which time he will pay off the total debt, and Roberta spends an additional $5,000 to make the needed improvements to convert the garage and storage room into the two studio apartments, calculate the new cash flow and cash on cash yield.

New Cash Flow

Net operating income: _____

Less existing debt service: _____

Less seller-held mortgage: _____

NOI less total debt service: _____

New cash flow: _____

New Total Investment

Cash down: _____

Remodeling expenses: _____

Total cash invested: _____

Find the new cash on cash yield as follows:

New cash flow ÷ total cash invested = new cash on cash yield

Convert the result to percent yield.

New cash on cash yield: _____

Answer: 39 percent return.

C H A P T E R

4

HOW TO MAXIMIZE YOUR BENEFITS THROUGH LOCAL OFFICIALS

This chapter introduces the reader to the local bureaucracy that affects real estate usage and ultimately real estate values. The goal of this chapter is to indicate which officials within local government are most important to real estate investors and how the investor can develop a working relationship with these people.

After some key terms are introduced, the chapter will discuss in detail the four most important governmental areas of real estate bureaucracy: the building and zoning department, elected officials, the planning department, and the tax assessment office, as well as how to build a working relationship with VIPs in these areas.

KEY TERMS

In this section, the following terms related to local officials are defined and explained:

- Building permit
- City manager

- Department of transportation (DOT)
- Public safety officials
- Utilities

Knowing and understanding these terms and issues related to them will help you to learn and apply the concepts presented in this chapter.

Building Permit

A **building permit** is the official authorization and license needed for construction within most communities. This is issued by the appropriate governing authority (usually the building department), which generally requires plans and drawings showing that the desired construction meets all the rules and regulations that apply. In almost every instance, a fee is paid by the property owner to one or more governing authorities. A building permit to construct a home can be very involved and could require separate approvals and inspections from many departments and agencies such as the fire department, water department, environmental agencies, Army Corps of Engineers, and state and county DOT as well as code enforcement for plumbing, electrical, structural, parking, and potentially health. In most areas of the country a building permit is required for any work that exceeds a base cost. This cost can be as low as $50 and covers virtually anything from minor repairs to major construction. If several contractors or subcontractors are involved, it is also likely that each will have to apply for permits separately. The ultimate purpose for these permits is to ensure that work is done according to the building codes. This is protection for the property owner.

It is not unusual for a building to have improvements or repairs that were done without a building permit, even though one was required. Investors should pay close attention to this, as like the building codes, the failure to get the required building permit before making the repairs or improvements may become the new owner's problem.

City Manager

The city manager (or county manager) is a professional hired by the city or county to be the head of business operations. This person is not an elected official but is hired by the city council or county commission, which consists of elected officials. These professionals often retain their position for many years and are very influential and powerful within the community.

Some communities function without a separate city manager, giving that job instead to the mayor. If this is the case, voters need to pay close attention to the experience any politician who is running for this office has in city or county management. Most elected officials running for the first time for any elected office fall short on experience, and they usually show it relatively quickly in their elected term.

Department of Transportation (DOT)

This authority controls and regulates the roadways in any community. Generally there is a DOT for the local city, another for the county, and a third for the state. If there are toll roads, such as turnpikes, there may be a DOT that specifically deals with those roadways as well.

Road systems are very expensive to build and maintain, and much of the effort of any department of transportation agency goes toward the planning of future needs for the road system. Therefore DOT offices are a wonderful source of growth information. New roadways are one of the primary events that can cause property values to either skyrocket or plummet.

Because any new road or major improvement to an existing one is very expensive, these systems are planned well in advance and can provide an investor with ample lead time to invest ahead of those who have not reviewed the future roadway plans.

Public Safety Officials

Public safety officials such as the police, firefighters, and other ancillary providers such as paramedics compose what is frequently called the department of public safety. These departments are an important source of information about an area. Every investor should know how safe a potential investment area of town is. Of these offices, usually only the fire department is directly involved with real estate concerns. Generally, all new construction must meet certain local or state fire codes, and it is the responsibility of the fire department to approve the plans and "sign off" on a set of plans. This signifies that the department has approved the plans pending the final inspections it will make during construction. The fire department also makes periodic inspections of existing buildings to ensure that the property meets the necessary fire protection and fire safety rules and regulations. Every investor should know whether a property he or she is considering purchasing complies with fire codes either currently imposed or about to come into being.

Utilities

Utilities (both public and privately owned) consist of water, sewage, garbage and trash removal, gas, electricity, phone, cable TV companies, and bus routes and other public transportation. Each of these utilities has its own structure and plans for the future; each also has its own department heads and bureaucracy. These utilities can affect the values of real estate in a community positively or negatively. Clearly, the most dramatic effect would be the lack of an essential utility such as water or sewage. Each of these departments or companies is an excellent source for information about community growth.

BUILDING AND ZONING DEPARTMENT

Personnel from the building and zoning department administer the rules and regulations that are contained in the city ordinances directed to the real estate within a community. Almost everything that concerns property will come under the jurisdiction of the building and zoning department at one time or another. Therefore, the people who work in this department (which may actually be separated into two departments, one for building and the other for zoning) are excellent sources for any information about property. Even if they cannot answer a question, they usually can direct the inquirer to the right source.

Building permits are issued by this department, and it is also responsible for inspections during building progress as well as for ensuring that property is used according to the laws of the community. Within this department will be all the data necessary to discover how a property *can* be used (zoning) as well as the process for making a change in the zoning that governs property use.

ELECTED OFFICIALS

In a typical community, there are several levels of elected officials, many of whom are very important with respect to real estate. It is helpful for real estate investors to know which of these officials are influential for their chosen type of property investments in order to maximize the benefits that can be obtained from these officials, both directly and indirectly. Virtually all elected governmental officials are chosen by voters from districts: state legislators from certain counties, county commissioners from certain parts of the county, city councilpersons or commissioners from various parts of the city, and so on. Generally an investor would want to know and have the closest relationship with the elected officials from the district in which the investor lives, and the next closest with the officials of the district in which he or she invests. Because elected officials vote on matters that affect the whole community, getting to know all officials is helpful. The critical part of getting the most out of a relationship with any elected official is more than knowing that person; the goal is for the official to know you. Because this process takes time, the reader should start with the most influential areas and expand from there.

But first, look at the total structure of the government for a given area. The following is by no means a complete listing of every possible elected official, but is does indicate where readers should focus their efforts to become an "insider" to the system.

> **Federal level:** U.S. congresspersons—both senators and representatives from the districts within the state in which the investor lives and invests
>
> **State level:** State legislators—both senators and representatives from districts in which the investor lives and invests
>
> **County level:** County commissioners, port authorities (air, sea, river, etc.), school board—all are important, but the investor should concentrate on officials who are given special duties within the county commission that gives them influence over specific areas of government that affect the investor the most, such as specific road projects or water and sewage expansions. In the absence of such circumstances, the investor should begin with the commissioner from his or her district and expand from there.
>
> **City level:** Mayor, vice mayor, city councilpersons—all are important, as are the county commissioners. The investor should be selective in the same way as with the county officials.

PLANNING DEPARTMENT

At both the city and county level, an investor should seek out the heads of the departments that deal with planning for the future. The development of new roads, widening of existing roads, building of bridges, development of new intersections, changes in zoning rules and regulations, and the like are all key factors in real estate growth. All road planners, for example, take into consideration many growth trends, and most of that information is available to any investor who will take the time to get it.

Road development involves very long range planning, partially due to the fact that new roads may require long and costly acquisition of new road rights-of-way and eminent domain procedures. Also, the raising of funds, detailed plans and development drawings, and selection of contractors can give an investor an idea about what is planned or being contemplated for the future.

TAX ASSESSMENT OFFICE

The department heads within the tax assessment division or department of a local government are helpful to know because this department maintains detailed information on all real estate in the county. Data on property owners, prices paid, legal descriptions, and much more are at their fingertips.

Many tax assessors provide much "data search" information to people within the real estate industry. Title insurance companies and real estate lawyers as well as real estate investors can and do use property records found in the tax assessor's files. Within these records information is maintained that allows investors to track the ownership of a property, discover the tax assessment, and acquire a wealth of other information about the property and the property owner. Many communities maintain public access to their records via the Internet. Find out how to access those records as soon as you can—they contain valuable data for all real estate investors.

It is not essential for a budding investor to get to know the tax assessor; however, because the tax assessor is another local VIP, adding him or her to the investor's sphere of reference is not a bad idea. The most important aspect of using the tax assessor's department for investment purposes is to know what data is available and how to obtain it.

Fortunately, employees at most tax assessor's offices are very patient in teaching newcomers how to get maximum use of the data available. All real estate investors should spend a few days at the tax assessor's office to learn how to tap this vital information source.

Of all the information that is open for the public to access, the property records maintained by the tax assessor's office are the real estate investor's best friend. Most of these offices are not accessible through the Internet, and the data contained within these files is critical as it shows the history of sales, property values in relation to each other within a community, as well as ownership records, square footage, address of owners, and often their phone numbers. It is important to recognize that the tax assessed values may not be market value, however, as different communities have limitations on how much a value can be increased. Get to know what those limitations are and how to use the values shown in the records to judge the market.

HOW TO BUILD A WORKING RELATIONSHIP WITH VIPs

This section will guide you through some steps you can take to build valuable working relationships with VIPs in these areas.

Crystallize Your Self-Image

Any real estate investor who wants to establish working relationships should start with development of his or her self-image. This is important because the goal of developing a working relationship is not just to know the mayor or the head of the building department, but *for VIPs to know the investor.*

Credentials are helpful, and a personal card showing the investor's name along with address, e-mail information, and phone number provides a future communication link. Equally important is quality stationary, which is an impressive reminder of who the investor is and how he or she can be reached. Almost any print shop can design and print these items at a modest cost.

Bringing the investor's name to the attention of important people is what is essential. Remember, the KISS strategy works all the time, so when it comes to name cards and personalized stationary, fancy is not the way to go—but quality paper stock and good taste are.

Identify the People to Meet

The local newspaper usually publishes a list of the local elected officials at least once a week. If that source is not available, then see the county clerk of the court, who has a record of all elected officials within the county. Names of federal and state officials are available as general information from the nearest state government offices. Obtaining the names of building and zoning department heads and the heads of utility departments may require a direct phone call to those offices.

Seeing people in their workplace—the public meeting—will also provide insight into the type of people they are. Such insight plus later research on the background of these people at the local city library will quickly put the investor at an advantage for that impending first meeting.

Develop a Plan

Every person on the **plan to meet list** will be responsive to the request for an appointment. However, a sound reason for the appointment is necessary to avoid the awkwardness of wasting a busy person's time. To solve this problem, you should approach the situation in a clear, straightforward, and truthful manner. After all, the goal is to establish a good working relationship with the VIP because you want to buy and sell and possibly develop property within an area in which the elected official or other parties have obvious interest.

Set Up Your First Appointment

Start with an elected official within the county sector of government. The commissioner from your own district would be the best place to start. You should already know what the commissioner looks like and have done some due diligence homework about that person's background. Information to be discovered about the person should include things such as:

- Family background
- Party affiliation
- Years in office
- Other offices or positions held
- Current responsibility and authority

To set up the appointment, call the official's office in a businesslike manner and provide the following information for the appointment secretary:

- Your name
- You would like a brief appointment that should not take longer than 15 minutes
- The reason for the appointment: you intend to make investments in the official's district and would like to meet him or her first

Tips for the First Appointment

The goal of the first appointment is to meet the elected official (or other party). The following tips will help you to begin a good working relationship.

Eight Tips for Success at the First Appointment

1. Be prompt.
2. Find something to praise immediately.
3. Look successful.
4. Ask a few questions about the future for the official's district.
5. Ask for the name of two people the VIP will recommend you should meet.
6. Tell the official that you will keep in touch.
7. Do not overstay the visit.
8. Follow up immediately with a thank-you note to the secretary and the official.

Some of these tips may seem obvious, but three are absolutely critical for long-range success in becoming an insider as quickly as possible. The first is the element of praise extended at the start of a meeting. A sincerely delivered compliment is sure to start any meeting on the right track. Flattery, unfortunately, often comes across as insincere even when it is given with the best intentions. If nothing worthy of a sincere compliment can be found after due diligence in reviewing the official's history and background prior to the meeting, then praise the helpfulness of the secretary, the decor of the office, the official's reputation, or perhaps his or her attending the local university (which would become evident immediately from the framed diploma hung on the wall next to the desk).

The second important element of the first appointment is the request for *two* names of people the official feels would be worth your meeting. I guarantee that any such request will be answered with more than two "important" names. Yet, asking for two people is reasonable. Regardless of the number of names actually offered, care should be taken to obtain their correct titles, the correct spelling of their names, and the best way to reach them.

Later, these persons can be contacted with the honest approach, saying that their names were personally given by "so-and-so." Name-dropping does play a useful role in becoming an insider.

The third and most essential aspect of any contact is the follow-up. The desired result for the first meeting is to begin the process whereby a working relationship is developed. Nothing will actually come from the first meeting unless the investor initiates an active follow-up program.

Keys to Make the Follow-Up Work

Follow-up occurs in several ways. The most effective follow-up involves the supportive people around the official with whom you met, which is why the thank-you note to the secretary is so critical. Establishing a solid contact with the "right hand" of the important person is often far more effective and beneficial than having a so-so relationship with the official. This is not as easy as it might sound, however, as many secretaries consider themselves the first and primary barrier that cannot be breached by anyone other than God. The very best approach is sincerity, which should not be difficult if the primary goals are kept firmly in mind.

The follow-up to the official takes time and should not be rushed. One excellent technique is to draw attention to a relevant newspaper or magazine article during the first appointment and then promise to send it to the official. This forms a solid link that serves two very good purposes: First, it sets up a natural follow-up that does not seem forced. Second, when the follow-up occurs it proves that the investor keeps his or her word.

After the first follow-up note, the next correspondence should be brief notes describing your meeting(s) with those who were recommended as important people to meet. This simple approach will let the official know that (1) you appreciated the introduction, and (2) you are living up to your word to keep him or her informed about your progress.

It should be obvious that if two people are recommended in each appointment, your sphere of reference VIPs will continue to grow for a long time. This method of personal contact is the best and is simply accomplished.

Long-Range Contact Development

Insurance salespeople are the best at long-range contact development, and their normal routine is a lesson for any prospective real estate investor. The following three steps will ensure the success of long-range contact development:

1. Clip positive articles and send them to interested parties. Anything that would be of obvious interest to any person you have met will do. Naturally this should not be overdone, but with little effort four articles per year can be found in some local publication that would be of specific interest to a person recently met or who is on the long-term contact list.

2. Put the contacts on a "personal" Christmas list. A personalized card that has your photograph on it will ensure that the official and his or her staff remember what you look like.
3. Maintain respect for the positions of the VIPs. It's okay if they call you by your first name—in fact, you should encourage it—but never drift away from respectful communication.

5

HOW TO BECOME AN "INSIDER" TO REAL ESTATE INVESTING

The primary goal of this chapter is to illustrate the importance of becoming both a spectator and a participant in the various policy- and decision-making events that occur in a community. There are few countries in the world that possess the open form of government practiced in the United States, and yet many people in the United States take this kind of government for granted and do not take advantage of the information available to them.

Many policy- and decision-making meetings are held within every community. Some of the meetings are **workshop** meetings, in which differences of opinion among developers and building departments are resolved, or discussions on upcoming events that are made public so that local residents can have time to make formal requests or prepare proper counterproposals. Other meetings are scheduled on an as-needed basis as a result of problems that come up in city council or county commission meetings. In almost every case an agenda is published in advance of the meeting.

Reduce risk by expanding knowledge. Expand knowledge by attending city and county council meetings and becoming involved in community affairs.

Risk is reduced in any form of investing through knowledge of the subject and the causes of its value changes. A key to success in real estate investing is knowing everything possible about the growth trends of an area, the local problems, upcoming new investments, and changes in zoning or other regulations or rules that affect real estate both directly and indirectly.

KEY TERMS

In this section, the following terms related to zoning, other matters related to local government, and the real estate marketplace are defined and explained:

- Consent agenda
- Feasibility study
- Highest and best use
- Homeowner's association
- Homestead exemption
- Indemnify
- Land use regulation
- Performance bond
- Rendering
- Tax-exempt property
- Unincorporated area
- Variance
- Zoning board

Knowing and understanding these terms and issues related to them will help you to learn and apply the concepts presented in this chapter.

Consent Agenda

Most city or county council or commission meetings follow a prepublished agenda that lists the events taking place or items to be discussed at the meeting. Some straightforward, everyday kinds of items that need to be voted on will usually be lumped together into what is called the **consent agenda**, in which they are voted on en masse. Any voting member can request that an item be removed from the consent agenda if he or she wants to hear discussion on that item.

Feasibility Study

A feasibility study examines the results that can be anticipated from any specific development or proposal. Such studies are usually done for the purpose of showing the success potential of a project with the goal to enhance the developer's chances to obtain financing. However, feasibility studies can also be made for presentations before various public forums.

Highest and Best Use

The best economic use of a property with respect to what is legally and physically possible at any given time is called highest and best use. A change in zoning or other regulations may dramatically change the highest and best use. When an investor can find and acquire a property that can easily and economically be converted to a new highest and best use, the property value can be increased dramatically.

Homeowners' Association

Members of an area of town or a specific condominium or cooperative building frequently form homeowners' associations to concentrate their influence within a community and for other mutual benefits. Representatives from homeowners' associations are frequent participants at public meetings.

Homestead Exemption

Available in some parts of the country, a homestead exemption is a law that enables a resident property owner to, on application, receive a reduction from the real estate tax assessment. Its effect is to reduce the annual real estate tax on that property by providing an exemption from tax for a base value. Often this exempted value increases because of years of ownership or residency in the community or for other reasons, such as age or medical handicap of the property owner. These exemptions often have several plateau levels that increase the amount of value of a property that is exempt from ad valorum tax assessment. Those may begin with every property owner who owns a home (apartments included), and go up based on age, if the person is a widow or widower, if he or she is blind, and so on. The tax assessor's office can give you the exact details for your community.

Indemnify

Indemnify means "to agree to hold harmless." For example, when Charles is given authorization to place a sign in a city right-of-way, the city may require that Charles indemnify the city against any claims or damages that are a result of the sign. In such instances, Charles may also be required to obtain a bond or insurance policy that protects the city from damages that could occur as a result of his actions.

Land Use Regulation

Most areas of the country have detailed land use rules that are frequently changed. Much of the discussion in the public forum deals with these and other regulatory changes. Many times these regulations govern population levels and density in areas of the community. In some states the state legislature has certain levels of control over some or all of these issues. These changes can be very comprehensive or only minor. The problem with them is that public notification in the newspaper may not be explicit enough for everyone to understand the real changes. Any land use regulation change in an area where property is owned should be reviewed in detail by all concerned property owners. Many land use changes have the effect of reducing land values.

Performance Bond

When construction work is contemplated, frequently the lender and/or the city or other governing body will require a performance bond, which ensures that if the contractor fails to complete the work, the insurer will complete the work. Property owners can also require the contractor to furnish a **completion or performance bond**.

Rendering

A rendering is an artist's illustration of a proposed development or building. The developer, in making his or her best case possible before the required boards and the public, often uses renderings that are designed to win over public and board support.

Tax-Exempt Property

Certain types of ownership within a community may be tax-exempt in that the owner is not required to pay real estate tax on that property. Property owned by the community itself would be tax-exempt, and if this property is declared surplus land, the city may place it on the market in an attempt to convert it from tax-exempt to taxable.

Unincorporated Area

An unincorporated area is a part of a community that is outside legal city boundaries. These areas are governed solely by county government and may not have all the public services that are available to other parts of the county. Property in an unincorporated area often has a greater flexibility of use because the county building and zoning rules and regulations are often more lax than those of the cities in that same county. For that reason industrial businesses, junkyards, and less attractive commercial businesses are frequently found in unincorporated areas.

Variance

A variance is an approval granted by the city or county commission to enable a property to be used contrary to a building code or sometimes contrary to a zoning regulation. A community board, called the board of adjustment or some similar name, may be the group that hears a property owner's request for a variance. A variance may be easier to obtain than a complete change of zoning, but each circumstance will vary. In general economic hardship is not considered a valid reason to grant a variance. Make sure you understand the local rules with respect to your request for a variance prior to making your presentation.

Zoning Board

A zoning board is usually made up of community leaders who are appointed to the position by elected officials such as city or county commissioners rather than being elected. A zoning board hears and votes on zoning issues within the community. The zoning board is often the first step for a variance or request for zoning change. Developers interested in major projects within a community often request zoning changes so that the project will have more flexibility than is allowed in the current zoning. As a zoning change request may precede the actual project by a year or more, following the proceedings of the zoning board (sometimes a combined building and zoning board) can give an investor advance information that could be very beneficial, for example, in acquiring property that may go up in value due to the proposed project.

KNOW THE PUBLIC PLAYERS IN REAL ESTATE

Consider for a moment the people who attend the different public meetings that are held in every community. First, there are the people who run the meetings: the elected officials, city manager, city lawyers, department heads, and appointed citizens. These are the people who establish policy, make decisions, and play a major role in the growth trends and other aspects that affect the value of real estate in the area. All these people are in a position to be helpful to the real estate investors in the area, so it is very important that some time and effort be devoted to getting to know these people as well as something about the positions they hold.

Second, and of equal importance to the real estate investor, there are the people who attend the meetings, who may include the following:

- Elected officials and their staff members
- Local developers
- Homeowners' association members and directors
- Local lawyers who specialize in real estate
- Other real estate investors
- Local residents who are concerned
- People in favor of what is being discussed
- People who are against what is being discussed

No matter who they are, many people attending a public meeting will be worth knowing. Some of them are the real "insiders" in the real estate investing circles.

Every meeting can provide information that can be used to improve your chance of success in real estate investing. The key is to know which meetings to attend, what to look for, how to behave in these meetings, and how to follow up and take advantage of the information you have learned.

The **schedule of topics** is informative about what will be presented at the meeting, but it is a good idea for an investor to attend several meetings without trying to be selective. Sometimes the agenda is not very explicit about the nature of the topic, and the investor may need to experience how the meeting is run before relying on this schedule as the sole criterion to attend or skip the meeting.

Following are eight steps for making the best use of the public forum:

1. **Contact the city and county clerks.** For each of the cities or counties of interest, find out the following information from these clerks about every meeting that is open to the public.
   - Name of the meeting (city council, zoning board, traffic workshop, and so on)
   - Schedule of the meeting—the date and time
   - Location of the meeting—address and, if needed, directions and where to park
   - Usual content of the meeting
   - Name of the chairperson of the meeting (mayor, county commissioner, chairperson of the zoning board, etc.)
   - Names of all members who will attend the meeting
   - Procedure for obtaining an agenda
2. **Compose a 90-day calendar of meetings.** Start with city council and county commission meetings, then go to the zoning board and workshop meetings later.
3. **Build contacts.** After attending a few meetings, the names and faces of the other "players" (those who are already insiders) will begin to appear time and time again. These insiders will eventually be known by anyone at the meeting who is observant. At breaks or through personal appointments that can be arranged outside of the public forum, you should add these people to your growing list of contacts. It would be very rare for one of these important people to avoid giving an appointment to a person who calls and says, "I saw you at the county commission meeting last week while you were presenting your development plan for the private airport, which I think would be a great economic plus for the area, and I wonder if I could meet with you for about 10 minutes one day this coming week?"
4. **Follow up with praise.** Not everything may appear praiseworthy, and you may find your elected officials voting on issues contrary to the way you might have wished them to vote. However, the goal

of all this work must be etched in your mind: *Make contacts and develop a working relationship with the insiders.* There will be time later to take a stand on something important to you. For example, a personal note to the vice mayor, who voted against the wishes of an angry mob that packed the council chambers, can praise the vice mayor for keeping his or her poise in the face of such adverse circumstances without any mention that the sender of the note was one of those angry mob members.

5. **Be aware of all potential adverse players.** These are the local lawyers, architects, land planners, department heads, and so on who do not feel the same way as you. There may be a time when they will be representing an angry mob that turns out to protest something *you* are trying to get passed. Keep in mind, however, that these professionals may *not* actually have the same convictions as their clients, even though they may represent the clients' views in their professional capacity.

6. **Learn the procedures of the meeting.** Each item that comes before any of these meetings will follow a set procedure. These procedures are worth knowing. The clerk who provides the agenda usually has the details on the procedures. Even if a zoning petition is never filed, knowing the details that go into petition filing can be important in following an event from start to finish.

7. **Attend the meeting with the goal to meet people and make a good impression on them.** It may be impossible to know who may turn out to be an important player when attending these meetings. This means that when attending these meetings it is a good idea to treat the meeting as though it was a "first appointment" with everyone in the room.

   Of specific importance will be the dress and demeanor of the investor. Many people will recognize you as a participant if you show respect for the speakers and the other people in the room and show sincere interest in what is going on. They may view you as an "insider" right away.

Do everything possible to make a good impression on everyone at the meeting.

---

8. **Avoid taking sides.** In some meetings emotions can get very hot, and because you weren't there last week, the issue may appear to be more one-sided than it really is. Also, more people who are against an issue usually turn out to voice their opinion than those who may be in favor of that same issue. For this reason an audience may be "packed" with people opposed to or in favor of an issue who are there for the sole purpose of using public opinion to sway the elected or appointed officials and their decision.

IMPORTANT THINGS TO LOOK FOR IN PUBLIC MEETINGS

It is important for a real estate investor to attend to both the people who are present at a meeting and the agenda items that are being considered.

The People

This has been mentioned before and is worth mentioning again. A successful real estate investor can increase his or her chances for success and reduce risk by knowing both who has great influence within a community and what events are being planned that are not general knowledge to "outsiders." This is where the "people" part of the public forum comes into play. Be observant of who is doing what.

Many cities televise meetings or air them on the radio. This can be a good way to understand what is going on in the community, but it is not a good way to satisfy the purpose you want to attain. It is very difficult, if not impossible, to know who is talking, and you rarely get a full view of what is going on at the meeting. Worst of all, the people at the meeting do not get a chance to meet you. Some public meetings can even be very entertaining and filled with gut-wrenching emotion, hardship stories, sex and violence, and other types of intense issues. They are rarely boring to those who are interested in real estate investment.

The Agenda

What is the issue before the panel or council, and how does it affect you or the property in the community? Often what is decided will have no effect at all on anything other than the problem being dealt with. To reduce the number of meetings you attend once you are familiar with the officials and other attendees and the various types of meetings, look for those that deal with the following topics. What to look for when these items are brought up at the meeting is described under each topic.

Zoning

What is the problem with the existing zoning, and who wants to change it? Sometimes the government wants a change in land use (and thus the zoning must be changed). Other times a property owner or prospective buyer requests a change of zoning to improve the neighborhood or to get a better economic return from an investment. Any change of zoning may have an impact, positive or negative, even on property distant from the location that is being discussed. Follow zoning matters carefully and get all the details. If a change is going to be made because a project will have a very positive overall result, then being privy to that information early might be all that is necessary to make an investment in the path of progress.

Planning

Like zoning, planning can have far-reaching effects. Usually planning changes are slow in coming to fruition and occur only after many public meetings and much political give-and-take. Planned changes can be so distant in the future, in fact, that changes often occur along the way that keep some aspects of long-range planning in a constant flux.

Variances

A zoning variance is permission to do something that is contrary to the usual zoning rule. Sometimes a workshop conference within a building department is all that is necessary to avoid a need for a variance, but when a variance request is made, the reason for the modification to the rules should be investigated to see if this would set a trend that could either be a benefit or hindrance later on.

Platting or Site Plan Approvals

Any developer who has a major project on the drawing board may spend years in the government bureaucracy getting approvals for plats and site plans, and such approvals are usually of major import. Being aware of approval processes right from the start is a real benefit for insiders.

Traffic Control or Road Work

Each of the DOT offices in an area may hold meetings that either are a part of long-term road and traffic planning or deal with specific plats or site plans that are submitted before them. No new hospital, school, or factory, for example, is built today without preliminary discussions about meeting the needs of affected traffic and roadways. Knowing where new roads, bridges, highways, and the like are to be built is one of the keys to getting the jump on the investment competition.

Taxes (Any Topic)

Taxes—just the very word should increase the attendance of any public meeting. Investors need to pay close attention to any meeting that brings up this subject as any discussion about taxes generally centers on raising them and not reducing them.

New Construction Works

When the state, county, or city plans new construction, all real estate investors should pay attention. A new hospital, expanded airport or seaport, new public buildings, or other public construction will have an impact on property values in the immediate area of the construction. As is true of any prolonged construction project, there can be a temporary setback to existing businesses in the area of construction due to disrupted traffic flow, noise, dirt, and other problems that come from a change in the normal conditions in the area. Although these disturbances are temporary, it is not uncommon for businesses to fail while such activities are under way simply because overhead costs continue to accrue even when business income falls to zero. Owners of now vacant stores may be forced to sell, all in the face of a temporary setback that a new investor can take advantage of.

In addition, the allocation of a major portion of public monies to one project may mean that other projects, some of which an investor may be counting on, will be cut or put on hold. This can have a compounding effect for the investor who has made financial commitments based on a different timetable.

Land Plan Changes

Like zoning, a change in the overall land plan is often very comprehensive and can take a long time to be worked out. Of specific interest is how the population density is altered. Most land plans control the number of residences that can be put in a community or area of the county. These density regulations may establish a total cap, that is, a maximum number of people or residences per acre. As vacant property is developed, this density regulation is often changed up or down to fit the other services available or changes in other kinds of development in the area. These changes can increase or decrease the value of property in any given area, so investors are cautioned to be very wary of land plan changes proposed near property they own.

Building Moratoriums and Water or Sewer Hookup Moratoriums
The nightmare of all real estate developers is a moratorium that will limit development. However, insider investors can use these moratoriums as an opportunity to purchase property that suddenly drops in value if the investor is able to wait out the moratorium. Often this works nicely when a major project is what the investor has in mind because the lead time to obtain plans and then permits can be lengthy.

6

BECOME A REAL ESTATE EXPERT IN YOUR AREA

T he purpose of this chapter is to acquaint investors with what they can gain from experts in their community. The chapter goal is to help investors begin their own quest to become an expert in their comfort zone.

After introducing some key terms, the chapter will explain five aspects of working with brokers and agents that you need to understand, including how to use brokerage methods to your advantage, what investors need from their broker or salesperson, how to interview brokers and salespeople, how to get maximum benefits from a real estate agent, and where brokers and agents tend to work against your best interests.

KEY TERMS

In this section, the following terms related to becoming an expert in your comfort zone are defined and explained:

- Deed search
- Short sale
- Exclusive listing
- Exclusive right of sale

- Licensed broker
- Lockbox
- Market analysis
- Multiple Listing Service (MLS)
- Open listing
- Preview
- Realtor

Knowing and understanding these terms and issues related to them will help you to learn and apply the concepts presented in this chapter.

Deed Search

A deed search is a search of property records. These records contain much information that is helpful to buyers and sellers alike. Brokers who have computer access to the county property records can easily access this information and can provide this data to prospective buyers or sellers. The data contained in property records may vary from place to place, but the usual information available should include the following:

- **Legal description:** A typical legal description would be "Lot 10 of Block 5 of Royal Hills Subdivision, Unit A, as recorded in Plat Book (PB) 22, page 108 of Winston County Records, North Dakota." This legal description follows the usual lot and block format of recorded (or unrecorded) subdivisions.
- **Street address:** The actual street address of the property, as well as the address of the owner, if it is different.
- **Owner's name:** The name of the person or entity registered as the legal holder of title to the subject property. This can be a person, a corporation, or another form of legal entity. When a name is followed by the letters *TR*, such as "Paula Robins, TR," this indicates that the property is held by Paula Robins as trustee for someone else. Other forms of ownership may also be shown, and include JTROS, which is short for "joint tenants with rights of survivorship." This is typically a husband and wife relationship, although it is not limited to married people. It means that each party listed as JTROS has ownership rights to the entire property and automatically gains the rights of a deceased party. Another common form of holding title is with an LLC, or limited liability corporation. Any form of title may have slightly different

ramifications depending on state laws, which vary. Foreign forms of title likewise can vary even though the format or name appears the same as that used in the United States. Because of the importance of how title is held it is a good idea to make sure to discuss the method in which you take and hold title with your lawyer prior to the closing. Question the different methods you can use and what, if any, positive or negative impact the form used has toward the attainment of your investment goals.

- **Owner's phone number:** This is not always available, but the owner's phone number can be a very important part of the information when it is provided. It is possible that the owner is a corporation that may not have a published phone number.

- **Date the owner acquired the property:** Generally, the deed search will show the date the current owner acquired the property. If the property was vacant when it was purchased and the owner built on it, the deed search should indicate the improvements made and the date of those improvements.

- **Price owner paid:** There are several different methods by which property records report the price last paid. In some cases, this is done by showing the deed transfer stamps that were affixed to a deed when it was recorded. This often occurs when local or state authorities require that a tax, in the form of deed stamps, be paid on a sale. To translate the amount of the stamps into a price paid, one would have to know the formula for such deed stamps. A call to the county clerk in charge of property records would be the quickest way to ascertain the formula. When stamps are required on the deed this is a form of a sales tax and is calculated as a percentage of the purchase price. It may be possible, therefore, for the seller or the buyer to increase the amount of the stamps to show a greater amount than the actual sale price. The only benefit this could have would be to hide the actual amount paid if the seller's intention was to "flip" the property to another buyer as quickly as possible.

- **Square footage or front footage of the property:** The total square footage of both the property and the improvements are frequently part of the property records. This data is used by the tax assessor's office in determining the tax assessment of the property. Commercial and other unique properties may be listed with front footage, the dimension that the property fronts on a specific road, waterway, or other important boundary.

- **Property tax data:** The most recent ad valorem tax amount would be the usual information provided, as well as the most recent tax assessment value. Property taxes can vary greatly, and a higher sale price does not necessarily mean a higher assessed value. This occurs for many reasons such as different tax zones or changes in the millage (rate charged on the assessed value) among cities or unincorporated areas within the county or different counties. Tax data can become a very important factor in choosing between two nearly adjoining properties that front on the same highway, for example, but are in different tax zones. In areas where there are restrictions to the amount a taxing authority can increase the assessed value, the amount of taxes may not reflect the market value of a property. A review of the complete assessment should have the full information that shows the assessed value prior to calculation of the discounted or reduced value.

  Homestead laws, which govern a property owner's personal residence, are laws that offer some reduction in the tax that owner is obliged to pay. These may have different levels of deduction based on whether or not the property owner exceeds a certain age or is handicapped in varying ways, widowed, or blind.
- **Previous owner's name:** When the current owner cannot easily be reached, it may be possible to contact the present owner through the previous owner.

Short Sale

A **short sale** occurs when a lender agrees to satisfy or recast an existing loan at an amount less than the actual sum of the loan that is outstanding, to facilitate the sale of the property. This previously not often used tool became widespread in the early 2006 to 2011 financial crisis when foreclosures were at record levels. Many times, though, the term *short sale* was used to entice a buyer to make an offer with the hope that the lender would actually agree to absorb some of the loss of value in the property. Often the market price of a property was deemed less than the actual balance still outstanding on the first mortgage (or combined total of several mortgages). In these instances, and faced with the prospect and expense of a foreclosure, lenders sometimes chose the quicker method of reducing the amount of the loan rather than have to deal with the upkeep, taxes and insurance, and loss of equity in a foreclosed property. One of the overwhelmingly compounded problems is that the bank or lender that is foreclosing on the property may not actually have any equity in the mortgage as that mortgage was bundled or packaged with other similar mortgages and sold to an outside investor. In those instances, the bank may simply be servicing the loan for those investors, in which case the bank may actually be profiting by not participating in a short sale.

Exclusive Listing

An exclusive listing is an agreement between a property owner and a real estate agent showing the terms and conditions whereby the owner will pay a fee to that agent if that agent, or any other agent, performs the contract (to sell, lease, or exchange a property, or all three). Any other agent is bound to work through the exclusive agent. The owner of the property may be bound to pay the listing broker in any resulting transaction even if that broker did not bring the buyer to the seller. On the other hand, in some situations the seller may exclude prospective buyers who have previously negotiated with the seller from the exclusive listing agreement so that the seller can sell to them without paying a fee to the exclusive agent.

Exclusive Right of Sale

An exclusive right of sale is an agreement that expands on the exclusive agent contract that obligates the seller to pay the listing agent a fee in the event of a sale, lease, exchange, or any of the three as per contract, regardless of who brings in the other party. This does not prohibit the seller from dealing directly with a prospective buyer, but it does legally oblige the seller to pay the fee to the listing agent even if the seller goes to contract with a buyer he or she found without the agent. This form of listing is the usual contract between sellers and real estate agents.

Licensed Broker

Any licensed real estate broker or salesperson will have a valid document issued by the state showing that the person has met the requirements to act as a real estate agent. State law generally requires brokers to have higher qualifications than salespeople do; but each is bound by state rules and regulations governing this profession. A licensed agent who acts as a salesperson (and not a broker) must have his or her license placed under the umbrella of a licensed broker. That broker is responsible for many of the actions of those salespeople working under his or her brokerage license. Most states require that licensed brokers or salespeople who are acting on their own account, or buying or selling their own property, must disclose the fact that they are licensed real estate agents.

Lockbox

A lockbox is a lockable container that is often placed on the front door of a listed property in which a key to that door is placed to provide real estate agents access to show the property. These boxes usually have combination locks that can be set with a special code for that specific box. In theory, the real estate agent who has the listing gives the combination to other agents so the property can easily be shown. In practice, many lockboxes are used with the factory combination (usually the initials of the manufacturer) or with simple combinations composed of numbers or letters that the agency uses for all its lockboxes. Sellers should insist that specific and unique codes be used for any lockbox used on their property to narrow the risk of unauthorized entry. Some of the more modern lockboxes send signals to the agency office or other designated location showing when the device was activated and the name of the individual or company having access to the property. However, owners who allow any form of unsupervised access to their property run the risk of theft.

Market Analysis

Most real estate agents, in their attempt to obtain an exclusive right of sale from a prospective seller, will make a presentation to the seller that should contain an analysis of the condition of the market and a probable market range for which the specific property should sell. This analysis should include the following details:

- Similar property that has been sold in the past 12 months
- Similar property currently on the market
- Average time the sold property was on the market
- Price comparisons on sold and available properties

- Market plan that the agent proposes to implement
- Information about the salespeople and the firm

Multiple Listing Service (MLS)

In most communities, the local board of Realtors has a publication called the Multiple Listing Service. All exclusive right of sale properties listed by the subscribers to this service are printed and distributed among the subscribing firms. Some of these services are limited to Realtors only, so prospective buyers or sellers who feel that the service would be important should find out if the agent they are working with has that service available to them.

Open Listing

This is a listing that occurs when a seller agrees to pay an agent a fee but the agreement does not establish any form of exclusive relationship. Sellers should be aware that this kind of listing does not have to be in writing to be binding and can exist under very simple conditions. Many courts have found that an obligation to pay a fee exists even though the seller thought otherwise. If an agent can prove that there was an *implied listing agreement* by virtue of activity, by showing of the property, by letters of registration, and so on, a fee could be due to that agent in the event of a sale, lease, or exchange. Therefore, sellers should document their intentions exactly when dealing with any real estate agent. If there is already an exclusive right of sale, the seller need only refer other agents to the listing agent to avoid the possibility of paying two commissions. Investors should ensure that any relationship with a broker is clearly understood by both parties. It is best for both parties to have a signed letter or other document that outlines exactly what the relationship is, or for that matter, to specify that no relationship exists if that is the case.

Preview

A preview is the act of looking at a property prior to showing it to a pro-spective buyer. Sellers should encourage a listing agent to hold **open houses**, which are specifically for other agents to preview the property, as well as to allow prospective investors to visit the property. These open houses should be supervised to prevent theft or allowing a thief access to the property to determine if it can be burgled at a later time.

Realtor

A Realtor is a licensed broker or salesperson who is a member of the National Association of Realtors, which has a local board of Realtors in the area. Realtors pay a fee to the association, which in turn provides training programs as well as many marketing and research services for those agents. Local MLS programs may be one such service. Realtors also must agree to function under a **Realtors Code of Ethics**. This code of ethics allows Realtors to police each other over and above the laws of that specific state.

HOW TO USE BROKERAGE METHODS TO YOUR ADVANTAGE

Real estate brokerage firms may deal in residential property only, commercial property only, or both residential and commercial property. Within these categories, firms generally specialize in specific geographic areas and often in specific types of property. The critical aspect that buyers and sellers should look for is the method that the real estate firm uses as the primary procedure to obtain listings in any given area.

WHAT INVESTORS NEED FROM THEIR BROKER OR SALESPERSON

Once the investor has a clear understanding of his or her own goals, these should be broken down into basic elements to be obtained. Factors that can be delegated to the real estate agent will be the foundation for the selection of the best agent for that investor.

For example, suppose an investor decided that to meet her goals she must acquire a number of small single-family homes that could be converted into freestanding office buildings. Her geographic area would be narrowed considerably to areas that either presently permit such conversion or would allow such conversion with a change in zoning. Because this kind of investment direction combines residential and commercial aspects of real estate, it is likely that the best real estate firm to assist in finding this kind of property would be one that deals in both residential and commercial real estate.

In the selection of members of any investment team, the following six elements are the most important services that a broker or agent can render:

1. Computer access to property records
2. Area zoning maps
3. Knowledge of zoning rules and regulations
4. Access to MLS listing services
5. Time to assist the investor
6. Willingness to be a member of the investor's team

HOW TO INTERVIEW BROKERS AND SALESPEOPLE

Every investor should interview real estate brokers with the idea of finding the salesperson best suited to become a part of his or her investment team.

Locating the right real estate brokerage firm is not that difficult. A drive through an area will provide the clue: "for sale" signs, in any part of town where such signs are allowed (some parts of town or certain subdivisions may not allow "for sale" signs to be placed in yards or on buildings). The second source is the local classified newspaper advertisements. A review of the firms advertising the geographic area and type of property desired will help in identifying which firms to contact.

Ask the following eight questions. Positive responses will be important in selecting a firm and a salesperson to represent you.

First, the firm:

1. Does the firm specialize in both the geographic area and the type of property you wish to purchase?
2. Does the firm encourage and support its salespeople in a farming method? This is a systematic program where salespeople are assigned (or choose) an area that they will "farm" for new listings. This can be very much like the investor's Comfort Zone and is highly productive. In the absence of such a system, salespeople tend to "shotgun" for listings in a more random and less effective method. Clearly, the office that encourages farming of listings will be the better choice for an investor in most instances
3. Does the firm have computer access to property records?
4. Is the firm a member of the local Multiple Listing Service?

Second, the salesperson:

5. Is there rapport between you and the salesperson?
6. Does the salesperson have the time to help you?
7. Does the salesperson understand your investment goals and needs?
8. Is the salesperson familiar with the geographic area and the kind of property you wish to purchase? Does he or she have sufficient experience in the kind and value of properties you are seeking? This is critical because a novice salesperson trying to work outside of his or her comfort zone of value and complexity will not be able to represent your needs to the level you need.

A negative reply to any of these questions will weigh against the selection of the firm or the salesperson in question. The most important question is number 5. Regardless of positive responses to other questions, unless there is a good rapport between you as an investor and the salesperson, a productive relationship will not develop.

HOW TO GET MAXIMUM BENEFITS FROM A REAL ESTATE AGENT

Many factors are important for maximizing positive results when dealing with real estate agents. Review the different areas of service the real estate agent provides and how you can increase the productivity and get positive results from the agent.

General Representation

Once a firm and agent have been selected to become a member of your investment team, you should immediately make sure that the agent knows the investment goals you desire to accomplish, will concentrate his or her efforts on the kind of property you want information on, and understands what you expect from him or her. It is also important to make sure that you have not exaggerated your financial capability and that the agent understands that he or she is not the only agent you are working with.

As the agent begins to locate properties for your consideration, be sure to explain to him or her why certain properties presented are not satisfactory or do not meet your criteria to help him or her better understand what you are looking for. Once you have found a property that is of interest to you, make sure the agent knows how to negotiate offers and counteroffers. Let the agent know that you expect him or her to maintain urgency about the offer without giving signals that you are anxious. The agent should also be able to absorb the heat that is generated in an offer-counteroffer situation and vent the seller's frustration away from you.

If you are selling a property, make sure the agent seeks all viable options and will network the property to all logical firms.

Dealing with real estate agents is a two-way street. Agents make their living by being successful at closing transactions and collecting the resulting commission from the sale, lease, or exchange. A good agent knows that high priority must be given to the time spent on qualifying a prospect. If the agent determines that a prospective investor is not ready, willing, and able to close a deal, then the agent may simply move on to another prospect. An investor who finds a hardworking agent should make an effort to keep that agent interested in serving his or her needs.

WHERE BROKERS AND AGENTS TEND TO WORK AGAINST YOUR BEST INTERESTS

Brokers and their agents are motivated to make deals. To make deals they get listings and sell, rent, or exchange property for a commission. In the vast majority of transactions they handle, they are employed directly by the sellers or lessors who list their property with them. Alternatively, far less frequently, they are hired and paid by the buyer or would-be tenant to represent that party's interests in the deal.

Often the culprit in the broker or agent working against your best interest is due to the lack of education by those people who don't truly understand the state law, which defines where their fiduciary responsibilities lie and what data they can legally withhold from the other party in the transaction.

The best way to make sure the agent is working for you is to have a "buyer broker agreement" that spells out such an arrangement. Ask the next broker or agent you interview if he or she can show you an example of such an agreement. Mind you, not all brokers or agents have ever seen one, and many wouldn't know how to proceed to respond to your question. If so, move on.

HOW TO MAXIMIZE PROPERTY VALUE

7

WHY REAL ESTATE VALUES RISE AND FALL AND HOW TO TAKE ADVANTAGE OF TRENDS

Few investors ever perfect the crystal ball techniques well enough to anticipate the day the value will start to drop or the day the trend will turn around. For that reason, this book can only take you to the point where, often in retrospect, you can understand what leads to a change. The purpose and primary goal of this chapter is to introduce the reader to the concepts that affect real estate values.

The basic elements that cause real estate values to go up and down are relatively simple and generally predictable once the rules of the game are clearly understood. In fact, some of these factors telegraph their coming well in advance of the actual event. Yet, despite the simple and uncomplicated history that illustrates past increases or decreases in value, many different factors often hide the obvious or cause sudden diversions from the predictable. The single elements that are hard to predict are the magnitude of the rise or fall and the impact it will have. The timetable for these two events will never be the same for different locations in the market. Some areas lag behind the early starters in the race (to the bottom or to the top), and often it is the latecomers that make the turnaround first.

KEY TERMS

In this section, the following terms related to property values are defined and explained:

- Concurrency
- Economic obsolescence
- Highest and best use
- Land lease
- Tax shelter

Knowing and understanding these terms and issues related to them will help you to learn and apply the concepts presented in this chapter.

Concurrency

This is a relatively new term that strikes terror in the hearts and pockets of real estate investors. Concurrency means **current services for current needs**. When a county or city government decides that the level of services (road, water, sewer, school, police, parks, and so on) cannot be maintained for the population currently in an area, the government labels these regions as areas that do not meet concurrency. As a result, owners of property in this area may not build on vacant property or add to improved property. Under certain circumstances property owners can "buy their way out" of the moratoriums by paying **impact fees** that should go into the county fund to help solve the deficient service or services. Most investors argue that the impact fee is nothing more than a property tax that is not levied equally on all the property holders in the tax area. All real estate investors must be very alert to any move on the local governing agency's part to impose concurrency rules.

Economic Obsolescence

Many buildings and most of what goes into a building will, at some age, reach a point of economic obsolescence. Refrigerators, elevators, and boilers and mechanical, electrical, and plumbing systems and so on will reach a point in time when they become outdated and will be a burden to the value of a property by virtue of the cost it will take to replace those items with modern equivalents. This cost can be so onerous that modernization of the building would be more costly than razing it and starting over.

Highest and Best Use

This is an economic approach to define the best use of any site or building. The highest and best use approach is to ascertain what can be done with a specific property, either vacant land or an existing building, to obtain the maximum value based on the current economic situation. The mathematics of this approach will vary greatly due to local restrictions, building setbacks, green area requirements (area to be used exclusively for landscaping and/or ponds), parking codes, and so on, to the extent that each property is apt to have a completely different end result. Because the highest and best use determination will require assumptions to be made for future rents that can be collected, as well as estimates for future operational expenses, it is very easy for an investor to exaggerate the ultimate highest and best use of a property. A conservative approach to rents and a generous operations budget will, on the other hand, produce a far more viable project.

The very concept of a use that will produce the greatest yield is often very impractical unless the result of that use is exactly what you are looking to do. For example, if you are in the business of selling automotive tires and you want to find a location in a new town to open an outlet, your highest and best use is based on a modifying criterion of what is important to an automotive tire business. Taxing authorities often use the highest and best use as a benchmark for the value of raw land by making an assumption as to what value the tract would have if it were developed to its highest and best use. This requires far too much assumption and often imagination to predict if no one actually wants to undertake that mythical development.

Land Lease

Land that is leased and not owned is a tool used by investors to maximize their return by reducing the capital needed to acquire a property. Often sellers keep the land and sell the buildings subject to a land lease. This can be a very attractive seller's tool to avoid paying a large capital gains tax on land that may have increased in value many times over its original cost.

Tax Shelter

Any investment or investment plan that will produce a legal way to reduce annual or ultimate income taxes is called a **tax shelter**. The use of tax loopholes or legal maneuvering of ownership, depreciation, and so on generally convert present income into currently tax-free income with the requirement that the tax must be paid in the future when the property is ultimately sold. Land is not a depreciable tax item, so many investors interested in the maximum shelter from an investment will acquire property with a land lease.

SEVEN REASONS WHY PROPERTY VALUES GO UP

There are seven primary reasons why property values rise:

1. Inflation
2. Improved infrastructure
3. Economic conversion
4. Increased bottom line
5. Capital improvements
6. Supply and demand
7. Changes in permitted use

Each of these seven factors can cause a rise in the value of some real estate in an area independently of other circumstances that may also have an effect on the value of that same property. In most situations a combined effect of more than one of these factors creates the local market for property. The reader should avoid looking at too big a picture because that viewpoint may distort the events occurring in any specific area. Real estate is local in nature, and most of the factors that govern its value are often contained within the local community. What happens in New York City may have absolutely no effect on what happens in Philadelphia. Even with widespread recession or depression, the economy of the local marketplace and some pockets of the country can be booming. Conversely, even when values are skyrocketing around the country, there will be areas where values are plummeting.

The key to getting the most out of market conditions is to understand the local nature of real estate and to avoid the national "big picture" and concentrate on the local comfort zone.

In the remainder of this section we will review each of the seven factors in detail.

Inflation

Inflation is an increase in the value of any object due solely to the increased cost of replacing that item. In the example of improving real estate, the cost of the combination of acquiring the location and then building the structure today in comparison to purchasing an existing building takes into account many different factors. The cost of the land, the design of the building, building permits and fees required prior to construction, and the actual cost of construction can be more complicated and costly than in the past.

Even with the long-term increase in the cost of living, inflation has not been universal in its effect on real estate values. Other factors, discussed later in this chapter, can cause real estate values to remain steady or even decline despite sizable increases in the cost of living.

Inflation works to the investor's benefit, as it may be the single element that drives up the value of an existing property. Clearly, it is easy to understand that in a zero-inflation economy property values would become stagnate, and new development could be more attractive than purchasing an older property.

Improved Infrastructure

The changes in infrastructure in a community produce the most predictable effect on the value of real property. It should be obvious that the building of a new hospital should have a positive effect on the value of surrounding property. The development of a major public attraction such as Disney World would have an even greater impact on property values in the surrounding area. Roads, public buildings, public services such as electricity, water, and sewer systems, police and fire protection, bridges, parks, schools, hospitals, businesses that offer employment opportunities, and so on have a major, usually positive effect on the value of a property.

The changes that can occur following the development or expansion of any infrastructure within a community can be anticipated, and the investor can take advantage of these changes due to their long lead time and the historical examples that are available. A long lead time from the early planning stage to the final completion of the project occurs with almost all public works projects and most major private developments. The public forum within which all such projects generally pass gives the investor ample time to examine all the aspects of the project. A historical review of other communities that have had similar projects can give very accurate predictions of the results of the new project.

Changes in traffic systems such as new roads, the expansion of existing road systems, and additional intersections or access to highways open areas that were not accessible before and can create the greatest increase in value over the shortest period of time.

Economic Conversion

Economic conversion is when the *use* of a property changes. This change can be voluntary, as would be the case if the property owner decides to make a change in the property to improve the income from rent or services, or involuntary, which would occur when the property owner has no control over an event that causes an economic change. An example of an involuntary change is a governmental change in the zoning or permitted use of the property. If this change allowed for use that would generate greater income, then that change would be favorable.

The voluntary change from one use to another with greater economic reward is one of three factors in which the increase of value is within the direct control of the investor. The other two factors, increased bottom line and capital improvements, will be discussed shortly.

Several good examples of voluntary economic conversion are as follows:

- An investor buys a small apartment building and converts it to offices
- A single-family home is converted into three apartments
- A vacant lot is turned into a U-Pick-It Strawberry Patch
- A motel is converted to antique shops

In each case the conversion is possible either because the zoning permits it or because the investor is able to obtain permission to make the change from the governing authorities.

Voluntary economic conversion is what development and redevelopment of real estate is all about. This form of real estate investment has the greatest success potential for two reasons.

1. The investment is based on current economic conditions rather than a long-term hold as would be the case with land speculation.

2. Because a conversion from one use to another that will produce a greater income is the basis of this form of investing, the investor would acquire the property at a reduced value and increase it to a higher value with solid, predictable results.

Naturally, the investor must have the ability to perform the due diligence needed to determine what kind of conversion will work in the area and then to follow through with the legwork to bring about the conversion. Much of this book is devoted to providing the reader with the knowledge of how to accomplish economic conversion.

Increased Bottom Line

An income property increases in value if the income it produces increases. An investor who is able to increase the bottom line (cash flow) of a property will increase its resale value assuming other factors have not changed. Good property management requires an in-depth understanding of many aspects of real estate and the people involved. Once a property has reached its maximum gross income possible, the operating expenses and cost of debt service are the elements that reduce income and thereby have an effect on the ultimate value of the property. The investor must pay close attention to and make every effort to reduce these expenses, especially in the following eight areas:

- Cost of debt service (principal, interest, or both)
- Utility charges
- Vacancy factor
- Carpet replacement
- Plumbing repairs
- Advertising cost
- Janitorial and cleaning costs
- Bad debt and collections

Capital Improvements

Value generally goes up when capital improvements are made. This assumes, however, that the total value of a property will be the combination of values of both land and buildings. When the land value increases to the point that capital improvements are superfluous to the total value, then they are not a factor in value enhancement. Also, in some situations the improvements are such that the actual cost can never be recovered—as might be the case in remodeling a home that does not appeal to prospective buyers and will likely be redone by any buyer.

Because the investor has absolute control over the improvements made to a property, care must be exercised in the planning of these improvements. If the sole reason for making the improvements is to increase the value of the property, such as adding apartment units to an apartment building or adding a bedroom or extra bathrooms to a single-family home when the market demands such amenities, then the cost of the improvement must be weighed against the predictable increase in value. If the increase does not support the cost, then the choice to make the addition may not be sound.

Remodeling properties, with or without economic conversion, does not always require major capital expenditures. Many investors have been very successful looking for structurally sound properties that simply need some tender loving care, which may be nothing more than a fresh coat of paint, some innovative landscaping, or minor decor changes and improvements.

Supply and Demand

The theory of supply and demand dictates that the value of everything will rise as the demand for that item, product, service, or property rises. The theory also provides that with a steady demand, values will rise as supplies decrease, or that values will rise as long as a supply decreases faster than the demand goes down. In real estate this theory has great limitations due to the local nature of real estate values. There can be an overabundance of one kind of real estate—for example, condominium apartments in South Florida and Southern California and resort areas along the Gulf coast. If the supply in those areas exceeds a reasonable absorption rate, then the values could actually decline. However, at the same time that Florida and California have problems with the condominium market, other areas of the country could be having a boom in condominium apartments. More difficult to assess is the fact that even within South Florida, Southern California, and other areas that may be "overbuilt" in a specific property, there would be a demand for specific locations and price ranges that are contrary to the general market.

Real estate values should not be viewed as a **national statistic**. Gold, silver, and stock in IBM are but three items that can be purchased anywhere, and the influences on their values are independent of any general location where the item is purchased. Real estate is absolutely local, and investors must be careful to distinguish between national events or circumstances that can affect the real estate market and national trends or statistics that may give the impression of a rise or fall in real values.

A general statistic that the media is fond of using when discussing real estate is **housing starts**. If there is a general decline in number of new housing units being built, this can give the impression that all real estate markets are in a decline. Because this statistic is based on a total marketplace, investors need to look at their own local marketplace to see what is happening. The very fact that new homes are being built suggests that somewhere there is a "hot" market. The likelihood is that within every community, except in severe recessions and depressions, there is some location and category of property in demand.

Any given market, such as a town or a collection of nearby towns or cities, can absorb only so much of any type of service. Successful businesses pay close attention to the market absorption for their product and avoid areas where there is excessive competition.

In real estate development there is a contradiction to the prudence of avoiding excessive market proliferation. There are, for example, more office buildings and retail commercial spaces in most communities than the current market for those areas can support. The result is a high percentage of vacant office and commercial space, which results in a reduced value of those properties with high vacancies and loss of rent potential.

The contradiction is that even in these areas, new construction of more office buildings and more commercial buildings almost always occurs. There are several reasons for this:

1. **Lag time:** Some projects take years to go from planning table to construction; many projects that were planned and begun in better times are caught in the middle of economic hard times and high vacancy percentages for similar uses.
2. **"New is better" theory:** Some developers believe that even if there are high vacancies in the same type of use, a new building, center, complex, etc., will attract tenants who will want to move out of older buildings in areas of town that are no longer viable for those tenants. This concept works at times but is in direct opposition to the supply and demand theory. Developers who go headlong against the traditional concepts of the supply and demand theory are taking a risk that may not be prudent.

Changes in Permitted Use

This book stresses the connection between value and permitted use. Land will produce benefits based on how it is put to use. For most real estate investors the simple fact that there are restrictions and limitations to use of land is the magic pill that will carry the investor to heights often overlooked by the vast majority of real estate investors.

Why are these magic elements overlooked, and where do you find them? First examine why they are overlooked. The mechanics of real estate use are tied to a combination of elements that include zoning, density, parking, setbacks, storm water retention, plus other elements that may be pertinent only to your area. All of these elements are contained in the local building and zoning ordinances and development rules of any specific community. They may not be the same as those of a neighboring community. There are apt to be other governing rules and restrictions that will affect a property in a positive or negative way that come from authorities outside the local community as well, and these may be a bit more difficult to ascertain. These would include uses that require special licenses, special health department approvals, constant or periodic monitoring, or restricted distances from schools, hospitals, or churches, as well as other uses that are subject to regulation by some government body.

As you discover and examine such regulations regarding land use, within them you may find those elements that will produce a greater economic level from that which can be obtained from the present use of property you may be considering for investment. As you go through this book, it will be these magic elements that are your pole vault to success.

NINE REASONS WHY PROPERTY VALUES GO DOWN

There are nine primary reasons why property values decrease.

1. Decline of neighborhoods
2. Adverse effects of infrastructure change
3. Governmental controls and regulatory changes
4. Economic obsolescence
5. Supply and demand
6. Lack of proper maintenance
7. Drop of income

8. Inability to obtain financing
9. Urgency to sell

Each of these factors can cause drastic decline in property values. In general, circumstances work together to the ultimate effect that eventually all of these factors can occur. In this section we will review each factor in detail.

Decline of Neighborhoods

Every property occupies a location within the community that is going through change because of a wide variety of events that occur, some of which may be beneficial to the community and that location, while other events may have adverse effects on the location.

When areas of town begin to experience a decline in the economic viability of property, property owners are faced with increasing vacancy factors, which lead to reduced rents. A reduction of income from any property often means that maintenance will be reduced, and the whole neighborhood begins to slip into decline.

The initial reason these slides begin is usually a lack of good long-range planning within communities. If the infrastructure of a city is planned around sound zoning ordinances and building restrictions, areas are less likely to suffer major declines.

However, to meet the needs of a growing community, less attractive facilities such as prisons, sewer treatment plants, airports, and city dumps must be taken into consideration. The construction or development of one of these facilities is likely to have an adverse effect on an area, which in turn can trigger the domino effect of loss of rents followed by a decline in maintenance, which in the long run causes greater loss of rents and the fast loss of overall value. Only when new economic conversion can be brought to such an area will the values rise.

The factors that cause a decline in a neighborhood are usually slow in coming, and thus may not be as obvious as one might think. For example, the subtle effect of the introduction or increase of crime in an area could be the side effect of a nearby neighborhood spilling over into adjoining areas, ultimately causing the decline of what previously was a part of the community on the upswing.

Even a major impact such as the development of a new airport will cause some property to go up in value at the same time it reduces the value of other land. Clearly the investor should study the history of other communities in which airports or other major public works were built or expanded.

Adverse Effects of Infrastructure Change

As a community grows and the infrastructure of that community is increased, there can be major adverse effects on property values within the community. The impact of an airport, as already mentioned, will present both positive and negative results in some property values. The adverse effects of some infrastructure changes are relatively obvious and very predictable. Existing and already developed residential property that is under a glide path of aircraft landing at a new airport, for example, should decline in value. However, undeveloped land at the same location, which prior to the airport was zoned for single-family homes, may be changed (if the governing bodies allow it to happen) to permit use that is more compatible with the location, such as industrial or commercial use in support of the airport. When this rezoning occurs, the value of some property can actually increase in the long run even though it may decline while development takes place.

New road construction offers many such opportunities. It is not uncommon for a major highway or intersection to take a year or more to be constructed. During that time traffic might be diverted to other roads, severely limiting access to existing commercial enterprises along the roadway under construction. Even if the access is only moderately limited, the noise and dirt caused by the construction can cause a great loss of patronage to the affected businesses.

Some property owners cannot hold out long when their highly leveraged investment begins to experience sudden vacancies, and even though they know (or at least hope) that business will return when construction is completed, the reality is that a customer that starts going elsewhere may be slow in returning.

Governmental Controls and Regulatory Changes

Bureaucracy has invaded virtually every aspect of the real estate industry—so much so, in fact, that the cost to obtain permits to do many small remodeling projects far exceeds the cost of the actual project itself. Governing agencies abound, and each seems determined to exert more control than the other.

The following are just a few of the types of governmental controls or regulations property owners must contend with:

- Building codes
  - Type of construction to be approved
  - Setbacks
  - Approvals and inspections by department
  - Bathroom sizes
  - Licensed and approved contractors
  - Fees
- Zoning ordinances
  - Site plan approval
  - Uses allowed or not allowed
  - Green area
  - Parking codes
- Health department controls
  - Materials used
  - Ground to be tested
  - Well water and septic tank approvals
  - Restaurant and food service inspections
  - Fees
- Fire department regulations
  - Plan approval
  - Fire protection provided
  - Maximum persons allowed
  - Inspections
- Setbacks
  - Site plan approval
  - Possible building height regulations
  - Possible establishment of green area
- Environmental controls
  - Tests and studies to disclose possible environmental problems with the site
  - Approvals required prior to building permit
  - Fees

- Army Corps of Engineers
  - Approval prior to building permits (if they are required)
- Department of transportation
  - Possible involvement of city, county, and state DOTs
  - Regulation of road access
  - Possible major impact fees
- School, hospital, or parks departments

A change in any existing rule or regulation that governs any of the above can throw the real estate development industry into a grinding halt. Building moratoriums occur even when a study is under way about a possible change in a rule or regulation.

An investor who purchases real estate today based on yesterday's rules and regulations may wake up tomorrow to discover that the property will no longer meet his or her investment needs. This factor has changed investor thinking about raw land and long-term speculation, requiring far more detailed study than in the past when any opportunity along the path of progress was a good and profitable investment. With even short delays in starting a project, the high cost of holding onto property can eliminate the economic benefits the investor anticipated.

Some communities make it known that they are anti-development. This is a political stand that is often well supported by the residents of an area. In such locations there is usually a trend whereby building rules and regulations are constantly tightened to the extent that new development becomes next to impossible or at least not economically feasible. The changes can be very subtle and not appear to have the effect they do. For example, a beachfront resort community in Florida has over the years reduced the building height allowed from 10 floors (for apartment buildings and hotels) to 45 feet in height. At the same time, the parking codes have been changed so that owners of commercial buildings cannot count the public parking areas provided by the city in front of those buildings as a part of their allocated parking. The end result is such that virtually every existing commercial building does not meet present-day codes. While the current use is grandfathered in, any thought of remodeling a structure may require the property to meet the current (and increasingly tougher) codes.

In contrast to this community's attempt to reduce density, another beachfront resort community, also in Florida, has gone the other direction and has become pro development. In this community, developers have had it their way for the past several years to the extent that too much development has been going on. Both of these communities now are struggling with properties that cannot be sold at anywhere near their all-time high values. The community that was anti-development saw developers throw the towel into the ring and move on to other areas to develop. In the community that opened the door to developers, they flooded in, and now there are buildings with hundreds of unsold condos, as well as unfinished projects that no one can touch because there is no financing available to build condos that will not sell.

All governmental controls are instituted in the name of public betterment, and to be sure the vast majority of such controls are effective in maintaining a high standard of development with public safety keenly in mind. Nonetheless, investors should pay close attention to the local trend.

Economic Obsolescence

Everything from design to the equipment contained within a building may reach a point at which it is no longer economically viable for that property. Constant repair and maintenance can add many years of life to each part of a building, and in fact the style or charm of an older feature may actually add to the value of a property. However, the cost to keep up an old elevator or maintain out-of-date plumbing may well exceed the relative cost of replacement with modern fixtures.

When a property is not properly maintained and the equipment fast approaches economic obsolescence, the value of the property is reduced by the anticipated cost to replace these out-of-date items. Many investors fail to consider the age of many of the parts of a building that will eventually need to be replaced. They consequently overpay for the property based on the current income and expense figures without taking into account the future cost of replacement.

Supply and Demand

The law of supply and demand is a double-edged sword that can cause increases in value as well as drive prices right into the ground. On paper the supply and demand theory of a market is rather simple and easy to adjust to. If the product in question is doughnuts, for example, a bakery can adjust to make the kinds of doughnuts that are in demand on a daily basis. The method of determining the demand is to look at the remaining stock at the end of the day and keep track of what sold out first and the number of requests for the types of sold-out donuts. The next day the situation is corrected, and new adjustments are again made based on the demands for that day.

Products that take longer to plan and fabricate, however, require more analysis to determine what kinds of marketing and design will satisfy the demands of the future marketplace. Fashion clothing is one of the most difficult products for supply and demand planning, and often the manufacturer must *create* the demand through extensive advertising and promotion.

Real estate is fixed and cannot be moved from where it is not in vogue to another part of town or the country where it would be in demand. Doughnuts and clothing, after all, can be moved from one place to another to adjust to market differences. The factor of permanent location, coupled with the magnitude of the investment, causes long recovery periods when the law of supply and demand drives property values down.

The following are two major factors of supply and demand that cause real estate values to go down, or at best to remain at the same level.

• **Overbuilt market:** The term *overbuilt* says it all. There is more of the item or product on the market than current demand can absorb in a reasonable time, and property values tend to drop. The difficulty here is defining a reasonable time. In the "hot" days of the California real estate market, it was not unusual for an entire subdivision of several hundred homes to sell out in a matter of a few weeks or months. In a moderate market several hundred homes may take several months to sell.

• **Tight money:** Tight money comes from causes such as recession and depression, expensive or unavailable financing, and lack of confidence in the market. If this occurs when the real estate market is also overbuilt, the market can decrease quickly and stay down for a long time. Because tight money has the effect of bringing *new construction* to a halt, the excessive number of properties on the market must experience a drop for the market to show any real move upward.

The availability of long-term financing is the absolute key to real estate development. Institutional lending is structured with three major control points imposed by the lender: restrictions on the type of loan issued, the interest charged, and the term of the payback of the loan all affect the ability of the buyer to repay the loan.

Lack of Proper Maintenance

A run-down home in a nice neighborhood is an obvious example of what poor maintenance can do to the value of a property. Worse, it can also affect the values of properties that adjoin it or are across the street from it. Worse still is the fact that this may be a trend that, if left unchecked, could result in the decline of a whole neighborhood.

The gems in the rough of real estate investing are single-family properties that are no longer adequately being taken care of. Inadequate maintenance happens for many different reasons, some of which are as follows:

- Absentee owner
- Owner has other, more pressing priorities
- Poor management
- Owner cannot afford the cost
- Tenant is overlooking his or her obligations
- Ownership dispute

In each of these situations, the end result can be the same: a deteriorating property. If an investor is able to find a property that is going downhill for one of the above reasons, that property may represent a sound investment that could be *turned around* relatively inexpensively.

Drop of Income

Income from a property can drop for many different reasons. Roadwork that shuts down traffic to a building or a chaotic financial meltdown of which the world is still feeling the impact will both do the trick quickly. When the drop of income causes the net operating income to drop below the fixed expenses for the property, disaster for this real estate and its owner is quick to occur.

Inability to Obtain Financing

When money goes into hiding, banks and lenders begin to shun the typical outlets to increase their own revenue. They look to the high-end loan, credit card loans, and the like that rake in tons of cash. They borrow cheap money from the government and the people who have some cash but nowhere to invest it. We live in a credit world, which is sad in one way because the only ladder out of a stagnate economy is to spend more to jump start it.

Maintaining high leverage in investments is a way to make it big when the times are good. But high leverage when things get tough is a quick way to the end of the rope. The only conservative approach is to always use long-term fixed-interest debt and to maintain a reserve of cash to carry you over the dry periods.

Urgency to Sell

Unlike a block of IBM stock, most real estate cannot be sold at a moment's notice. It is well known that the instant a person *must sell* is the very moment when the wolves arrive at the door.

Real estate investors look for situations where the seller is highly motivated. The greater the motivation to sell, the better the deal the investor is likely to get. This is so important that when there is a hint of urgency, there can be great excitement directed at getting a bargain deal. What should not be overlooked is that if the seller knows and understands how to use this urgency to his or her advantage, the end result desired, which is the sale of the property, can be accomplished.

Bargain sales are often a compromise between the price and terms of the transaction. A highly motivated seller may reduce the price but get all cash, or get the full price by offering easy terms or taking another property as all or part exchange in the deal. Each of these is an alternative that sellers will have to sort out to decide which will move them closer to their goals.

Smart investors watch for property owners who must sell when the seller's motivation is strongest to make a deal. And all investors try to avoid ever reaching the moment when they are forced to sell quickly.

C H A P T E R

8

THE PHRASE "LOCATION, LOCATION, LOCATION" IS "WRONG, WRONG, WRONG"

The real key and primary goal of this chapter is to illustrate that the *importance of a location* to the investor's intended use is what is critical. Of this, the actual location is only one-third of the equation. The other aspects are the use that can be put on that location and whether the governing authorities, or the laws and rules of development in the community, actually approve that use. This chapter will show the reader how to distinguish good locations from poor ones according the criteria of the ultimate use. But for land speculators who have no actual use in mind, this chapter will also show you what elements you need to look for to maximize values in the future, because what is most important is the discovery of the subtle differences between a good location and an *important* one.

Each of these factors is relative to any given need. A vacant commercial lot, for example, has a different economic value for different users *even though they may have the same type of use for the property.* This means that one hotel chain may be able or willing to pay more for a site due to the nature or clientele of the intended hotel in comparison to what another hotel chain could or would pay. Each hotel company would evaluate the geographic locations they might consider purchasing based on their concept of what is essential for their brand. Often the criteria have more to do with market dominance than physical attributes. This is why it always seems that if one drug store, bank, or fast-food business acquires a corner of an intersection, another will pop up across the street on another corner.

On the other hand, timing can be the element that makes or breaks a decision between several alternatives. Because time is a function of value, an investor should weigh the added cost of the time it may take to convert one of several seemingly ideal land acquisitions into a desired development. Clearly, if all other aspects were equal, a two-year battle to obtain the required permits to build would send the investor running to the property that needed little time to proceed.

It is often in retrospect that we say "location, location, location"; after all, location is a critical aspect of any decision process to buy a property for investment purposes. There are many factors that, for your specific goals to be met, you need to consider, and the following statements should be carefully reviewed before you buy any real estate.

Seven Truths About "Location, Use, and Approval"
1. No single location is perfect for every use.
2. The best location for a Burger King may not be any good for your intended use.
3. Even supersmart investors have had to throw in the towel trying to fight the establishment in attempts to receive approval for what they want to do, even when the zoning indicates the property is suitable for the investor's intended use.
4. If you do not know what you want to do with a tract of land, then perhaps you should not buy it.
5. Always have an exit strategy in mind and use it to help you purchase according to the needs of your goals.
6. Remember, even a landfill trash dump is a sign of progress, but it may not enhance the value of the land around it.
7. It is possible that the existing use is hiding the many potential uses for which the property is better suited.

KEY TERMS

In this section, the following terms related to location are defined and explained:

- Centers of employment
- Centers of entertainment, education, and recreation
- Access (visual and actual)
- Corners
- Crime statistics
- Demographics
- Approvals
- Impact fees
- Traffic count
- Population shift

Each of these terms plays a role in the ultimate determination of the importance of any given site or location as it relates to the specific investor's need and use. Knowing and understanding them will help you to learn and apply the concepts presented in this chapter.

Centers of Employment

One of the first elements I choose to look at in a community is where the centers of employment are and what kinds of employment opportunities they represent. For example, diverse employment opportunities may present a greater diversity in the mix of employees who will wish to live in an area, or high-tech employment centers may offer a greater spending capability because they attract people and other job opportunities. Employment centers also are a governing factor in traffic flow and allow predictability in what times of the day the traffic is heavier or lighter and which directions traffic is most advantageous for your use of a site. Depending on the nature of your planned investment, property that is located between the employment centers and the bedroom communities will have a more stable future, and as both the bedroom communities and the employment centers are already visible and in place, the predictability of traffic flow is already established. However, this fact may offer opportunity outside this area due to rising congestion and lower-cost land beyond either the bedroom communities or the employment centers. In this instance, the investor would look to what other factors will come into play that will help funnel traffic in certain directions. Natural boundaries such as a shore, river, mountain, swamp, or other geographic block can make the investor's choices easier to make.

Centers of Entertainment, Education, and Recreation

These three elements have similar draw factors that channel people to and from them. It should be obvious, however, that their impact on your goals will differ. Some centers may satisfy both entertainment and recreation, as Disney and other theme parks tend to do. A new university or a new branch of a state university system can provide all three elements for the students it serves and the staff and faculty it employs. As these kinds of ventures can take many years to develop and millions of dollars spent in the community, I recommend that all investors pay close attention to such expansions. The best way to do this is to stay in touch with colleges and universities in your state to be early on the list of potential investors who learn about these things long before they are announced in the local newspaper.

Access (Visual and Actual)

When it comes to most real estate, and in particular commercial real estate, poor access, either visual or actual, can mean the difference between a great location and a very poor one.

The question of access goes beyond the site itself because the kind of access may vary depending on the actual use. For example, the values of homes within a subdivision may vary greatly depending on the type of access to the subdivision. If the roads leading into the subdivision are private, well landscaped, and at the same time not traffic ways leading through the subdivision to some other area, then the property values are almost sure to be higher than those in an adjoining subdivision that has access off a major highway crossing the area.

Some commercial properties have excellent visual access, such as frontage on main highways or turnpikes, but by the time prospective patrons of businesses find an exit from the highway and locate those businesses, the advantage of visual access may be negated. At best, a possible user or tenant for such a location would have to weigh which of the two accesses of that site, visual or actual, was the most important.

Corners

In every commercial site at current or future intersections, there are two types of corners: the near corner and the far corner. (See Figure 8-1.)

As you approach an intersection, the first corner on your right, no matter which direction you are traveling, is called a **near corner**. This corner is the first one you approach and the closest to you as you enter the intersection. The **far corner** is the second corner on your right that you come to when driving straight through an intersection.

If all corners of an intersection are the same size and access to the sites from the traffic ways is equal, the two far corners, as defined by the most trafficked of the two streets making up the intersection, will generally have the greatest value. This is because as traffic approaches an intersection, the farthest corner on the right is the most visible and the driver has more time to position himself or herself to turn into the business at that location. This visibility and ease in access gives the driver a second or two longer to anticipate turning into an entrance at that corner. This is important to drive-in restaurants and gas stations, for example, because when all four corners are developed, the far corners will have that extra second or two of advertising pull. One disadvantage that can occur with any corner is that the governing Department of Transportation (DOT) may limit or prohibit a **curb cut** from the road to the site. This limitation or restriction results from a possible traffic hazard that could be caused by people trying to turn from a fast-moving traffic lane into the site. If the site has sufficient frontage on the highway, a **right-turn storage lane** into the site becomes critical. This storage lane gives high-speed traffic time to decelerate before making the turn to the right. While this may appear complex, several factors are important.

Figure 8-1   Example of corners

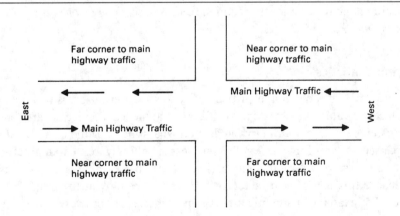

First, if the property does not have enough frontage on the highway, access could be greatly restricted or prohibited altogether. Second, even if there is enough frontage, the road right-of-way may not allow sufficient width to construct the turn storage lane. Third, the cost of such construction with possible deduction from the site itself to contain the lane could be more than the use would warrant, provided the DOT would approve such a storage lane in the first place.

Some DOT authorities have taken an interesting position about medians and permitting U-turns at intersections. I have noticed that in areas that previously had median cuts, or no medians at all, traffic access to a business located along such a traffic way was relatively easy. Then along comes some super-DOT, and medians are added, with no right or left turns permitted. Individuals wishing to pull into the parking area of their favorite businesses may have to drive half a mile to make a U-turn, or go around three blocks or more to get to the other side of the street. All of this has an impact on the access to a property you may want to purchase. As a redo of the medians will likely be in the planning for several years, make sure that the property you are interested in purchasing will not be adversely impacted by plans for future changes that are already approved. If you own a property on any street that presently has easy access, stay on top of this issue so that the moment the DOT starts to plan a beautiful median with a mile of unbroken trees, remember this section in this book and voice your disapproval. Demand to know why they are going to take away your customers' easy access to your property.

An investor who has immediate use for a site should obtain the necessary approvals for the needed turn storage lane or permits for curb cuts and ascertain that the cost for the required work is acceptable *prior to the closing on the purchase of the site.*

Crime Statistics

There should be no doubt in anyone's mind that high-crime areas will greatly reduce the value of a property. An afternoon at the local police department's statistics department will provide data on what type of crime is going on in a particular part of town. Very few businesses willingly locate in high-crime areas, and when a "good" neighborhood goes "bad," values go down fast. Because this is a proven factor, it is important to look at the trend in the area. For example, a site might be 100 percent perfect in every aspect, and the area may even have a moderately low crime rate; however, watch out if this area adjoins an economically declining neighborhood.

One factor that can cause a sudden rise in crime rate is a dramatic change of traffic patterns. While new roads can turn a property into a gold mine, those same roads can cut off a part of town that was on an upward move. Access can become difficult, and in some cases the area may be isolated from other parts of town that are "okay." Overnight this "good" area can shift into a declining neighborhood.

When new roads, bridges, overpasses, changes in intersections, and so on, are in the planning stages for areas near property being considered for investment, the investor should carefully review all potential changes.

The local DOT offices can provide information on what future works are already planned and approved, as well as on potential changes that, although not yet planned or approved, are moving ahead without opposition. That lack of opposition generally is simply that no one knows what is about to be made public.

Demographics

Demographics are elements that pertain to the characteristics of an area. It will contain information about the people who live in the area and will include race, sex, age, number of people per household, population density, wage-earning strength, employment statistics, percentage of white-collar and blue-collar workers, and percentage of residents that are unemployed. Most of this information is available through various local planning offices or within the development departments of local utility companies. Many county tax assessor offices track this data and make it available to anyone who is interested. A real estate investor will look at the area that surrounds any possible comfort zone or investment location to see the pattern in that location. The review of statistical information is most useful when comparisons of time and location are taken into consideration. By plotting several years of demographic change, a **trend** may emerge, which will be like a crystal ball in foretelling the future of the location.

Approvals

Ownership without use is, although this sounds like a contradiction, against the law. It seems that many communities have become more sophisticated in their attention to detail, and as it is generally a trend to become anti-development, because those who got there first don't want any more changes now that they have had their way, the government in power looks for ways to maintain that power and the control that comes with it.

It is sad to say this, but much that goes on in community planning and growth is not something that the public really wants. It just happens because the public is often ignorant of the impacts and the complications that result from poorly thought out progress.

Impact Fees

Some communities have discovered a new way to "tax" property owners without calling it a tax. They call it an **impact fee**. These fees are charged to investors or property owners generally prior to development of a specific property. However, some communities assess these impact fees on a less predictable basis. Generally, the impact fee is levied because the development of a property causes an adverse impact on the rest of the infrastructure of the community. This impact may be an increase in traffic on roads not designed to carry the number of cars currently traveling on them, or the creation of more demands on utilities or other public services than can currently be met.

The importance of these impact fees is that often the investors may not be aware that a major hidden cost could await them before they are able to develop the "ideal" site they were lucky to find. These fees can be very high and could make the property no longer ideal.

As would normally be sufficient to discover a concurrency problem, investors should check with building departments in the local community for any outstanding or pending impact fees. If there are such fees due, the investor needs to anticipate the amount of this added cost and determine if the site is still cost effective for the intended use with the added expense.

Traffic Count

Traffic counts are studies of the number of cars that pass a location or intersection during a 24-hour period. Usually the counts are done over a period of a week or month, and the average number of cars per day is determined. The direction in which the cars travel can be very important to determine which of the far corners would be best for a user who needs maximum exposure and easy access to traffic. Many different governmental departments take traffic counts. By contacting the different DOTs within an area, an investor can find out if there has been a recent traffic count for any specific area. Usually the best information is obtained through a study of traffic counts around the area and not just a review of one count right in front of the prospective location.

The time of day and direction also are important as to when peak traffic is strongest. Some businesses thrive better in afternoon and early evening traffic, while others prefer the morning to midday.

Population Shift

Population shifts for many different reasons. Some communities have seen a move from the cities to the suburbs and a change back to the inner city. Some population shifts can be anticipated, and investors can plan future investments based on a clear understanding of what causes population to shift. The reader has already been introduced to many of the reasons for population shifts. In a very simplistic look at population shifts, people tend to move toward a less complicated way of life and away from problems, such as a move from the cities to the less densely populated suburbs or to a more rural area. As the problems and complications of life have followed them to the suburbs, however, and life is now a battle with traffic and distances, people tend to seek the less stressful nature of living close to employment and services. This factor opens doors for urban redevelopment, which is something I do not recommend that any novice investor consider.

HOW TO DETERMINE THE IMPORTANCE OF LOCATION

The importance of any property to a specific investor, at any given point in time, is controlled by three circumstances: the purpose for the investment, cost versus income produced, and contributing factors that affect value. A review of each of these three factors illustrates the steps an investor can take to determine the importance of a prospective location from his or her point of view.

Purpose for the Investment

There are two basic real estate investment strategies:

1. Buy what you need when you need it.
2. Speculate on long-term value increases.

Each of these strategies has many followers. The real estate developer can be either or both depending on the development, but many commercial investors whose properties include but are not limited to fast-food restaurants, gas stations, and franchises of any product or size fall into the immediate user investor category and rarely speculate on the outcome of sites they acquire.

If the investment is for immediate use, the investor has the least chance of making a mistake if proper due diligence is undertaken. The property's value now can be determined far more accurately than what it might be ten years from now. The long-term effect of future roads and master plans, to name just two potential steering forces, are very critical to both methods of investing. Despite the importance of such effects, most immediate users who buy what they need now often overlook the review of these longer-term trends and discover too late that had they looked under a few more stones, they would have found that the "ideal" location was actually in a trend of decline.

Flexibility becomes the critical factor for the speculator who buys a tract of land in anticipation of future needs. These needs may not be predetermined, or the purpose may be solely directed toward a profit in a future sale. The best long-term plan for any site is to anticipate more than one possible use for the property. As economic trends change, other factors develop that can turn the future factory site into a golf course community. The greater the flexibility, the less the risk in any long-term land acquisition.

Cost Versus Income Produced

In every investment, the desired return on the investment must be considered. In the case of the immediate user, the economics are relatively easy to calculate because the investor is dealing with a current situation. The capital investment needed to buy the property, and if required, to construct buildings or other improvements, can be estimated, and income and expenses determined through recent experience. As long as there are no hidden impact fees or moratoriums on construction, the cost versus income produced can be accurately anticipated. A comparison of available properties can be made that could lead the investor to the best property to buy.

For example, suppose the Burger Magic fast-food restaurant franchise company knows the gross income one of its restaurants should produce with a given set of criteria (such as traffic count, demographics of the area and of the traffic, and trends for population growth for the area). Property selection would be a relatively simple matter of adding all known costs for the construction of the facility to the acquisition cost of the site:

	Site A	Site B
NOI anticipated	$180,000	$160,000
Cost to build facility	$400,000	$400,000
Cost to acquire land	$600,000	$400,000
Total cost	$1,000,000	$800,000
Yield on investment	18%	20%

Yield on investment is calculated without debt service:

$$\text{Yield} = \text{NOI} \div \text{total cost}$$

In this example, site B would be the better investment if all factors were more or less the same. An improving trend for B would make it a great buy.

Do Not Rely on Long-Term Projections

Short time spans in projections are important because too many unknown factors can affect the property over the long term. Smart investors like to get a 20-year picture of what "seems" to be happening from growth and development trends, but the range of future projections and pro forma plans on which one would make a decision should be limited to no more than five years from the day the operation or use would begin.

The real estate speculator who buys land or improved property antici-pating an increase in value must spend the most time at due diligence. The total cost to hold onto a property includes more than the initial capital spent to acquire the property. These holding costs include financing cost, impact fees, tax increases, and additional capital investments to maintain a tempo-rary improvement. While the speculator takes the greatest risk when acquir-ing a property that may take 10 years or more to reach the level of value the investor wants, with prudent planning some or even all of the holding cost can be covered by the property itself. For example, in acquisition of large tracts of farm land that is clearly in the path of growth from expanding towns on two or more sides, it may be possible to rent out the land to farmers or plant a tree farm that can provide income during the holding stage. As an experienced investor in such tracts, I have been successful in that strategy, even to the point where I could sell off a prime corner of a much larger tract to recoup all of the up-front costs to acquire the bigger tract.

Contributing Factors That Affect Value

There are a multitude of factors that affect value. These factors range from
zoning and rezoning to density changes, traffic counts, trends in the area and
surrounding neighborhoods, and master plans for future development. These
factors are most difficult for the investor to compile, but all information
necessary to ascertain the likely trends for an area is available to investors
who seek it out.

When speculation is the investment purpose, the investor should study
the trends that are developing in any given area without a specific use in
mind, looking instead at a number of possible future uses. The immediate
user compiles the same data, but this investor applies the study to a specific
use and makes investment decisions based primarily on the cost-versus-
income viewpoint.

Important locations from the speculation point of view must be based
on the growth trend that is currently evident as well as the historic patterns
of growth for the area. Some communities seem to grow naturally toward
residential or commercial use. The long-term investor must look at neighboring cities to see which of the two divisions of use is moving toward the
intended investment. It is not uncommon for one community to be expanding
with residential use toward another town that has industrial growth closing
the gap. This can occur because the major job market is the growing industrial sector and the neighboring city is the residential source for workers.
When these two growth sectors collide, the residential area could be affected
adversely. Therefore, if the trend is a dynamic commercial growth, the investor should look to that part of the market for the greater profit potential. On
the other hand, if the commercial expansion is reaching its growth potential,
then the residential sector may prove the better opportunity. But remember,
other criteria may affect this, perhaps a natural barrier such as a river or
highway, that may cause one use to stop expanding.

C H A P T E R

9

THE SECRET TO POTENTIAL INCREASES IN VALUE IS ZONING

The primary goal of this chapter is to show the reader how to interpret zoning ordinances, use them, and change them to the investor's advantage. Many real estate investors recognize that a real estate developer will pay more for a tract of land that is ready to go with the kind of project the developer wants to build. Because there is no guarantee of approval or even the time to get a project approved, developers often prefer to let someone else take that up-front risk in time and effort. Therefore, be mindful that one way to profit is to take a property from one zoning category into another that offers more potential.

KEY TERMS

In this section, the following terms related to zoning are defined and explained:

- Density
- Grandfather provisions
- Planning and zoning board

Knowing and understanding these terms and issues related to them will help you to learn and apply the concepts presented in this chapter.

Density

Every residential zoning provision has some regulation that governs the maximum occupancy density of development for any given property. In these cases, the density may be defined in terms of the number of "families" that can live per acre on a tract of land. In rural areas, this limitation may be set as so many families per number of acres, such as "one residence per five acres." In more urban areas the density may use other formulas; one that is quite popular is the FAR, or floor area ratio, which generally is applied in different formats. It is important to understand all the ramifications when dealing with this kind of density formula. The result is to give a developer the maximum square footage of a building that can be constructed on a site. For example, in the advent of a FAR of 4, without knowing any more we can assume that the development can create 4 times the square footage of the ground floor area, which is allowed by taking into consideration setbacks and other limitations or regulations that would be applied. If those limitations established a ground floor of 10,000 square feet, then the FAR of 4 would allow the developer to construct 40,000 square feet of building. Whether or not that would also include required parking is another matter that the building department would have to define.

In the case of multifamily property, it is usual for the density to be established with a set number of units that may not be exceeded—such as 12 units (family units) per acre, or through a more complex square footage allocation per number of bathrooms or bedrooms constructed. The square footage allocation is a more restrictive form of density, as it can greatly limit the number of units that can be placed on a property depending on the size (number of bathrooms or bedrooms) contemplated.

Grandfather Provisions

Grandfather provision are allowed violations to current zoning ordinances or building codes because the existing structure was built prior to the existing rules and regulations. These provisions present hidden hazards for investors because while they may be allowed now, a needed change in the building (desired expansion, repair, or rebuilding due to a fire or other casualty) may require that the entire structure then meet the current rules and regulations.

In some cases, the change can be as simple as a change of use, say, from an office building to retail stores. The only protection an investor has to ensure against these hidden hazards of grandfathered provisions is to follow these two steps:

1. Check the zoning and building codes as they apply to the property in its as-is condition. If there has been a change in codes or zoning that allows the property to continue in use in this as-is condition, this may be due to its "grandfathered" status. Have the city officials give you a letter that outlines your obligation if you purchase the property and want to change the use away from its grandfathered rights.
2. No matter what the results are of item 1, insert a provision that the seller warrants that no conditions are grandfathered in that would otherwise be building code or zoning ordinance violations, and if any do exist, the seller will adjust the price to pay for bringing the property up to present codes.

Planning and Zoning Board

This board comprises citizens of the community who have been appointed by the city council or county commission (depending on the level of the local authorities in question) who review planning and zoning matters and give their recommendations to the city council or county commission for further disposition. When the investor initiates a petition to change the zoning of a specific property, this board is usually the first step. The procedure before the planning and zoning board may vary between different local communities, but in general, the stages are as follows.

The Six Stages of a Rezoning Petition
1. A petition or application for the zoning change is filed with the city or county clerk (depending on the governing body). A fee is paid to start this process. A checklist of required information accompanies the petition. Usual material includes the following:
   - Legal description
   - Owner's name and address
   - Recent survey
   - Existing zoning
   - Zoning requested

2. A workshop session may be requested by either or both the community staff or the petitioner to consider the reason for the change requested. This is advisable because many potential difficulties may be modified in advance of the actual submission of the formal petition. These workshop sessions also give the investor insight as to how the community staff will view the intended project that to move forward, needs a change to be made in the development rules.
3. The petition is placed on a future agenda and is properly advertised according to the state laws for such events. It is customary that these rules require a 30-day advance public announcement and written notification of property owners within a certain distance from the property.
4. On the day the petition is presented to the planning and zoning board, the petitioner has the right to make a personal appearance (or have professionals do this with or for him or her) to present his or her case. The public, having been notified of the petition, can come to the meeting and speak out for or against the petition. It is not unusual for the audience to be predominantly against the petition. Generally, the staff members who have participated in the workshop sessions or other meetings with the developer will voice their approval or disapproval and give their reasons for their decision.
5. Depending on the local rules, the petition can be deferred to another meeting, sent to workshop meetings to iron out problems, approved with or without conditions, or passed on to the council or commission without the approval of the planning and zoning board. The final approval must come from the elected officials within the city council or county commission.
6. The investor or his or her representative appears before the commission and the requested change is voted in or out or held over for further review. If it is approved at the first "reading," generally it will require at least two meetings to confirm a zoning change, and even then a third meeting may be required. These delays are a safeguard so that a new zoning change has sufficient time to be opposed.

USE REZONING TO INCREASE VALUES AND LIMIT RISK AT THE SAME TIME

While zoning establishes the basic use for any given location, there is generally some flexibility within the zoning ordinances, or the investor can seek to create flexibility, giving added investment potential. If the flexibility in the actual zoning still will not permit the desired construction or use, the investor may want to attempt to change the zoning of the property to a classification that would allow the desired construction or use.

Some Communities Encourage Development

Some communities encourage real estate development and tend to have a good "let's work it out" attitude within the building and zoning departments. When an investor encounters this kind of cooperation, variances or zoning changes are easier to accomplish than with a community that is against all changes. An investor should quickly discover which of these two attitudes prevails. It is possible that one community can be closed to all changes while a neighboring town can be open to reasonable changes that will bring growth and employment.

Reduce Risk by Obtaining a More Flexible Zoning

The name of the game is to increase value and at the same time reduce risk. Because a zoning change is likely to ensure an increase in value, if an investor can tie up a property knowing the value will go up when the zoning is changed, then the investment will have very little risk. However, the risk will not be zero because of the cost and time involved and because not every petition for rezoning is successful. The key to obtaining required changes is to know and understand the local political attitude about granting variances and zoning changes and to have an in-depth working knowledge of the zoning ordinances.

THE INVESTOR'S SIX STEPS TO OBTAIN A ZONING CHANGE

Following are six steps you can take to increase the value of an investment property by obtaining a zoning change.

1. The Property

Find a property in which a slight increase in zoning category will produce a profit by allowing a new use or uses of the property that make it more valuable to buyers. The type of property that will work best for such an investment is determined by the market and availability.

2. Preliminary Homework

Sit down with the city manager and/or one of the city council members you know and discuss the proposal. Explain the intended use for the property and what must be changed to permit that use. The first meeting may provide clues about what these people feel their city really needs. If the original plan does not fit within those needs, you may wish to shift the plan so it has a better chance of being approved. Working with the flow can be more productive than fighting city hall.

3. Tie Up the Property

Contracts to purchase with contingencies that give the buyer an out or use an option, can work well in allowing the investor to have control over the property without having to buy it until the zoning has been altered to the investor's best interests. The investor should have a firm agreement with the seller before proceeding with any rezoning petitions. Once the process has started, the property value can increase simply because the idea becomes public knowledge.

4. Have an "Out" in the Contract

If the final decision to buy into or walk away from the deal depends on a zoning change or variance, it is essential that the investor has some kind of out or escape clause in the agreement that will give him or her the option to close on the transaction or not. To do this the investor must make the contract contingent on success in obtaining a zoning change. An example of a provision conditioned on rezoning follows:

> The buyer, at his expense, will promptly file a petition with the proper governing authorities to change the current R-3 to R-4 Zoning. This change allows the site, which presently can contain 30 multifamily units not to exceed a total of 35,000 square feet of living space, to contain 40 multifamily units not to exceed a total of 50,000 square feet of living space. This contract is conditioned on the buyer obtaining this rezoning without conditions, or if conditions are imposed as a part of the rezoning, the buyer must be in agreement with such conditions to the rezoning. The buyer has a period of 260 days in which to obtain this rezoning, after which, if not successful as aforementioned, the buyer may elect to withdraw from this agreement and have any and all deposits refunded, or the buyer may elect to proceed to close under the terms of this agreement as though the zoning conditions had been met.

Making the contract conditioned on actual approval of building permits to build the intended structure moves the investor into an even stronger position. This will take longer than just getting a zoning change, and many sellers are reluctant to allow their property to be tied up for such a long time. The time issue may be dealt with by giving certain plateaus in the transaction, each of which has its own timetable. For example, a contract that allows the investor 180 days to get the rezoning and an additional 180 days to get the building permit may facilitate the transaction by giving the investor incentive to move the process along. At the same time, once the zoning change has been obtained, the seller knows that the value of the property has been increased even if the investor is unable to get a building permit, and it is unlikely that the investor would get to this stage and then abandon the project (although this is still possible if some problem has arisen such as the investor's financing drying up).

5. File the Rezoning Petition

The investor should now proceed to effect the changes required by way of a variance or zoning change. A variance, when it will work, is often easier to get than a full zoning change. However, this will depend on the situation and the kind of cooperation available from the planning and zoning department and the city or county commission.

6. Close on the Contract

Close according to the contract once the petition for change is granted and approved by all the required governing bodies. This action gives the investor a vested interest in the property that will make a sudden shift by the local governing bodies to rezone the property very difficult.

HOW TO DEAL WITH THE REZONING PROCESS

Unlike learning to fly an airplane, there is no school that teaches the process for obtaining rezoning. The actual procedure to follow may vary depending on the community and the local disposition toward the specific rezoning being changed and what will replace it. This book illustrates the importance of this procedure and gives the reader the necessary fundamentals, but each local community is so different that some "on-the-job" training is not only helpful but also critical. Because getting to know the workings of the local bureaucratic process is a necessary task for successful real estate investors, the reader will find that attending both planning and zoning board meetings and city and county council or commission meetings will provide lessons that can be later copied when the investor becomes the petitioner when his or her own rezoning petition is filed.

A check with the clerk at city hall will generally provide a schedule for all public meetings held by the city and county departments. Agendas of these meetings are not always printed in advance, but the clerk usually can provide the information over the phone a day or so in advance of the meeting. If matters concerning variances and rezoning are to be presented, the investor should attend the meeting.

At the meeting, the investor should make a list of all the board or council members. The city lawyer is usually present, as will be other officials who tend to the tasks of recording the session, handling paperwork, dealing with security of the session, and so on. At times, department heads or their assistants from different sections of the local government are present when their input is required to provide insight about an item on the agenda.

The investor will be able to get background information on each of these members from the city or county clerk. This background information may give clues about topics of mutual interest that will aid the investor's approach in making personal contact with members who may later be influential or helpful in giving advice on a zoning problem or voting on the rezoning petition soon to be presented.

Review the following section of a multifamily zoning ordinance.

SECTION 47-13.1.0. "R-4-C" DISTRICT*

Sec. 47-13.10.1. Purpose of district.
The R-4-C district is a planned high-rise, high-density hotel and tourist residential district. It is intended for locations, such as parts of the beach, where it is desirable to encourage hotels and motels and other tourist-related facilities because of the importance of the tourist industry to the city and also to preserve and enhance the appearance and image of the city. Because of the relationship of such areas to non-tourist residential areas, traffic and transportation facilities, beaches and parks, and other community facilities, special provisions are required to allow such areas to be utilized for high intensity tourist facilities and insure a development consistent with a high quality tourist resort area. Those provisions depend on the details of site and building design and include the use, appear-

ance, height, bulk and location of principal and accessory buildings, and the location and design of landscaping, open space land and water areas, recreation areas, parking areas and other features. Therefore, review and approval of a development plan are required to insure such provisions will be provided. (Ord. No. C-77-166, § 1, 1-3-78)

Sec. 47-13.10.2. Uses permitted.

No building or structure, or part thereof, shall be erected, altered or used, or land or water used, in whole or in part, for other than any use hereinafter set out:

(a)   Any use permitted in R-4, if approved by the planning and zoning board, except hospitals and nursing homes.

(b)   Accessory buildings for use as convention facilities, restaurants, bars, nightclubs, and recreation facilities located on the same site as a hotel or motel of one hundred (100) or more guest rooms, when approved by the planning and zoning board. Prior to approving such use, the board shall make a finding that such use is consistent with a high quality resort area and that the location will not be detrimental to nearby properties.

(c)   Commercial or private recreation facilities such as pitch and putt courses, tennis courts, shuffleboard courts, boating and similar, provided the planning and zoning board finds that they are consistent with high quality tourist residential use of nearby property.

(d)   Museum or cultural facility, including commercial art galleries, studios, and similar. (Ord. No. C-77-166, §) 1, 1-3-78)

Sec. 47-13.10.3. Special accessory uses.

(a)   Hotels, apartment hotels and motels having fifty (50) or more units may have restaurants, nightclubs, dining rooms, or bars which are of such design and size as to cater primarily to the guests of the main use, subject to the provisions of all ordinances of the City of Fort Lauderdale and subject to limitation of sub-paragraph (c) of this section. Patio bars and food service areas shall also be permitted, subject to the foregoing limitations and subject to the prior approval of the planning and zoning board, which shall consider the following factors:

(1)   The location of the proposed use on the property;

(2)   The impact of the proposed use on the abutting properties;

(3) The adequacy of the parking for the proposed use; and

(4) The compatibility of the proposed use with existing land uses in the surrounding neighborhood.

The planning and zoning board shall grant, deny, or approve with specified conditions, the application for the proposed outdoor use.

*Editor's note—Ord. No. C-77-166, § 1, enacted Jan. 3, 1978, repealed former Section 47-13.10, §§ 47-13.10.1—47-13.10.10, relative to the R-4-C district, derived from Ord. No. C-74-73, § 1, adopted July 2, 1974, and enacted in lieu thereof a new Section 47-13.10, §§ 47-13.10.1—47-13.10.10, pertaining to the same subject matter.

There is much about a parcel of land that might have this zoning that is not said in the above ordinance. There are many rules and regulations that need to be ascertained from the building codes, which are separate from the zoning rules. The building codes will determine issues such as just how much parking must be available, what kind of garage (if one is needed) can be used, setbacks, traffic flow, and so on.

10

DEALING WITH BUILDING CODES AND RESTRICTIONS

Building codes and restrictions have a profound impact on real estate values. The primary goal of this chapter is to show how these codes and restrictions affect the current and future values of property and to discover how to deal with the local building department. The key is to discover how to avoid and overcome problems that occur due to possible violations of building codes. Building codes and restrictions, which include zoning ordinances, tend to become more restrictive over time. These changes may cause older properties to be in violation of the new codes. This can create a "time bomb" of expense when the unsuspecting investor acquires a property that must now be improved to meet these codes.

KEY TERMS

In this section, the following terms related to building codes and restrictions are defined and explained:

- Building department
- Building heights
- Encroachments

- Fire codes
- Green area and landscaping requirements
- On-site water retention
- Parking codes
- Property setbacks
- Deed restrictions
- Site plan approval
- Compatible use
- Survey
- Utility and access easements

Knowing and understanding these terms and issues related to them will help you to learn and apply the concepts presented in this chapter.

Building Department

Virtually every community has its own building department or shares one with a neighboring city. The building department reviews building plans and issues building permits for construction. It also maintains records of past construction when permits were issued. Because the permit may indicate the estimated cost of the improvement or construction, it is possible for investors to double-check statements given about the cost of such improvements. The building department also inspects construction to ensure that the work continues per code and as the submitted plans indicate.

During construction, periodic inspections are made, and until the work has been approved, that affected portion of the construction cannot continue.

Building Heights

Many communities have height restrictions as a part of their zoning ordinances. Some fire codes limit the height of buildings for certain uses. However, building codes can also restrict height by applying economic restrictions and interpretation of code restrictions.

Economic restrictions occur when the cost to build higher floors becomes disproportionate to the income potential from the added structure. Building code requirements for elevators, interior fire stairwells, types of construction, sprinkler systems for fire protection, and the like become more expensive the higher the elevation. This added cost may not be offset by added income from the extra space constructed, thus effectively limiting building height.

Building codes can also limit building height through **interpretation of elements of the code**. For example, some communities have a shadow law that is part of the building code restrictions. This provision may prohibit any building from casting a shadow during certain hours of the day on adjoining or nearby property. If the investor desiring to construct a high-rise building owns enough property to contain the shadow, however, the restriction of height caused by the shadow law would not apply.

Encroachments

When a building or other structure extends past a property line onto, over, or under the adjoining property, an **encroachment** occurs. Some encroachments are obvious and appear on the survey. Sometimes encroachments are less obvious, such as a septic tank drain field that crosses a property line but is underground and not visible until, for example, the neighbor digs it up while installing a swimming pool. There are six primary reasons encroachments occur:

1. **Improper survey:** An error is made with the location of the property boundary, and as a result of this error construction is completed in the wrong place.
2. **Miscalculation during construction:** Measurements in plans are misread, property lines are incorrectly drawn, or another mistake is made that unintentionally results in the encroachment.
3. **Division of property after structures are in place:** A property owner cuts up a farm or other property for sale as separate lots, and one or more of the buildings encroach over the new property lines.
4. **By design:** A building may extend across a boundary on purpose to serve the needs of both property owners or for some other reason. This may have been okay at the time the encroachment was created, but a problem can exist for new owners unless an easement was granted for the encroachment.
5. **By nature:** If a property line is a natural boundary such as a river, a change in the river can create an encroachment.
6. **Due to regulation changes:** If there has been a change in setback requirements, it is possible that an existing building may be in violation of the new rules.

When an encroachment occurs without the property owner's permission, legal proceedings may be initiated by the owner of the property being trespassed. All investors need to be sure before they buy a property that there are no encroachments onto other property.

Fire Codes

In many communities, building plans are reviewed carefully for compliance to fire protection codes. Because fire protection has improved due to new technology and more stringent fire codes, most structures over 10 years old may not meet the current regulations. Unlike other building codes that may allow the structure to be grandfathered "as is" without the requirement to upgrade to current standards, most fire codes become absolute requirements, and many unsuspecting investors have discovered, after the closing, that the state requires their newly purchased building to have fire sprinklers installed in every enclosed space within the building. And it may not be just the cost to bring the building to current standards that hurts—this kind of construction can require the closing of the building for a period of time, which may mean the loss of income from rents when the new investor needs it the most. Worse still, the building may take some time to recover the possible loss of tenants.

Normally when there is a major change in a fire code that would require an existing building to install fire sprinklers, the owners are given several years to comply. A property owner who has not complied in hopes of selling the property to save a $50,000 cost, for example, may be a highly motivated seller. If this is the reason for the sale, and the investor *knows* of the fire code regulations, then he or she need only take the future cost into consideration when negotiating for the building.

Green Area and Landscaping Requirements

There is a growing trend for cities to require more green space and landscaping around buildings. Green area is the amount of land area that cannot be used for anything except landscaping or sometimes water retention (ponds or lakes). This is often stated in the form of a percentage of the property—for example, "25 percent of the land must be green area." In some circumstances it may be possible to use this green area or to design it to be functional, such as gardens that separate buildings, tennis courts, putting greens, and other public areas for apartment buildings. Sometimes the required green area is a calculation based on several factors, such as the square footage of the building and/or its use. Landscaping requirements can be very detailed, even to the exclusion of certain kinds of plants or the requirement for specific plants to be used. Because many communities are trying to improve the aesthetic nature of some commercial areas, in particular vast parking lots, it is possible that an investor may suddenly discover a city requirement to plant trees and other landscape areas around the parking lot that serves a just-acquired shopping center. This is another "time bomb" expense that is easy to check in advance.

On-Site Water Retention

As storm drainage is often inadequate to handle major rainfalls, many communities have enacted strict water retention rules. What this means is that a property must be able to provide on-site percolation of rainwater when adequate drainage to a storm system is not available. It is surprising how much area it takes to accomplish this, and many projects are not economically viable to meet the needs of these codes.

Parking Codes

Parking codes are part of the building rules and regulations and govern the size of spaces allotted for vehicles in open or garaged parking areas. The codes generally provide different layout formulas that allow 90-degree parking as well as angular or parallel parking formulas. Drives and traffic ways for entrance and exit from the parking areas to highways and roads are also controlled. Some communities allow parking to consist of a surface that allows water to percolate into the ground, whereas other communities do not. The amount of parking and its purpose can be a limiting factor that needs to be considered early in the planning stage of any building or development. Factors such as the number of handicapped parking spaces, compact car areas (smaller spaces that allow more cars to park than with normal parking sizes), and loading zones are carefully controlled. The number of parking spaces needed to meet *use* requirements is also critical. Restaurants and other such facilities generally need to have a minimum number of parking spaces that relates to a formula of "service area" or number of customer seating. Doctor's offices and many other office uses generally must meet other minimum parking codes in order to qualify for an occupational license.

Property Setbacks

Most communities have required setbacks from one or more property lines. Setbacks are the distance structures must be situated from a property line. These distances are generally shown within the zoning ordinances for each specific kind of zoning and may vary for front, rear, and side boundaries. Corners are usually treated as two front setback lines.

Generally, the only structures that can be constructed within the setback lines would be walls and fences of limited height, driveways, utility lines, landscaping structures, and walkways. Each of these items must be constructed according to code. Encroachments into setback areas can create a building code or zoning violation and potential title problems later on, so every new construction should be watched carefully so that it does not violate these setback boundary lines.

Deed Restrictions

Other restrictions can be added to the deed that limit building design, prohibit "for sale" signs, prohibit animals over a certain size, require white roofs, limit or prohibit the sale of tobacco on the property, and so on—there may be no logic to a deed restriction. Usually these restrictions are designed by the developer of the subdivision or the seller of any property to enhance the area by creating stricter standards than the local zoning or building codes establish. The problem with deed restrictions is that they may not be evident, despite the fact that to be valid they must have been properly recorded and would therefore have become a part of every deed unless limited by state statute or by the restriction itself. A deed may contain a clause that references deed restrictions that were recorded on a past date without actually listing the deed restrictions. Failure to check those deed restrictions can become another hidden "time bomb" investors may face.

Deed restrictions require someone to enforce them to be effective over a long term. In the beginning, the developer, who is still selling within a subdivision, is the truant officer watching for violations. Later, long after the developer is gone, the trend is to ease away from the deed restrictions, but another property owner can—and sometimes will—insist on strict adherence to a deed restriction. Any seller can place a deed restriction when transferring a property; therefore it is necessary to check all transfers within the time limit that a state may establish after which deed restrictions automatically become invalid.

Site Plan Approval

The site plan is an architectural drawing that shows the footprint of the building, and sometimes the elevation views that show what the building will look like, with all roadways, traffic flow, parking spaces, utilities, fire protection, and landscaping indicated. Once the site plan has been approved, the working drawings for the building can be completed and presented for the building department to review prior to approval of the building permit.

Compatible Use

There is a fairly new catchall term that many building departments or city and county commissions use when they determine that a proposed project should not be approved and they cannot find a code or building regulation that will prohibit it. The term is *compatible use*. No matter what the actual verbiage is, the concept is that a new building or project should be compatible with the existing buildings or projects in the neighborhood. This sounds good, but a strict application of this kind of rule would dictate that in a slum only slums could be built. Property owners need to be careful of arbitrary and vague rules.

Survey

The survey is the licensed surveyor's drawing of the property that becomes the initial layout for all plans. Most building permits require surveyors to locate and verify that the corners of structures and all subsoil work (plumbing, electrical, septic tanks, drains, and so on) have been placed in the proper location with respect to the survey. When this is done correctly, it prevents encroachments. A survey may be a subdivision of a residential neighborhood that shows roads, lots, and blocks of area where houses or other structures can be built. The survey of an individual lot may simply be identified as Lot 9 of Block 25 of the Cummings Heights Subdivision. The overall subdivision and possible out parcels may be shown as part of what was a 10,000-acre ranch. The survey of the ranch may be identified by a metes and bounds survey that is linked to a government monument some distance from the actual boundary of the ranch. These government monuments exist across the country and are the prime points of beginning of many metes and bound surveys. As land is surveyed away from one of these monuments, surveyors may choose to begin at a point located on an adjoining survey. However, in modern times many surveys are made with the surveyor taking his starting point from a marker or survey monument at an adjoining property. These markers are often pipes in the ground surrounded by cement, and they may not be permanent and may have been set in the wrong place from the beginning. A survey that has an incorrect "point of beginning" will have incorrect boundaries and will be likely to result in future encroachments.

Utility and Access Easements

An easement is the right granted by a property owner to one or more parties for the use of a portion of a property. Utility lines such as water, sewer, phone, gas, and electric lines all pass through, over, or under property. Sometimes there is a utility easement that runs across part of a property. This easement was granted at some time in the past by the owner of the property at that time. It might have been a requirement to get a building permit, to plat the property, or to give a concession to the utility companies to ensure service to the property. Access easements often are a roadway or pathway that when in use is clearly visible. A previous property owner often grants these easements to himself or herself before selling off a portion of a property that would otherwise block entrance or access to the remainder. Properties in recreational areas that have beach, lake, or river frontage may have public or private easements that cross the property.

All easements should show on a recent survey, and the actual document showing the grant of the easement should be recorded in the county records. However, if the surveyor has not done a good job in checking the recorded documents at the local property records archives or if the survey occurred prior to the recording of the easement, the survey can be in error.

PRECONTRACT CHECKLIST

All investors who have already gone to contract on a property should use the following checklist prior to closing on that property. *Review this list prior to every offer made to acquire a property.* If there are items on the checklist that should be part of a contingent provision, make sure your purchase, lease, or option contract is clear on that issue.

Remember, a seller may be motivated because he or she knows something the investor should know.

---

1. Does the property look the same as it was represented both verbally and visually?
   a. Improvements:
      Was construction done according to code and with proper permits?
      Check the date of improvements.
      Building plans should match the actual improvements.
   b. Property boundaries:
      Walk them off according to the new survey.
      Compare them to the old survey.
   c. Encroachments:
      Do any encroachments appear on the recent survey?
      What has been done about any old encroachments?
2. Review possible or current building or zoning violations.
   a. Check for existing violations.
   b. Check for pending or future violations that will result from code or zoning changes.
   c. Be sure to check long-term required changes:
      Fire code changes
      Landscape changes or additions (green area requirements)
      Sign changes (type and size of signs allowed)
      Road access changes
      Traffic changes
3. Review property tax assessments:
   a. Are there property assessments that have not yet been paid?
   b. Have future assessments been discussed but not yet levied?
   c. Are impact fees or replatting costs required before improvements are made?
4. Review the deed and association rules for any restrictions.
   a. What are the deed restrictions?
   b. Are current deed restrictions in violation?
   c. Is this property part of any association?
   d. What are the association restrictions?
   e. Are there any association rules violations?
5. Have the title examined by competent advisers.
   a. Is the title clear of any liens?
   b. Review exclusions in the latest title insurance policy.
   c. Are there outstanding clouds on the title?
   d. Do the *legal description and dimensions* match both the title and visual inspection?

6. Have the building inspected by competent advisers.
   a. Roof—check for repairs and problems.
   b. Structure—check for cracks and code violations.
   c. Electrical—check for code violations and problems.
   d. Appliances—check for function.
   e. Gas lines or tanks—check for code violations and problems.
   f. Termites—check for damage or insect presence.
   g. Plumbing—full and comprehensive inspection.
   h. Pumps and sprinkler systems—check for function.
   i. Check zoning and code compliance.
   j. Compare property lines to survey.
   k. Other (per local conditions and codes).
7. Review all documents under which the buyer has obligations:
   a. Mortgages and notes
   b. Insurance policies
   c. Leases
   d. Warranties
   e. Deeds and deed restrictions
   f. Employment contracts
   g. Service agreements
   h. Work orders
   i. Other

11

DISCOVER THE MAGIC OF ECONOMIC CONVERSION TO MAXIMIZE VALUE

The goal of this chapter is to introduce the reader to the dramatic concept of economic conversion and to illustrate its use.

Economic conversion takes place when the investor acquires a property that has one use (or no use at all) and converts it to something else. When done properly this change increases the economic potential of the property, thereby increasing the property value. Several examples are changing a motel to an office complex, developing a vacant lot into a U-Pick-It Strawberry Patch, altering an apartment complex into a time-share resort, upgrading a restaurant into a nightclub, and converting a five-unit apartment building into a seven-unit complex. Sometimes the change is very subtle, such as the change of a general office building to an all-medical practice, but the result is always increased income potential. This increased income potential may be temporary, as an interim use, or it could be a use that will have a long life for the property and its owners. Keep in mind that no use can be considered to be permanent simply because any use tends to be outlived by the building, the location, and the land itself.

KEY TERMS

In this section, the following terms related to economic conversion are defined and explained:

- Property expert
- Leverage
- Risk

Knowing and understanding these terms and issues related to them will help you to learn and apply the concepts presented in this chapter.

Property Expert

Real estate is local in nature and statistics. This point is critical and no investor should overlook this aspect. All real estate investors should continually be reminded that real estate investing is unlike any other kind of commodity or market investment. There are no two identical pieces of property. When there are very similar properties, their values will rise and fall in a very close relationship.

Anyone can become the property expert in his or her area. All it takes is before you in this book.

Becoming an expert in real estate is very easy. Readers of this book can become property experts within their community if they apply the principles contained herein. The length of this process would vary, of course, but even a modest effort would be successful within six months. There are very few categories of investing where the novice can become an expert in such a short period of time.

Leverage

Leverage in financing terms is the result when money is borrowed at a cost that is less than the yield the property generates. Under some circumstances, an investor can borrow 100 percent of the funds needed to build or buy a property. In this case, if the property will cover its expenses and pay the debt service, then that investment is leveraged 100 percent. In this event, even a break-even property will eventually amortize the value of the debt, which alone could be a substantial return on the invested capital. Leverage is, however, a double-edged sword. The investor that pushes leverage to the point where the slightest slip in revenue can move the positive return into a negative outflow of cash runs the risk of owning an alligator that simply eats up the cash flow. This does not mean this is the end of the world, because the solution might be a few months or even a year away and grander things lay ahead. Yet, the conservative approach is always a sound one, although over a long term virtually every investor is apt to hit a snag somewhere along the path to wealth.

Risk

Risk is relative to each person and each transaction. When investors have completed their initial due diligence, much of the risk may be reduced. Most investors get into trouble not because they take risks that are too great for them to handle, but because they make mistakes in their investment plans and have lost sight of their original goals. Nonetheless, if the investor over-estimates the income potential and/or underestimates the operating expenses, then the deal could be headed for problems and, in retrospect, the transaction can be seen as full of risk. The whole idea about investing in real estate is to reduce risk by learning everything possible and important about every investment. This concept will become more evident as you progress through this book. There is a concept, which I term as "building your comfort zone," that will give you confidence. It is the best way to become comfortable with your abilities to invest in real estate, and will make you shine as an expert in your area.

WHEN TO USE ECONOMIC CONVERSION TO CREATE VALUE

Economic conversion is used in one or a combination of the following situations:

    1. **The investor has a specific use in mind and looks for a property that will meet those needs.** For example, some investors look for fast-food operations that have gone out of business because they have discovered that a conversion of that kind of location best suits their completely different

business. Another developer is successful in converting large old homes into corporate offices. Another investor has found conversions of well-located apartment buildings into seasonal furnished rentals to be highly lucrative. Land developers prosper because they know how to turn vacant acreage into housing developments and commercial ventures. Each of these examples has its own nuances that the individual investor has tailored for his or her unique purpose of use.

2. **An opportunity surfaces that if grasped will automatically increase the value of the property.** This often means changing the zoning from one use to another to broaden the market appeal, but many times the zoning may already allow the new use. This occurs because many investors are visually oriented. They see a tract of land that is surrounded by single-family homes; therefore, they presume the land is zoned for single-family homes. However, the reality could be that the land has an industrial or other commercial zoning.

Many investors specialize in taking a vacant tract of land, working through all the governmental paperwork to get approvals for a change of use, and then selling the property to developers who would rather pay a profit to the first investor because they can now move ahead into a ready-to-go property.

3. **There is a change in market demands and reduced value of an existing property.** In this case, the owner should look for a new use or change in the existing use, or a new type or category of tenant that will increase the value of the property. For example, when a neighborhood declines, rents fall and property loses value. Property owners can become *stuck* in this kind of market condition and be unable to sell their property. It can be very frustrating to watch property values quickly erode, and most property owners feel there is little they can do except drop the price further. Continually dropping prices establishes a trend that can be very hard to stop, and the already declining neighborhood may decline even further. Worst of all, the few tenants you may have will become unhappy the moment they learn that you are offering space in the building at half of what they are paying. If your goal is to get rid of the tenants you have, that will surely do the trick. Mind you, your tenants may be part of your problem in renting the remaining space to start with. What the property owner should do is make a positive effort to find a use that stabilizes the decline. When this is done, the trend will be reversed and property values will start going up. In severe situations, this may require a collective approach with a block of property owners to find

out what change would make a turnaround possible. Sometimes a rezoning will help.

4. **There are community changes of any kind.** Many types of change can create the need for different use and greater economic return because of it. New roads, bridges, airports, schools, hospitals, and so on all can have profound effects on the neighborhoods in the area—both positive and negative effects. The same increase in community infrastructure can cause some property values to go up and others to go down. A change in zoning may be the right step to stabilize or increase values. Because most infrastructure changes take a long time to occur, the investor who is well informed about future plans for the community can be ready to take advantage of opportunities long before they are visible to the general public.

NINE STEPS TO MAXIMIZE THE EFFECT OF ECONOMIC CONVERSION

The following steps will help you to use economic conversion for maximum benefit in your real estate investing.

1. **Ascertain what your present zoning and development rules will allow at your existing property or the property you want to buy.** Often buyers or property owners already have the zoning they need to make economic changes but fail to recognize this because they do not see other properties in the neighborhood undergoing those changes. I see this as mass blindness, and it is very common in real estate ownership. The fact is few people have any idea what can actually be constructed on their property or the property across the street.

2. **Find out what the local market for that area needs.** Is there a void of certain services in the area? This is easy to find out, but it requires time and a little effort. The process is to drive through town and pick out the neighborhoods that you would consider to be prosperous. Make note of the kinds of businesses that are in and around these neighborhoods. Do these same kinds of businesses and services exist in your area? If not, consider why. Is it because the demographics are so different—for example, high-end beauty salons may not do well in your area because of the price of those services. In this case, think of a comparable business that would be more appropriate for your area's demographic—for example, are there more affordable salons? If not, then there is a potential void. The same thought

process works on every successful business or service found in some of the "in" communities in your part of the world.

3. **Ask if the local government will be receptive to a zoning change to meet the market need if your property's current zoning does not.** Some communities have zoning laws that are very antiquated, and the local officials know it. Nothing may be done to change those laws, however, until a property owner comes to them and asks if a property can be changed to some less restrictive zoning that will produce a benefit to the community. Change is the nature of zoning laws, and economic conversion can live and prosper because of it.

4. **Work with local zoning authorities to find out how you can turn the property into an asset for the community as well as yourself.** No elected official will object to a well-presented plan to improve the nature and economic strata of any neighborhood. Once that is understood, it is a good idea to pay a personal visit to the representatives in local government that are accountable to your area. Ask them what you can do and how they can help you to achieve this goal. If you are not lucky and are dealing with an area that is so anti-change that nothing positive can come from such visits, then consider moving (at least your investment interests) to another area.

5. **Check with local lenders to find out if the void you want to fill can be financed.** Financing can be the single most important factor in any economic conversion. Unfortunately, with the recent downfall of sound thinking within the lending profession and industry, many lenders are shy about making any loans at all. This makes it harder on everyone. Actually, this is the good news. The harder it gets for everyone, the easier it is for the dynamic investor—you—who knows that perseverance will win out in the end.

6. **Lock up the property in a contract where you have an out clause.** Once that is done, you can spend more time and perhaps some money to pursue the needed changes. Much of this book is dedicated to the techniques of "locking up" a property so that you beat out other potential investors by having a lock on the deal while you are pursuing the economic conversion process, while at the same time you have the safety net of the out clause if the conversion cannot be accomplished.

7. **Make sure you have the best property locked up.** This might become the revelation of the week. You have found the need and the void you can fill, and you have a great property locked up—but is it the *best* property in the area to use to make the economic conversion? If not, do not hesitate to lock up another property or two so you can cherry-pick the best property.

Don't be sorry for the seller that you have to say no to. Be happy for the one you say yes to.

8. **Run the economics of the "big picture."** Will the new use bring tenants that will occupy the building and give you the return you need? This will cause you to do more homework. The best way to assess this is to look at properties with the same usage or business that you want to create. If they are for sale, then great. Go over the numbers that show why that price is being asked and how much the associated expenses are. Feel free to pick the owner's brain. Then ask, "Why are you selling?" Learning the reason can be a wonderful way to evade risk and failure.

9. **Close only when you are ready to start the conversion.** The closer you are to the actual remodeling or changes needed, the better off you will be. A long delay between closing and the conversion will result in increased costs of financing and holding or maintaining the property that are not met by the increased income from the conversion.

AVOID TWO COMMON PROBLEMS WITH ECONOMIC CONVERSION

Two problems that may occur with economic conversion are a seller who does not allow you sufficient time to attempt to make the conversion and a conversion that takes a year or longer to produce revenue.

What do you do when the seller insists on a contract that does not allow you a reasonable time to back out of the deal? You must educate the seller about the problems that beset your investment plan. Many property owners are unaware of the issues that confront a real estate developer or investor. Sometimes it is not the seller that has a problem accepting an agreement that has "escape" provisions for the buyer, but the seller's advisers. A smart and experienced Realtor can help pave the way for an investor who expects to need time to check out the property or to obtain necessary approvals prior to moving forward with the transaction.

A second problem is, how do you tie up a property for a year or longer and still have an out? The key is to let the seller know what is going on. In the case of rezoning for economic conversion, the investor should include the seller as much as possible. After all, the seller is motivated to help the buyer get what he or she wants as a condition to the contract. There is a problem with this, however, if the process is drawn out and takes longer than expected. Sellers have a tendency to feel that they are being taken advantage of in these situations. Establishing a good rapport with the seller will help reduce this problem. It is wise to do whatever you can to reduce the risk of spending time and money to obtain approvals only to end up without them. A sizable deposit that is refundable to the investor if his or her time, hard work, and money are unproductive might be necessary.

Who holds the buyer's deposit is a matter of negotiation between the parties. Sometimes the buyer actually gives the seller an option payment that remains with the seller no matter what, or if the transaction closes, it is applied to the purchase price. Actual deposits that pertain to the transaction are held in escrow, generally by the buyer's or seller's lawyer but also possibly by a third-party escrow company.

MAKING ECONOMIC CONVERSION WORK

The key to making an economic conversion work is to know what kind of property is convertible and what to convert it to. At times, the answer is simply to expand the present use to generate additional revenue, or perhaps to upgrade the quality of what is offered to increase the revenue. For example, if the property is doing well as a rental apartment building and the rental vacancies in the area are low, it is likely that the property value could be increased by adding several more units. However, the additional income to be earned must give a desired return to the investor. A likely downward turn in the overall yield after the addition of units because of the added expense and the capital cost to make the improvements would strongly indicate that this is the wrong choice to make.

If the addition of rental units can be done in such a way that the yield goes up, this would clearly be a good choice, but this still may not be the only route to pursue. What else could be done? This is the question that each investor must continually ask. The answer will be found in several different places. Start with the current zoning and go from there.

- What uses does the current zoning allow for that location?
- Are there any restrictions from any source that would prohibit such a use?
- Of the uses allowed, which will return the most for the cost to accomplish it?
- Which use can be put into effect the most easily and in the shortest time?
- Would a change to another zoning be more effective?

C H A P T E R

12

EASY AND INEXPENSIVE WAYS TO INCREASE PROPERTY VALUES

The goal of this chapter is to illustrate easy and inexpensive ways an investor can increase the value of real estate. In every instance, by using creative purchasing techniques, the investor can actually implement the necessary steps to increase the value *before* the purchase is closed and paid for. Because the seller pays the carrying cost for a property up until the date of closing, by using the "seller's time" the investor can often save on the cost of the improvement.

After defining and explaining some key terms, the chapter describes six quick and inexpensive steps you can take to boost property value:

1. Upgrade the land.
2. Enhance the landscaping.
3. Clean, fix, and paint the improvements.
4. Make the entrance appealing.
5. Give care to the interiors.
6. Establish your own new value and publish it.

KEY TERMS

In this section, the following terms related to ways of increasing property values are defined and explained:

- *R*-factor insulation
- Municipal trash pickup
- Wholesale buying power
- Local cleanup codes

Knowing and understanding these terms and issues related to them will help you to learn and apply the concepts presented in this chapter.

R-Factor Insulation

Insulation within a building can have a dramatic effect on air-conditioning and heating costs. If a sudden change in the energy cost for a building has a beneficial effect on the "bottom line," the value of the property can jump by a multiple of 10 times the savings or more. For example, if insulation can cause a monthly savings of as little as $75 per month, the annual savings would be $900. An increase in the annual cash flow of $900 would be a 10 percent return on an investment of $9,000 (and hence make the property worth this much more)—and it is likely that the actual cost to install the insulation would be only a fraction of this added value. In addition, many local power companies offer refunds to property owners for adding insulation. This incentive allows the investor to receive a refund from the utility company for a portion of the cost of the insulation.

If the investor has included certain "fix-up costs" as part of the initial investment, the seller will actually be paying to increase the value of the buyer's new investment. An example of this would be a purchase agreement that shows a total down payment of 20 percent of the total purchase price; however, $5,000 of that amount is to be spent by the buyer for improvements to the property. The provision may have been negotiated into the agreement, for example, after the buyer's first offer of 15 percent down with the seller holding the balance in the form of a purchase money mortgage was rejected. By adding the extra $5,000 the seller can see that the buyer should have a greater equity in the property. Because the buyer anticipates spending money on the property right away in any case, adding this $5,000 cost to the down payment is no hardship. At the same time, the seller sees the buyer's added investment in the property as additional security to the mortgage the seller is to hold.

Municipal Trash Pickup

Many communities have "bulk" trash pickup. This kind of trash pickup may require a phone call to the proper authority to get the service, or it may be on a monthly or other long-term schedule. Because this service is usually a part of the existing utility charge, scheduling a cleanup of a property so that this "free" service can be utilized can save in private trash hauling charges. A call to the city or county department that manages trash pickup will provide the necessary details on this kind of service. If there is no "free" bulk pickup, there may be a "for hire" municipal service that is inexpensive.

Wholesale Buying Power

Wholesale vendors, which would likely include landscape nurseries, generally do not sell directly to the public, but for a real estate developer and investor, the situation changes. All it may take to have access to the wholesale marketplace (not just for landscaping but for all building materials as well as interior decorations and other products) may be a city occupational license and a state sales tax number. The usual requirement to get a city occupational license is to have a business address (in a zoning that permits business locations) and to meet other simple requirements for the type of license. Prior to showing up at the city occupational license office, it would be a good idea to check the requirements for different categories of professional licenses. Usually there are no special requirements, such as state tests or other educational qualifications, for occupational licenses for the following: interior decorators, remodeling counselors, and providers of landscape decorations, painting services, and the like.

The state sales tax number is obtained through the local state sales tax office—check with your state revenue department for the requirements. Once a state sales tax number is obtained, periodic reports may need to be filed, but having this number will allow the holder to buy wholesale and not to pay the state tax (depending on state rules on certain items or services) for "pass-through items" that are going to be resold. Even if the investor elects or is required to pay the state tax, many wholesale operations use the state sales tax number to distinguish qualified buyers from people looking to avoid paying sales tax.

Local Cleanup Codes

When a neighborhood is in a run-down condition, it is not unusual for junk to pile up in yards, cars to be left abandoned or junked, and so on. If no one complains, the local authorities may not be aware of the situation and therefore not enforce local ordinances that either require the property owners to clean up the place or provide automatic municipal service to remove the debris and junk. To determine what ordinances apply, call the local code enforcement departments of the appropriate city, county, and state involved. Each may have a separate department that would control different aspects of the situation. For example, the state health department may have control and power to clean up a potential health hazard (rotting garbage, rats, vagrants living in unsanitary conditions, etc.), while the county may have control over abandoned cars and the city control over excessive plant growth on vacant property. It is the right of every property owner to seek the help of local officials in maintaining the values of the neighborhood.

UPGRADE THE LAND

Obviously, cleaning up is the first step if the property needs it. As has already been mentioned, the investor should go the extra step and get neighborhood property cleaned up too. Then start with the basics. The following ideas can give vacant land a sudden boost of value.

Get a Temporary Use for It

As long as the use is not detrimental to the property, the sudden new look that a vacant property has when it is put to use attracts new interest, which can reflect in increased value. With rural land, a temporary use could be to turn the plot into a U-Pick-It Strawberry Patch. If the investor is not agriculturally inclined, a drive around the area may turn up a farmer who would love to enter into a joint venture for a season or two of strawberries. One solid benefit to the landowner may be that the property is cleared of unwanted shrubs and growth that would otherwise be costly to remove (if not impossible due to landscaping regulations that may not apply to farmers). In the end, the farmer may even be asked to leave the property freshly planted with thousands of "free" timber seedlings obtained from the state agricultural department.

A temporary use can turn into a permanent use once the user discovers that the site is economically viable for his or her purposes. An example of this is when the owner of a commercial site lets a local new car dealer turn the vacant site into a parking lot for excess inventory or for used car sales, and the car dealer later wants to make the site a permanent one.

File for a Rezoning

Yes, this step may be both simple and inexpensive. Not all rezoning requires months and expensive efforts. Check with the local authorities first, make sure the land is tied up in a long-term contract as a safety factor, and then go for it. Because the contract will not be closed until some time in the future, the normal carrying cost of the land, such as taxes and insurance, will remain the obligation of the existing owner and thus are not part of the investor's rezoning cost.

Demonstrate Pride of Ownership

Pride of ownership is evident when the owner makes an effort to maintain a property in top condition and shape. This means all property owned, not just the property that has been purchased for a fast turnover. When an investor is working within a small community, the way that investor maintains his or her property becomes public knowledge in a short period of time. In a large city, this fact may take a bit longer to be known to the general public, but within real estate circles it still gets around quickly.

Taking good care of everything you own, from the shoes on your feet to the car you drive, becomes a matter of pride in appearance as well as respect for the items you own. Investors who let property run down generally show a lack of "tender loving care" in their whole lifestyle. Pride of ownership need not be extravagant or lavish; all it takes is to be clean and neat, with good taste for the occasion, and to make sure that everything you own is well maintained.

ENHANCE THE LANDSCAPING

Many investors view landscaping as a long-term investment that takes years to pay big dividends. While this is true, there are circumstances in which, with good planning, a change to the existing landscaping can provide dramatic and valuable changes to the property almost overnight. Even simply pruning existing trees and shrubs and removing weeds will result in an immediate and very noticeable improvement in the appearance of a property.

One way to quickly upgrade land is to plant trees on it. This is an improvement that has the most benefit when it is done as early as possible to give the new trees time to become established and grow. When planting trees, take care in choosing where the trees will be. Ask yourself, where would I plant around a building that might be constructed here? It is relatively easy to mark off setbacks and to put the bulk of planting in these areas, usually closer to the property lines than the future building area will be. Some trees are easier to transplant than others, so plant those easiest to transplant in areas where they may need to be moved.

It is important to remember that landscape enhancement does not mean just plants. It can also mean rocks, mulch, cutting and removing plants, and changing the location of existing plants. All of these can create nearly instant value. The cost can be little more than a couple of weekends of work.

Many communities have landscape codes that regulate the kinds of plants that are preferred or even required for new landscaping projects. While these codes may not affect a redesigned landscape, it is a good idea to check with the local authorities to ensure that no building codes are violated. In addition, these same officials can provide valuable information about the kinds of plants that will grow best in certain areas of town.

Each state and most counties have agricultural departments that offer free or very inexpensive tests of soil, information on plant illnesses, and so on. In some areas there are reforestation projects in which a landowner can get free trees if he or she agrees to plant them according to the rules of the department. While this may be a long-range project, the very fact that this step has been taken *now* may attract a long-term investor who will view this as a positive way to increase the value of the property.

An older property may have excess trees, shrubs, or other plants that hide the natural beauty of the property or make the buildings dark and unattractive inside by blocking light from the windows. Because mature trees and other plants can be very expensive, it may be possible to swap these for new, more appropriately sized plants and landscape material from a retail landscape company, which will then move the mature plants to a location where they are desired. Another option is to move these trees or other plants to another location on the same property. This adds the beauty and value of mature plantings where they are needed without incurring the expense of buying them.

In some instances, mature trees are so valuable that they can be sold for a substantial profit. One lot I purchased as a site for a commercial building I planned to construct had five medium-sized oak trees right in the middle of it. Prior to closing on the lot (my deal was predicated on my obtaining permission to build a 30,000-square-foot single-story building), I put a sign up announcing the advent of the building. The sign showed an artist's rendering of the future building in hopes of attracting future tenants. A few days later I had a call from another developer asking if he could buy the trees and how much would they cost. This was my first time making money from trees that I had anticipated I would have to pay to have removed. There was plenty of time to prepare the trees to be moved (the roots had to be properly pruned around the root bulbs that would go with the trees when they were removed from the ground) during the six months it would take to get the appropriate approvals to build the building.

Now, when I purchase land, I pay close attention to what plants, if any, can be moved and how much landscapers will pay for them. Some trees and shrubs are easy to transplant as long as the proper technique is followed. Towering palm trees, for example (palms are one of the easiest of all trees to transplant), can bring a very attractive price.

CLEAN, FIX, AND PAINT THE IMPROVEMENTS

The first impression a prospective buyer gets of a property may mean the difference between a sale with a profit and no sale at all. The buildings or other improvements on a property can usually be given a sudden *new appearance* with a three-part process:

- Clean
- Fix
- Paint

Investors who are handy with one or more of these three tasks will find the actual cost to spruce up a property is more a matter of time than money.

The word *fix* is an important factor to consider from two points of view. Novice investors should shy away from property that needs a lot of fixing up unless there is ample capital to handle any hidden problems and the investor wants to expand his abilities and is willing to pay for the lesson if mistakes are made.

Small items that need to be fixed should be completely repaired with high-quality materials.

Most important, however, is that small items that need to be fixed should be properly fixed. It pays to do it right and to use high-quality materials. Broken toilet seats, doors that stick, cabinets that will not open or close, plumbing that drips, and so on are all minor things that investors will find in any property—and they can be fixed without much cost.

Pitfalls in the Cleaning-Fixing-Painting Routine

There are four major pitfalls when it comes to cleaning, fixing, and painting:

- Time
- Money
- Hidden problems
- Permits

Work on even the simplest-looking job can drag into six weekends in a row. Other demands on your time or a change in the weather that sends the workers home should be anticipated. The old saying "Make hay while the sun shines" works here. When the weather is good, clean, fix, and paint the outside; the inside can be done without worrying about inclement weather.

The cost for extra labor and materials can easily exceed original estimates, and it is not unusual for a simple remodeling project to become a major reconstruction project. Taking it slow and easy at first is one way to keep out of trouble and limit overruns of the time you have to give to the project and the money available to pay for it.

Never plan for any remodeling that requires the removal of any structure or built-in fixture (walls, windows, plumbing, or cabinets) until the structure has been carefully examined. This may require that a section of a wall be opened up to see if the removal will be as simple as it may appear. There may be elements now visible that you had not anticipated—such as a roof support or plumbing or electrical lines. Even a coat of paint can hide everything from valuable flooring and antique furniture to major problems such as termite damage, lead paint, or other problems.

Check the building plans before you start any work. If the seller does not have the building plans, this should be a big "red flag" that something is wrong. Check with the appropriate city or county building department to see if they have a copy of the original building plans. These might be stored on microfilm or microfiche from which a specialized copy machine can enlarge and reproduce the plans on paper. However, for buildings that are older than that technology, there may not be building plans available.

Even if you do not anticipate making any changes or upgrades to a property, you should make every effort possible to obtain a set of the "as built" plans, plus any plans that were used to make changes in the original structure. Use these to ascertain if work has been done that may not meet present building codes, or that was done without a permit.

Any time you wonder why you need time to make proper inspections and do your due diligence, come back and reread this chapter. Keep in mind too that the seller may not know of any such problems and be entirely innocent in passing on to you such nightmares, so it is up to you to take the steps to avoid them.

MAKE THE ENTRANCE APPEALING

A redesign of the entrance to a property can also make a major difference in the appearance that is instantly appealing, and that single factor can increase the value of a property overnight. A new walkway or a new front door can turn a dull, drab property into a fresh, vibrant one that beckons new buyers.

One of the very best single expenditures is the "front door appearance." New door hardware, a new brass mailbox, and a new brass doorknocker on a freshly painted or new door can be all it takes to give an overall impression of quality throughout.

Before you tackle the task of redesigning an entryway, I recommend that you drive around the neighborhood, as well as around neighborhoods in a higher-quality area of town, and pay close attention to entrances that are appealing to you. Take along a digital camera just in case you see some knockout designs that could easily be reproduced.

Often what is needed to turn an old entrance into a new and appealing one is a change in the landscaping near the entrance. For example, planting flowering plants along both sides of a walkway from a sidewalk to the front door may be the key. Alternatively, perhaps giving the walkway a slight serpentine double curve may enhance its appearance. You could even add a wall of plants with a gate that leads through it near the front door to create a semiprivate courtyard. A mixture of elements such as potted plants, a bench or two, and other decorative items are special touches that can turn this entrance into a work of art.

GIVE CARE TO THE INTERIORS

Tender loving care is usually what the previous owner did not do, which is why the price is so low and the investment a sound one. Turning around a property that has not been cared for can take a little more than just cleaning, fixing, and painting. It may also take some care to add finishing touches.

There are some quick and easy things that can be done to give the interiors of any property a fresh and more valued look. The idea is to look for the hidden treasures that can be found within some properties. These make fix-up and the return of tender loving care evident.

Look Under the Carpet

Do you find hardwood floors, tile, or marble under the carpet? These may be much easier to bring back to their natural state than to recarpet. These are gems, but watch out—under old carpets can also be rotten floorboards, termite damage, and worst of all, asbestos. The key is to know what you are dealing with in all eventualities. If the gem is there, then that is your bonus. If a problem is encountered, get an estimate on what it will cost to deal with the problem, or walk away from the deal by using one of the outs in the purchase contract.

Check Under the Paint

Solid brass that has been painted over a thousand times does not look very nice—until all the paint is removed. Doorplates, hardware, railings, and countless other brass items found in older properties could not be replaced today for less than a fortune. Removing the paint and polishing them will add evident quality at very low expense.

Tap doors, woodwork, and built-ins such as a buffet or bookshelves with a plastic hammer. Solid building material has an "expensive" sound to it, and solid wood doors and other fixtures in good shape can be restored. (Solid-sounding walls might indicate block or heavy plaster, which are more costly than cheap wallboard or other more modern materials but not as good building products.)

On the downside, if there is old paint it is important to check to see if it contains lead. Ask at a paint store for lead tests that can ascertain if this problem exists.

Make Sure the Property Smells as Good as It Looks

Unfortunately, many property owners do not seem to notice the smell of their pets or other pervasive odors they may have grown accustomed to. However, any unpleasant smell will turn buyers off quickly and must be dealt with immediately. A partial solution just is not enough.

The introductory smell, that is, the first smell people notice when they enter a home, can be very important in the potential sale of the property. Dog and animal smells are definite "turnoffs" and should be eliminated. Mildew and other problem smells may be more subtle, but they also must be dealt with as soon as possible.

How to Remove Odors

If there is a pet smell or other pervasive odor, the first step of course is to get rid of whatever is causing the smell. This can be difficult at times (especially if the source is your live-in father-in-law's cheap cigars or a beloved but as-yet-unhousebroken pet llama). Once the source has been dealt with satisfactorily, the solution to the problem is to get rid of or thoroughly clean whatever is "holding" the smell. This can be the carpets, an old sofa that was the dog's bed, or drapes that have soaked up the smell over a long time. Once the fabric that contained the smell is removed, then the whole place needs to be cleaned with a strong cleaning solution—but one that does not introduce new smells that are equally difficult to remove. Check with your local hardware store to obtain cleaning supplies for the specific problem at hand. Be sure to request cleaning chemicals that will not replace one smell with another that is equally offensive.

Do not attempt to mask any nasty smell with the perfume smell that some chemical cleaners tend to have. Baking soda in water may be a good rinse to remove smells that remain from cleaners. For example, mildew and mold can be removed with a chlorine-based cleaner. However, after using them you also have to clean out the chlorine smell. Let the chlorine dry, and then wash the area again with a box of baking soda dissolved in a bucket of warm water.

Replace Stale Smells with Fresh Ones

There are several acceptable, if not desirable, smells that can be introduced into a building that will help overcome any kind of old smell. Paint is one, but be careful: this does not apply to all paint. Some paints produce vapors that are unpleasant or even harmful. Safest generally are latex water-based paints, but ask your qualified paint expert (not the clerk from the hardware department who is assigned to the paint department for the day) which paint has the nicest "freshly painted" smell.

Another wonderful smell is leather. One new piece of leather furniture can give a whole room a great smell.

Remove and Prevent Mildew

Removing mildew smells is not as difficult as it once was, thanks to several different cleaning materials that kill mildew. The real problem is not the existing mildew, because with proper treatment it can be eliminated; the problem is to keep it from returning. Mildew grows best in a dark, warm, and moist environment where there is poor air circulation. The remedy for mildew, then, is circulating air, sunlight, and a dry environment. Roof and plumbing leaks can leave the insides of walls just damp enough to become ideal mildew hide-outs, but not so sopping wet that the actual leak is noticed. Mildew inside walls may not be seen for a long time, but the smell is very evident to any newcomer to the property—although the owners may have gradually grown accustomed to the smell so that they no longer even noticed it.

The key is to stop the leak in order to eliminate the mildew. Fans to circulate air in the area will help, and together with mildew remover sprays that are available in any good hardware store, mildew can be beaten. In hot, humid areas it is a good idea to keep air circulating in a closed-up house to keep mildew from getting a foothold, and once mildew is present a dehumidifier may be the only way to solve a chronic problem.

Appeal with "Memory" Aromas

In addition to the general cleaning, painting, and touches such as leather furniture already mentioned, there are several "memory" smells that can produce a good aroma within a home. These smells can evoke pleasant memories in buyers and become a type of subliminal sales tool. Various smells may have different levels of appeal to different people, but in general the following smells are most likely to produce a positive reaction from a prospective buyer. Each of these smells can be "made" within the house, and each has a relatively short duration.

- Freshly baked bread and/or cookies (frozen dough is available in grocery stores)
- Fresh hot cocoa
- Fresh coffee being brewed
- Freshly made popcorn
- A boiling pot of water with a spice added (pick only one—cloves, cinnamon, or vanilla)
- Fresh roses or orange blossoms (very few)
- An apple or peach pie being baked (or reheated)
- Cooking chocolate or peanut butter fudge
- A citrus-scented candle burning

Remember, a little of the above will go a long way. For the best results, choose one such "memory" smell and do not mix it with another. No matter how much you may love the combination of popcorn and citrus-scented candles, multiple smells suggest that you are trying to mask something unpleasant.

ESTABLISH YOUR OWN NEW VALUE AND PUBLISH IT

There is nothing subtle about this approach, as it is bold and direct and generally works. Once the property is on the way to being cleaned, fixed, and painted, and the TLC starts to show, a well-prepared sales brochure with the new price can let everyone know what you think about the present value of the property. Neighbors, by the way, may be the first to agree with you if that new price makes their property look good too.

The best way to find out how to make a great-looking property brochure is to look at some that professionals have already created. A check with several Realtors in the area should turn up several examples.

FINDING THE BEST PROPERTY FOR YOU AND HOW TO PURCHASE IT RIGHT

13

SEVEN TYPES OF REAL ESTATE YOU SHOULD CONSIDER OWNING

here are seven principal categories of real estate: farmland, land speculation, single-family homes, multifamily properties, commercial and industrial properties, retail shops and shopping centers, and lodging. This chapter reviews key terms that are pertinent to those categories, then illustrates the usual advantages and disadvantages each category presents. The primary goal of this chapter is to acquaint the reader with the various kinds of property in which one can invest and to show how each property can serve different goals, depending on the method of acquisition and holding period of the investor.

KEY TERMS

In this section, the following terms related to choosing property for real estate investment are defined and explained:

- Downside risk
- Pattern of growth

- Single-purpose use
- Multipurpose use

Knowing and understanding these terms and issues related to them will help you to learn and apply the concepts presented in this chapter.

Downside Risk

Every investment has a downside risk, which is the worst-case scenario under slightly exaggerated negative circumstances. If an investor is looking at vacant land as a growth investment, the downside risk might be that the value of the land does not reach the level the investor would like. However, even if the property is never more than farmland, it should have a value. If the value of farmland is above the price paid for the site, then the downside risk is not great. If the investment is income property, an acceptable downside risk may be a break-even point—that is, the point at which income matches total expenses, including debt service. Each investor must decide for himself or herself what is an acceptable downside risk to balance the upside potential.

Pattern of Growth

The trends of growth in any given area develop collectively into a **pattern of growth**. The word *pattern* is appropriate because real estate development occurs in set growth areas and generally does not radiate from a center equally in all directions. Instead, development follows new roadways, surrounds lakes, moves around parks, and so on. Industrial areas often are blocked together, whereas expensive single-family home projects may sprawl out around golf courses. When a community is viewed from the air, these patterns are often more obvious than when seen from the ground. Investors need to study the pattern of growth for any area they intend to invest in to ensure that the property being acquired fits into the current and pending pattern.

Single-Purpose Use

Any property that has only one likely use is a **single-purpose use** property. The key here is, what makes that property a single-purpose use? It might be zoning, which determines that the land under the home is zoned for "single-family homes," or it could be that the building design is clearly for a fast-food operation, and so on. Obviously, no property is absolutely single purpose, because with the right amount of money and time, any building can be altered to accommodate another use. Even in very restrictive zoning such as single-family residential zoning, other uses are usually possible—for example, churches, schools, and parks. In general terms, single-purpose use refers to the reasonable use of the property as zoned and built.

Multipurpose Use

This use is clearly flexible due to the zoning and/or the building design. When this flexibility is obvious, there is never any problem in seeing the multipurpose nature of a property. What is important is that all real estate investors need to sharpen their vision of property to see what is not so obvious. Economic conversion depends on the investor being able to take a property with one use now, and a price based on that use, and turn it into a property with a greater income potential at a cost that makes the investment successful. An example of this is a single-family home situated on a lot zoned to permit professional offices. The visual fact is that the home is just a home. However, if the home can be used as office space, this would expand opportunities.

FARMLAND

Farmland and the next category, land speculation, can possibly be the same tract of land. The difference is the motivation and purpose for acquiring the property. Farmland is valuable and can produce a cash flow when purchased with that in mind. The economics of the acquisition must be carefully examined, however, because farmland has a high maintenance cost. Farming is a business, and like all businesses, the investor needs to know what he or she is getting into.

However, having said that, not all farmland goes through the same annual process of preparation, planting, and harvest. Some farms, such as tree farms that grow landscaping plant material, have a limited amount of preparation but often require years of growth until the first batch of trees or shrubs can be sold. Once this process begins, it is a rotation procedure of selling some plants while others mature.

Tree farming also comes in another category, and that is trees grown for wood, both for use in construction and furniture, as well as wood pulp for paper and other chemical production. Tree farms of this nature have an even longer time between planting and cutting, but if the purpose is coupled with land speculation, this kind of investing can be ideal for both a growth of value and an extra cash bonus when the land is cleared for other development and the wood is sold.

Ranch land has similar benefits, except that the cattle or other animals living on the land can be sold off at any time, which offers some protection to the investor should market conditions warrant a move to sell or a wait for a better market.

Advantages of Buying Farmland

It should be clear that the greatest advantage of buying farmland is if you are a farmer (or want to become one). Non-farmers who purchase farmland can be successful if there is strong evidence that the land is in the path of growth that is taking place at that moment. I have a lot of experience and have had success in purchasing that kind of farmland. I was able to tie up the land with long-term debt, then lease it to farmers (often the same people I bought the land from), which helped with the debt payments. The key to this kind of investing is to be sure that growth is on its way. Then realize a profit and don't hold the land too long, because as growth arrives, the neighbors will want to change the allowed uses of your portfolio of farmland to the point that it may never be used for anything other than farming. I have seen that happen with land I bought, but I sold the land in advance of any zoning changes happening.

Disadvantage to Buying Farmland

The time factor of dealing with farmland with an ultimate exit strategy for it to be sold to a developer adds an extra quotient of danger to the original investor. Land that an investor acquires anticipating that he or she will hold it for a long time runs the risk of undergoing local administrative changes as to its allowed use. As there is a trend to keep farmland in that use category, future development potential might disappear or require major litigation expenses to obtain a more liberal use. Nonetheless, a conservative approach with land that shows potential within a more reasonable time period can produce a real winner of an investment.

LAND SPECULATION

Land speculation is investment in land with the hope that it will increase in value enough to either cover the cost to hold it or provide a desired return over and above the total invested capital.

Land speculation requires considerable due diligence. Investors must determine the pattern of growth in the community and tie that together with the future infrastructure planned by the community. When the investor sees that new roads and other planned projects (whether by local or state government or for private or public use) will have a beneficial effect on an area that is slightly beyond and in the path of an established growth pattern, then investing in land in that area should be considered. If the long-term cost to hold onto the property can be financed by an arrangement with the seller at below-market rates or with soft terms, the investment would have greater appeal to the investor.

Advantages of Land Speculation

The economic advantage of land speculation is that the greatest increase of value in real estate comes from taking vacant land, which has the lowest basic value along the chain of real values, and turning it into a pyramid of values that includes everything from commercial sites to parks. When circumstances are favorable to land investment, there can be little risk if the investors have the time and carrying ability to hold the land. The key to land speculation is the ability to properly assess the growth patterns of the community and to get a good picture of future developments that are in the works or on the planning boards.

Disadvantages of Land Speculation

It is not uncommon for local governments to have a 180-degree switch in their ability to follow through with future plans. The plans themselves can be changed as well. For example, moving a proposed interstate highway a few miles to the east can put an investor's 300-acre tract on the wrong side of the highway. Worse still, relocating the road network to the other side of town or canceling the project altogether can shift attention away from the area. This could have such a negative impact that even farmland goes down in value in that part of the county.

Long-term investing in land is much more difficult and can be far more expensive than investors think. Liberal estimates in carrying costs must be taken into consideration because costs go up. Taxes can increase substantially to the point where they double or triple the estimated increases. Local governments can impose building restrictions or moratoriums that can limit if not prohibit reasonable development until utilities are brought to the site— utilities that may be charged as costs to the property owner.

SINGLE-FAMILY HOMES

Many real estate investors swear by single-family homes. Buying single-family homes as an investment generally fits into three different investment strategies:

1. Buy, fix up, and sell.
2. Buy and rent (with or without fix-up).
3. Buy, live in, slowly improve, and then sell.

There is no "best" of these three, as each method will have a different appeal depending on the goal of the investor and the market where these properties are situated. Some investors may apply more than one of these methods at the same time. They may buy one home to live in while slowly improving it and others to fix up and sell, while renting out still others while the market improves. The term *buy* here is meant to include other techniques of acquisition that give the investor the same or a similar position to sell even though the investor may never actually take title to the subject property. An example of this would be if Frances obtains an option to buy a property that she leases in the meantime. During the lease, Frances improves the property and then sells her option to Bob, who takes title to the property. The technique of using options is explained in detail in Chapter 17.

How to Buy Single-Family Homes

The key with buying single-family homes is to cover the carrying cost. Once the investor knows that there will be no cost to hold onto the property, time generally will ensure appreciation of value and an ultimate profit. This will, of course, depend on the investor's due diligence to ensure that the area is not in a decline and that there are no pending public or private works that can adversely affect the property in any way. Downside risk in single-family homes will depend on the terms of the purchase and the cost to carry the property (taxes, mortgage payment, property maintenance, insurance, and property improvement). If the home has the flexibility for a future economic conversion to some other use, then that can be an added bonus to what may already be a good investment.

Advantages of Single-Family Home Investments

There are many advantages to buying single-family homes, but the best is the fact that single-family sellers are often the most motivated of all sellers because of the many different reasons people may *need* to sell a home, such as the following:

- They are transferred to another work location.
- They need a larger home due to family growth.
- They need a smaller home due to a reduced family size (because children have grown and left home or as a result of a divorce or death of a family member).
- They have economic problems and cannot afford to keep the property anymore or are undergoing a foreclosure.
- They have a balloon mortgage due.
- They have bought another home already.
- They need to raise cash to take advantage of another investment.
- They can no longer (or no longer want to) maintain the property.
- They wish to dispose of a gift or inheritance.

In each of these situations, there is a motivated seller. If the real reason the owner wants to sell is something like because the property has termites or a structural failure, then the seller may be motivated, but the property is not worthwhile for the investor.

Downside risk can be slight when investing in single-family homes as long as the investor is able to carry the debt incurred to purchase the property and provided that the investor is reasonably comfortable that he or she can survive one or more of the top reasons people sell homes. The financial meltdown that began with the over-lending practices of the early 2000s created a massive problem within the lending profession that extended into Wall Street and beyond. Easy money was made available to just about anyone who wanted to purchase a home or several homes at a time either for investment or to live in. Lenders were quick to make these loans because they were packaging them into bundles to be sold to institutions that then sold actions, or percentages of the bundles, as securities to hedge funds. The whole thing was a tightrope walk that did not require much to send its investors into the chasm of bankruptcy. Therefore, prudent investors pay attention to the marketplace and are advised to remember how quickly a market can fall when there are no buyers, and even if there are, the lenders turn their backs on them.

Disadvantages of Single-Family Home Investments

The potential profit may not be all that great if the investor is looking for quick growth. If the investor wants to build an income stream by buying and then renting out the homes, he or she will discover quickly that the property maintenance problems that come with owning several single-family homes may not warrant the purchase of this kind of rental property. There will be exceptions to this, of course, but in general, the best reason for buying a single-family home and renting it is to "buy time" and let the market improve while the property is slowly enhanced and upgraded, using, whenever possible, the tenant's rent money to accomplish those goals.

MULTIFAMILY PROPERTIES

Any property that has more than one family unit is considered a multifamily property. The smallest would be a duplex (when this word is used to mean two units, often side by side or one on top of the other). From this point, the size ranges to large rental complexes with hundreds of apartments.

How to Buy Multifamily Properties

All income-producing properties have the advantage of potentially being able to support debt from the income they produce. This factor leads investors to the principle of using other people's money (OPM). The introduction of OPM into the picture gives the investor an edge in the ultimate financing of the investment. Unlike the situation with vacant property and single-family home financing in which the investor's financial strength is the most important element lenders consider, all income properties are viewed from the point of view of the property first, the investor second. If the property is represented fairly to the lender and the income and expenses shown are accurate, then the lender will evaluate the property based on this income stream. The current trend for lenders is to establish a conservative value on the property and to lend a much lower loan-to-value ratio than was prevalent in the late 1990s. Stronger borrowers can obtain higher loan-to-value ratios.

The key to buying any income property is the ability to establish a sound financing package on the property that does not place excessive burdens on the cash flow from the property or the investor. To achieve this it may be necessary for the seller to work with the investor to create a composite of financing that gives this end result.

All rental apartments thrive or die because of the OPM scenario. When there is a shortage of apartments for a particular market, then the vacancy factors approach zero and the property owners can be more selective about the type of tenant they rent to. This factor, the type of tenant in the building, is very important because it will establish the ultimate direction of the building or complex. When a rental market shifts to the point where there is a shortage of tenants, then owners can no longer be as selective about tenants because they are dependent on OPM to meet their debt service and other obligations to keep the property.

Fortunately, multifamily property investors will quickly discover that one of the easiest trends to spot within any community is the rental market. All that is necessary is to drive around the community, make a list of all rental properties that have vacancies, and ascertain rental prices and how selective property managers are in acquiring tenants.

If the investor sees that selection is tight and rents are on the increase, then this is a good sign that there is a shortage of rental units in the market and that opportunities may exist in that sector of real estate.

An element of economic conversion that can be nicely applied to multifamily units is the upgrade from one level of rent to another. This occurs when former property owners have let the property run down to the point where rents had to be decreased to keep the units filled. This factor can snowball, and the situation can deteriorate progressively to the point that even reduced rents cannot maintain high occupancy.

If these properties are in a good area of town or in an area that is returning to a former higher quality, then the remodeling of a run-down apartment complex can be a profitable venture. The important element that must be determined carefully is, how run-down is it? As stated before, major fixing up is not for the novice investor because of the many problems that can lurk behind, for example, the surface crack that the investor thinks needs only to be filled.

Potential Advantages of All Income-Producing Property Investments

The most obvious advantage of owning income-producing property is that the investor can grow wealthy in the long run simply by holding onto the property and letting the OPM pay off the debt—even if there is no immediate cash flow.

Multifamily properties serve a basic need, which limits the downside risk. They provide housing to those who cannot afford or do not choose to buy single-family homes. In any given marketplace, there are members of the community who are moving to and from property ownership. This causes a chain of events in which some people are upgrading their living accommodations, while others are moving into more modest and less expensive quarters. When the labor market is strong and there is a low percentage of unemployed workers, the rental market is at its strongest.

Disadvantages of Multifamily Property Investments

The disadvantages of multifamily property investments center mostly on the management problems that come in dealing with tenants. Apartments can be very management intensive, although not as much as hotels and other "business" forms of accommodation rentals. On a small scale, the key to minimal management problems is in the selection of tenants and in keeping the rent at slightly under the going market. The rent lost by not staying just above the going market, which is a tactic that a well-managed facility may choose to follow, can be offset by the increased occupancy and reduced management problems.

COMMERCIAL AND INDUSTRIAL PROPERTIES

Income-producing commercial and industrial properties range from office buildings to warehouse complexes and everything in between. If the property is a building that is not used for habitation, it is most likely a commercial or industrial property.

Commercial and industrial properties fall into two basic categories: single use and multiuse. If IBM, for example, occupies an entire building or complex, it is clearly a single tenant, but the use could be multiple to the extent that the building may house offices, repair facilities, a medical clinic, and so on. Note the difference between single tenant and single purpose, as in the case of a fast-food restaurant. This too is a single tenant, but the use is greatly limited, and without major remodeling it is a single-use hamburger restaurant.

Multiuse buildings are more often also multitenant buildings, which spread the obligation of the rent over several or many different tenants. When the single tenant is very strong and has a top credit rating, the single-tenant building can be more attractive than multitenant buildings. However, when the single-tenant building is vacant, the vacancy is 100 percent until a new tenant can be found.

The tenant is often a net or triple net tenant: when rent is quoted as **net** or **triple net**, the owner of the building usually passes on other expenses and cost to the tenant over and above the actual rent. Because the terms *net* and *triple net* are not universal in their meaning, a prospective tenant or new investor should obtain an exact definition of other obligations tenants are to pay. One cannot assume that *triple net* means that the tenant pays everything—even though this is exactly the case in some leases.

When the tenant pays rent plus building maintenance, taxes, and insurance (the common basis for triple net) plus all other costs that may be assessed against a property, the cost to the tenant is established *as though the tenant actually owned the property*. This type of rental situation is highly sought after by many investors because the investments require very little management. Only a straight **land lease**, where tenants lease the land and then construct their own building, requires less management.

Advantages of Commercial and Industrial Property Investments

Advantages are the ease of operation and generally favorable acceptance by institutional lenders. As with all income properties, the income stream of the property will be a major factor in the ultimate value of the property and the basis for financing. When an investor can take over a property that can be improved or converted to a higher income stream, then great profits could be generated.

Disadvantages of Commercial and/or Industrial Property Investments

Some disadvantages are the result of the lag time that occurs in the development of this kind of property. Shortages of office space or commercial buildings encourage investors to build more. As the time from initial idea to finished building may be several years, the shortage may suddenly become a glut on the market, and a slow rental market may result. If some other economic decline happens during this same period, the end result can be a major decline in commercial rents in a wide area, and real estate values can fall very quickly.

The downside risk in commercial and industrial buildings is the strength of the tenant. This factor has become even more critical as some of the "best risk" tenants have seen some very hard times and even the giants of industry are no longer thought of as risk-free tenants.

Commercial buildings are often classified into A, B, and C categories. A category buildings are usually high-rent office buildings that generally are in the prime commercial centers of a community or city center. B category can be any type of use that has few if any services, may not have prime location in the community, and is often a local tenant or franchise that leases smaller facilities for its specific use. C category is other commercial uses such as small strip stores and independent retail and service uses.

RETAIL SHOPS AND SHOPPING CENTERS

Retail shops and shopping centers seem to be everywhere, and even in bad economic times new shops are built, even when whole shopping centers are less than half filled. There are some very good reasons for this, which makes this kind of investing very profitable if the circumstances are right and the investor sees the opportunities in time to take advantage of them.

This category of property differs from the preceding category in that the majority of rentals in a multitenant situation will be retail and service-oriented shops rather than office space. Some shopping centers and retail shop areas also have offices for rent, but in strictly defined commercial projects, such as office parks and office buildings, the only retail shops found will generally be limited to restaurants, sundry shops, print shops, and the like designed to serve the needs of the workers and businesses in the offices rather than outside customers.

A typical business district in almost any town in the world is apt to have individual shops lining the main streets for several blocks. In older cities, it is not uncommon for many differently designed buildings to adjoin each other, giving cities a "quilt" look. To counter this look, many cities now have design codes that must be strictly followed to prevent this hodgepodge appearance and to bring a more homogeneous look to the commercial areas. One such town, Boca Raton, Florida, has a code that requires that buildings have a colonial Spanish look along the lines of certain existing buildings. Cities in many areas of California have similar design codes.

Finding retail shops and shopping centers is relatively easy. First, the areas are limited, usually along main streets, which makes the area easy to check out through deed records in the courthouse or deed searches by members of the real estate industry. Many of these buildings may be for sale even though there is no sign out front announcing that fact. Why? Most property owners do not want their tenants to know the property is for sale. This means that the pickings will go to the investor who digs up the information and acts on it.

Advantages of Retail Shop and Shopping Center Investments

In established areas, it is relatively easy to see the trends and flow of traffic. It does not take long to tell which area is improving and why, and which area is losing ground and why. Of these trends that investors look for, two are significant and can open the door to profitable investing if the trend can be spotted and a deal can be made:

1. A decline in rents with increases in vacancy factors due to a temporary situation.
2. A moderate to strong rental market area that is about to experience an event that will have a strong positive impact on rental space.

Each of these trends will lead to a stronger rental market in the relatively near future. The investor who gets in on the ground floor of these trends will have the first chance to acquire the better locations that may be offered for sale. Selecting the property to buy will depend greatly on the ability of the investor to deal with the complexity of renting out retail shop or shopping center space. Buying large retail space is not for the novice investor unless there is sufficient capital to hire managers with shopping center management experience. However, small strip stores or small buildings with several shops can be a good way to get into this category of investing relatively safely. Because these buildings often are in need of repairs and can lend themselves to remodeling to upgrade the look and hopefully the rent, there can be substantial room to improve the income generated from such investments.

The biggest advantage in this kind of investment is that it serves a general need of the community, and if the investor has chosen the location well, it is doubtful that there will be a high vacancy factor.

Disadvantages of Retail Shop and Shopping Center Investments

The main disadvantage is in dealing with the tenants. It is important to be as selective as possible and to upgrade the quality of tenants when possible. It can be tempting to fill a vacant space with a tenant that is less than ideal, yet the investor should set a goal to maintain a certain status in the building or on the street. One slip from this goal, by introducing the wrong kind of tenant into the area, can start a downhill slide that will eventually cause other vacancies.

Take an inexpensive city map of an area that you know well. It may even be the area around your ultimate comfort zone. Go over the map and mark off the different areas you are familiar with into the five categories described in this chapter.

When you pick an area to be developed as your **comfort zone**, it is important to ascertain how the different categories of property evolved. What was the trend that resulted in the present situation, and how are the different property types faring at present? An understanding of this pattern is essential to begin to remove risk from your investments.

LODGING

The lodging industry is a mammoth one that stretches around the globe. There are hotels and motels that cater to almost every demographic aspect of humankind. Room rates run a wide spectrum, and as one would expect, a well run and moderately financed hotel or motel can be a "cash cow" that produces a steady income.

This industry tends to go through some major swings in development, though this is less so for the high-end properties that continue to maintain their position through constant upgrades and frequent remodeling. The Ritz Carlton and other five-star hotels around the world can, however, fall on hard times when their location is compromised due to some crisis that affects travelers to the area. The more modest hotels that are not full-service properties but have limited amenities for their customers proliferate in areas where the market for high-end properties is already met by one or more five-star properties and the predominance of customers fall into the "sleep and leave" category.

Interstate properties that fill up every night and are empty by 11:00 in the morning have certain inherent management problems in dealing with a heavy turnover on a daily basis. Nonetheless, a novice real estate investor can find this kind of business a nice way to go because historically the hospitality business is nearly etched into stone. There are franchises one can purchase that pretty much ensure a measure of success if the location is approved. Operation of a hotel is not overly difficult if the hotel is a limited service type. Food and beverage service is one area that can create many problems to the novice investor, and except for a buffet type of breakfast that many of the "Express" hotels and motels offer, food and beverage service is best avoided.

Advantages of Lodging Investments

If the investor's principal goal is to work for himself or herself, then work is what you will find in any hotel or motel. Even small operations can hire an entire family, including in-laws. In virtually every part of the country where there is substantial population there are hotels and motels for sale. Many of the smaller ones, say fewer than 100 rooms, are of an older category that fits into the limited service line. Older hotels or motels often have single-loaded corridors, which are rarely built today, as the rooms are designed back-to-back and have a single window and door in front that open out to the corridor. People walk in front of the window, which forces the room's inhabitants to keep the drapes closed to maintain privacy. Investors should avoid investing in hotels that have single-loaded corridors. Double-loaded corridors are the typical design where rooms are accessed through a door that opens to the corridor and have windows in the wall opposite the door that can provide a view to the outside—of the ocean, for example—or open to an interior airshaft. Some properties may have a mix of both single- and double-loaded corridors.

Disadvantages of Lodging Investments

The biggest disadvantage in investing in hotels or motels is the inability to control competition. The ideal location on an intersection of two major interstate highways that happens to be five to eight hours' driving time between four major population centers might seem perfect for a new franchise hotel. Unfortunately, eight other hotel companies may have thought exactly the same, and suddenly there may be eight new hotels looking for customers that only occasionally fill five of them up to a 70 percent level on an annual basis.

Hotels can be very hard to finance, especially if the investors have little experience in their operation. This forces a motivated seller to hold a purchase money mortgage, which can be good for the buyer, but those kinds of financing are often for short terms and at a higher interest than the business can support.

14

DEVELOP YOUR OWN INVESTMENT COMFORT ZONE TO ENSURE SUCCESS IN REAL ESTATE INVESTING

Focus, knowledge, due diligence, and clear goals are key factors when pursuing any investment category. Real estate investors should focus their time and effort to a narrow market area, which ideally will be close to where the investor spends the majority of his or her time, and decide exactly what kind of investment real estate they wish to buy.

The first step is for the investor to form an investment comfort zone in a part of town that meets the guidelines of this chapter. Once this has occurred, the investor can begin working in that area. In a short while, by following the plan outlined in this book, you will begin to see opportunities. The primary goal of this chapter is to illustrate five steps that any investor can take to establish his or her comfort zone and to show how that zone will be critical to the investor's success in real estate investing. After introducing some key terms, this chapter will show you how to establish a geographic territory, become the expert of that territory, document what you investigate, build the investment techniques required, and act on opportunities.

KEY TERMS

In this section, the following terms related to developing a comfort zone in real estate investment are defined and explained:

- Goal orientation
- Priority of time
- Sphere of reference
- Search for the void

Knowing and understanding these terms and issues related to them will help you to learn and apply the concepts presented in this chapter.

Goal Orientation

A major factor for attaining success in anything is the strength of a person's focus on his or her goals. As important as focus is, the reader should understand that without a well-defined goal, success will continually slip away.

Proper goal orientation requires work and practice, and continual fine-tuning must take place along the way. In real estate investing the adjustments occur as investors learn about their own aspirations, future desires, and abilities and expand on each. In each situation the individual will discover that it is too confining to set goals within the current reach of those abilities. Every goal process *must* include the improvement of the individual's abilities so that greater and more challenging goals can be set, attempted, and achieved. Some of the most successful people in any form of endeavor are continually learning, and they take pride in this process. People who think they know it all already know all they will ever learn. In contrast, the person seeking success should make an effort to learn something meaningful every day, and then apply that new bit of knowledge as soon as possible. This is the formula for happiness as well as for success.

These wonderful phrases lead to success: "I didn't know that, will you teach it to me?" "I need to learn how to do that. What would you suggest I do?" "Boy, you make that look so easy; would you show me how to do it?"

When you don't know something, admit it; then ask how to learn it. People will respect your desire to learn.

Priority of Time

When the goal is clearly in sight, and the steps to get from start to finish are well planned, the proper use of time becomes a critical step in the attainment of that goal. If time is not valued, a goal may take too long to attain, and frustration and disappointment can become stronger than the desire to attain the goal.

A common error is to underestimate the time it will take to attain a certain intermediate step. For example, one of the elements of creating a comfort zone is to become an expert on the property and events that are going on within that zone. This is not an overnight process. In fact, it is a process that continues for the entire time of involvement in that investment zone. However, the process must start somewhere, and a certain definite time must be set aside for the process to occur. That time should build rather slowly to allow the investor to adapt to the new and growing sphere of reference.

Sphere of Reference

As the comfort zone develops, investors will see and feel the growth of the sphere of reference around them. If the reader faithfully completes The Real Estate Investor's VIP List of sources of "insider" real estate information introduced in Chapter 15, for example, this sphere of reference will be 1,000 percent greater than it was the day this book was opened.

Step-by-step this sphere grows. The **sphere of reference** is the envelope of everything that goes on around investors over which they have some control, or if not control, direct contact. The process is not automatic, however, as to gain benefit from the natural process, investors must follow up on the growing contacts around them. Keep this firmly in mind when the line for the name of the secretary is completed in the Investor's VIP list. Much is accomplished through the VIP's secretary.

Sphere of reference must be treated as a two-way relationship. While it is important for you to expand the number of VIPs in your community, it is even more important that the people you add to your list recognize that you too are a VIP. This factor alone will launch you into the real estate "insider's club" quicker than you dreamed possible. It is easy to get to know someone, and a bit more difficult to make sure *they* got to know *you*. You attain that status by working at building your reputation in this "insider's club."

Search for the Void

Any endeavor will have its best chance for success when it fills a void. Remember the supply and demand theory of economics—well, it is similar with opportunities. The greater opportunity is the one that, when taken, will fill someone's need so there will no longer be a void. Think of an opportunity as a black hole, a star whose gravity is so great that even light cannot escape. We know black holes exist even though we cannot see them. It is the effect that they exert on surrounding celestial bodies that exposes their existence. So it is with opportunities. They are really there all the time, only we often do not recognize that there is something about that location, or property, or use that has not been fully, if at all, taken advantage of.

Have you noticed how often two competitive businesses suddenly appear, one right after the other, at an intersection of two busy streets? Drugstores, banks, fast-food restaurants, and many other kinds of businesses suddenly have noticed a void in a neighborhood and rush to fill it. This kind of "filling the void" is more a copycat situation, but it is worth paying attention to because being the second (or even third) to recognize the opportunity might even be better than being the first.

As you move from this book into the real world of real estate investing, you will begin to automatically notice these voids. Often they are very subtle, however, and you have to train yourself to see what is missing and how you can fill the need.

The void is not always a need that is completely unmet; it might be something as simple as giving sparkle to an otherwise great property by making aesthetic changes to the buildings. Investors who purchase tired, out-of-date shopping strip malls know from experience that a fresh, modern look can turn around a property that otherwise is a candidate for a wrecking ball.

ESTABLISH A GEOGRAPHIC TERRITORY

The first step is to decide *where* your investment comfort zone will be. It is important that the zone meet the following five minimum criteria.

- **Your comfort zone should be convenient to where you live and/ or work.** This should be obvious, but many investors are drawn away from where they live or work by that nasty "greener grass syndrome." You might find diamonds in the rough 100 miles from where you live or work, but my bet is that if you apply the techniques in this book you will also find them in your own community.
- **Your comfort zone should not be a deteriorating neighborhood.** A deteriorating neighborhood is usually obvious, but there may be plans in the works not yet publicized that are about to shake up a stable neighborhood. One such event might be the closing of the only major employer in the community, or a new superhighway that is going to slice through the neighborhood, cutting it in half and making it either inaccessible or undesirable. Whatever the situation, the investor should avoid spending any time in a deteriorating neighborhood. In fact, if you live in one, my suggestion would be to get out as soon as possible. Where you live can have a profound effect on your mental outlook. Living in a negative area of town will affect you negatively. If you look hard, and even use some "sweat equity," you can move to an improving neighborhood more easily than you think. Live and work in positive surroundings.
- **Your comfort zone should contain affordable properties.** Affordable properties do not mean properties an investor thinks he or she can afford at this moment. By the time you have completed this course, you will have discovered it is possible to buy properties and profit from them even though they may seem out of reach, pricewise, at this moment in time. *Affordable* means property that is priced from the middle of the specific market for the area to the lower end of that same market. If the price range is from $150,000 to $250,000, then the affordable range is from $150,000 to $200,000. That is the area in which there can still be improvement in value, and it may present an opportunity to investors.
- **Your comfort zone should be expandable.** At the start, your comfort zone should be large enough to allow you to begin with a range of properties so that you can slowly expand your zone to several hundred property owners. The basic reason for this is to give you a wide choice of properties from which to select, while at the same time limiting the size of the zone with which you start. This will enable you to focus attention on a narrow part of town. The actual number of property owners will vary depending on the category of real estate on which you have decided to focus. If you

want to concentrate on small B category commercial retail buildings, this category may not be as expansive as buying single-family homes to remodel and resell.

  • **Your comfort zone should be within one community.** In the beginning investors need to concentrate their efforts on one governmental process. Different communities, even though they neighbor each other, often have different procedures, rules, ordinances, and possibly worse, a different attitude about real estate developments. Investors should concentrate on one closed area so they can get to know it like the back of their hands before moving to another. If there are two different possible comfort zones and all the criteria are similar except for the governmental attitude toward real estate development, then select the community that works with rather than against property owners and real estate investors.

BECOME THE EXPERT OF THAT TERRITORY

The fortunate part of real estate investment is that nearly everything of importance occurs locally and generally slowly. This localized and slow-to-mature nature of things makes it possible for any determined investor to become an expert in any given area in a relatively short period of time. But even though becoming an expert in real estate matters is very simple and basic, most property owners have never taken these steps.

This chapter and the rest of Part 3 detail the steps you can take to develop your investment comfort zone and how to get the most out of your zone. The steps are simple, and all that is needed is well-planned use of what limited time is available. Following is a list of the information investment experts strive to obtain about their comfort zone. Keep in mind that many of these factors change from time to time, and thus a constant review of the current circumstances is required.

Twenty Facts Experts Know About Their Investment Comfort Zone
  1. Geographic layout
  2. Street names
  3. Subdivision names
  4. Zoning rules and regulations
  5. Local ordinances that affect real estate
  6. Price ranges by subdivision and/or by street
  7. Rental market data and rents charged
  8. Future road plans

9. Future utility plans
10. Future developments that are in planning stages
11. Local employment statistics
12. Employment trends
13. Major impacts that will affect employment trends
14. The "how" and "who" of local government
15. The "what," "how," and "who" of the local building department
16. Private and public schools that serve the area
17. Bus and other local transportation routes
18. The "what," "how," and "who" of public records
19. Names of prominent business leaders in the community
20. Sources for local financing

And where does this data come from? The sources have already been discussed. There are just a few, and the most bountiful of all is the deed search that would be accomplished by a Realtor or at the tax assessor's office (see Chapter 15). Every item mentioned in the list is part of the public data that is available. It is up to the devoted investor to utilize the public information sources disclosed in this book to extract the data that can provide the path to his or her own success.

DOCUMENT WHAT YOU INVESTIGATE

With the advent of the digital camera, it is possible to create a visual archive of your entire comfort zone. Over the years this archive will need to be updated because real estate changes its appearance as buildings are removed, landscape matures, colors are changed, and so forth—but a single digital flash stick may actually be all you need to maintain this data. If you maintain your data on a single flash stick (say 8 gigabites), be sure that you back up the information to a hard drive or another flash stick. Also get used to having file folders that have descriptive names that hold specific data. For example, all the property information for Dolphin Isles Subdivision should be compartmentalized within one folder. You might have subfolders in the Dolphin Isles folder, such as: "Owners Data," "Sold Property Info," "Active on the Market," and so on. Another folder might be "Building and Zoning" with subfolders for building codes, contacts, and planning and zoning meetings.

Keeping records of zoning ordinances and building rules and restrictions is as simple as going to the appropriate community office (city and/or county building and/or zoning departments) and purchasing the document.

An alternative approach would be to check the Internet for those departments to see if the data is available in a downloadable file. The advantage with the Internet form is that it will usually indicate the date of the last update. This is important because any building and/or zoning ordinance is subject to changes.

BUILD THE INVESTMENT TECHNIQUES REQUIRED

Part 4 of this book, "How You Buy Establishes How You Profit in Real Estate Investing," will help you build the techniques that will become the tools for building your investment portfolio. As with any tool, practice with each technique will hone the edge and will give the investor confidence in both the technique and his or her ability to use it.

Just as no single tool can be used for every purpose, so it is with real estate investing techniques. By now the reader has been introduced to various techniques that investors use through the examples in this book. By the time you finish this course, how and when to apply these techniques to best attain the desired results will begin to be evident. However, continued study beyond this course is recommended because the real estate environment is constantly changing. Tax laws that affect real estate depreciation or tax consequences in the event of a sale or other disposition of the property go through frequent changes by the Internal Revenue Service, and adjustments in investment plans may be needed to keep abreast of the current events. Periodic Internet searches using keywords such as "government perks for real estate investors" will help you locate news on current real estate issues.

ACT ON OPPORTUNITIES

As you begin to get the feel for your comfort zone, there will be a sudden shift in what you actually see. It is almost like looking at a forest and not recognizing one species of tree from another. They are all green, and while some may stand out as pines, the rest may look more or less the same. Finding that sugar maple may be an impossible task—until you learn what a sugar maple looks like. The same perception happens in the investment comfort zone.

Opportunities in real estate are rarely so obvious that they have a sign out front that announces them as the "opportunity of the day." Frequently it is the subtle, not so obvious potential for economic conversion that guarantees a profit.

When you get to know the geographic territory like the back of your hand and have a firm grasp of the 20 facts mentioned earlier in this chapter, opportunities will stand out like sugar maples growing among pines.

Avoid the following pitfalls when building your comfort zone:

1. Don't look for shortcuts.
2. Let failure work for you, not against you.
3. Don't let anyone tell you that you can't succeed.

Avoid shortcuts. The key is to keep working at the process and to continue to build your very important sphere of reference. But remember that building a sphere of reference only works if the particular reference gets to know and remember you. This requires follow-up on your part. If you are looking for shortcuts, you will find many, but they are all pathways to some other destination, and not to the goal you seek.

Failure is what I call "the French word," as it is soft and alluring if you say it slowly while at the same time thinking of an evening in Paris as you stroll along the river bank. . . . There is nothing harsh or sinister about the way the word sounds. Then why is everyone so frightened of it? Fail is what people, even successful people, do a lot of the time. In fact, if failure occurs just a little bit less than half the time, that can be a signal that you are really on your way to a huge success. People who are not successful in working their comfort zone lack success because they do not take chances. It is usually not that they shirk responsibility and hard work—quite the opposite; they often work harder than others trying to avoid a situation where they may (heaven forbid) actually *fail* at something.

Think of everything as small bits and pieces that guide you to success. If your goal is to buy a small income property, for example, then look at the elements that can lead to that goal:

1. Get to know the area.
2. Look at everything on the market.
3. Find a Realtor who is compatible with this goal.
4. Build your comfort zone until you know more about it than the property owners there.
5. Make offers.

6. Get counteroffers.
7. Fine-tune those counteroffers until you get an acceptance.
8. Work with cooperative sellers to **close a deal**.
9. Start over again so you can close more deals.

These steps contain intermediary steps that have to be accomplished, but each is a move in a positive direction. Frequently the drive toward the goal loses momentum at items 4 and 5. Somebody steps in the way—a broker, a lawyer, or a negative seller who actually says no to your offer. None of these people are roadblocks; they represent road signs to make you stop for a while and see if something can be done to work out the deal or to move on to another property and another seller. There will always be another seller.

The unfortunate aspect of life is that there are more negative people than positive people. The nice part of life is that positive people generally attract more positive people around them. It is simple mathematics, if you think about it. Because there are more negative people, and because positive people attract more positive people, then make the shift and get in on another simple fact of life:

Positive people enjoy their success, while negative people never believe they have attained enough of it.

15

SECRETS TO GETTING THE INSIDE TRACK TO REAL ESTATE VALUES AND TRENDS

The primary goal of this chapter is to introduce the reader to the main sources of "trend" information and other real estate data that will help the investor keep track of the local real estate market. In addition, this chapter provides hints on how to use that data to discover potential investment opportunities.

Many private and governmental organizations spend millions of dollars collectively on research and studies that can be of great benefit to the local real estate investor. In addition to this data, there is a vast wealth of public information about real estate. This data can give the investor a full and complete history of virtually every real estate transaction that has taken place within recent times. The data is usually so complete that it is easy for investors to discover prices paid, payoff dates of mortgages, cost of improvements, names of current and past owners, and much more. All this information is generally available to the investor willing to ask for it.

KEY TERMS

In this section, the following terms related to real estate values and trends are defined and explained:

- Deed search
- Legal description
- Tax assessment

Knowing and understanding these terms and issues related to them will help you to learn and apply the concepts presented in this chapter.

Deed Search

There is a record of virtually every real estate transaction. This information is recorded in the official records of the county in which that property is located. This information is very comprehensive and usually includes the following data:

- Previous owner
- Current owner
- Current owner's address (often different from the property address)
- Property address
- Legal description of the property
- Tax folio (number used by tax assessor)
- Assessed value (for both improvements and vacant land)
- Square footage of land area
- Tax assessment
- Data on improvements: square footage, date constructed
- Price of last transfer(s)

Legal Description

This is the description given to every property that distinguishes it from another property. In subdivided property, this description is written as **lot, block, and subdivision**:

Lot 5 of Block 20 of West Highlands Subdivision, in East Ridge County, Texas.

Rural property may be described in **metes and bounds,** which is a descriptive form that gives actual measurements from a known starting point.

From Marker 107 on State Road 17 West 270 degrees a distance of 82.4 feet to a point of beginning, thence Northerly and parallel to the right-of-way of State Road 17 a distance of 200 feet, thence West 270 degrees a distance of 1200 feet, thence South 180 degrees a distance of 200 feet, thence East 90 degrees 1200 feet to the point of beginning.

The above metes and bounds describe a tract of land that has 200 feet of frontage on State Road 17 and is a rectangle that is 200 feet by 1,200 feet.

    Section, township, and range descriptions are common for large tracts of land. The entire United States is divided into township and range lines. Each crossing forms a grid that encloses 36 sections. A section consists of a square that is approximately one mile on each side (there will be very slight adjustments in these sizes due to the curvature of the earth). Each section is divided into quarters, and each is quarter further divided into quarters or halves. A section of land consists of 640 acres.

    The following legal description refers to a tract of land that is 40 acres in size:

The North East quarter of the South West quarter of Section 36, Township 49 South, Range 41 West.

Tax Assessment

The tax assessment is the amount of money charged by the local taxing authority against the property. This sum generally includes several items that are lumped together from the different taxing authorities within the county. These may include school board, hospital district, city taxes, county taxes, and special assessments. Most of these amounts are based on a percentage called **millage,** which is then multiplied by the assessed value. The underlying assessed value is an evaluation that may not actually reflect the real value or the market value of the property. It has been customary in many parts of the country for the assessed value to take into consideration age (and therefore depreciation) and other factors with the result that a property built today may have an assessed value greater than an identical one built 20 years earlier.

    All property owners can challenge the assessed value if they have reason to support what they feel is an excess evaluation. When property assessments are generally less than the market value, property owners usually do not contest the evaluation. After all, as tax assessors are quick to point out, you would not sell the property for the tax-assessed value, would you? However, because property assessed values rarely equal the market value, the relative assessment of one property should be in balance with all other properties of similar criteria in the area. The owner of any property assessed more than the average value of similar properties would have a very good reason to contest the higher tax evaluation.

To contest an assessed value properly, the property owner should gather as much information about the assessed values for all property within the general area of the subject property and isolate properties most similar in size (lot size and property square footage). The subject property should have an assessed value in line with these other properties, despite the possibility that none of the assessed values may match real or market values. Investors should acquaint themselves with the procedures to contest tax-assessed values, as most tax assessment departments have an annual deadline for any tax dispute.

COMPILING TREND INFORMATION USING THE REAL ESTATE INVESTOR'S VIP LIST

There are four important questions when compiling sources of trend information:

1. Where can this source be found?
2. What data can be obtained?
3. Who is the best source?
4. How can the information be used?

Examine each of the following sources with particular attention to the answers to these four questions. Enter the information you gather in The Real Estate Investor's VIP List at the end of this book for use as a primary source of the contact information you will use to compile the trend information you need to meet your real estate investing goals.

Once you are in touch with the appropriate person, ask specific questions about what information is available and how to obtain the information. Each locality may vary greatly in how information is disseminated to the public. In general, the following list of information to be gathered will serve as the starting point for each of the sources:

Source Checklist

1. Name of source.
2. Address, phone number, and fax number.
3. Names of persons in charge of future planning and agendas.
4. Names of persons in charge of complaints.
5. Are there any meetings open to the public?
6. If so, what is the schedule?
7. What are the office hours?
8. What information is available that would be helpful to real estate investors?
9. Is there a charge for the data? If so, how much?
10. Can this person recommend other information sources that would be helpful to real estate investors?
11. Can you be put on a mailing list?

PUBLIC SOURCES OF REAL ESTATE TREND INFORMATION

Useful public sources of real estate trend information for investors include the following:

- Airport, sea, river, or lake port authorities
- Banks and savings and loan institutions
- Building and zoning departments
- Chamber of commerce
- County-recorded documents
- Government planning offices
- Industrial development board

Each is explored in detail in the following sections.

Airport, Sea, River, or Lake Port Authorities

Where Can This Source Be Found?

Local airports, sea, river, or lake ports may not be found in every community, or there may be several within easy commuting distance. If there is one or more within a drive time radius of an hour and a half, the investor should make contact with the appropriate management offices of each to ascertain who is in charge of future planning for the facility.

What Data Can Be Obtained?

Growth and business trends for airports and water ports are very important because they can give long-range signals that are important to real estate growth or decline. Because the expansion of this type of facility often involves very long-range planning and government funding, the data often is very comprehensive and extends well beyond the actual port facilities themselves. For example, to substantiate a multimillion-dollar federal loan or grant request, the data submitted may contain statistics on every aspect of the local community including new business patterns, population growth, long-range travel patterns, and much more. Expansions of any kind of port may also require other infrastructure to be developed, such as railways, new or expanded road systems, hotels, rental car facilities, local transportation, and other service businesses. In a growth pattern, everything tends to give cause for some other business to grow. In a decline, the sudden disappearance of businesses rarely will come as a surprise to the investor who has been following the information closely.

Who Is the Best Source?

Start at the top. In most cases, port facilities are under some sort of local government control: generally, a county commissioner is appointed or elected to oversee the operations, or a professional manager is hired to run the day-to-day operations of the facility. If there is a commissioner (elected or appointed), that is the person to contact first. If there is a manager below the commissioner, the investor would ask the commissioner (or the commissioner's secretary) to introduce him or her to that manager. This may be accomplished over the phone.

How Can the Information Be Used?

In the beginning, the data collected may have no direct bearing on what an investor is doing. The long-range goal is to make the initial contact and find out the details of the situation. As the investor begins to collect information from different sources, a pattern will begin to evolve. The most important part of this evolution will be the growing confidence the investor gains by virtue of becoming an expert on the area.

Some information may be instantly useable. Learning of a new expansion or major cutback would obviously give the investor a lead in the marketplace.

Banks and Savings and Loan Institutions

Where Can This Source Be Found?

Pick the biggest three lending institutions in the comfort zone or nearest to it and start there. The major lenders are a good start. Later on, the investor may be introduced to other lenders from different sources. This building of contacts is an excellent way to establish a position in the community as a real estate investor.

What Data Can Be Obtained?

The first data to obtain from lenders is the kinds of property they make loans on. Other useful information would be:

- Is the institution expanding or cutting back?
- What parts of town are lenders expanding to?
- Who is in charge of their REO (real estate owned) department?
- Who is their best loan officer?
- What are their lending rates and loan charges (points and other out-of-pocket expenses)?

How Can the Information Be Used?

Again, the major goal is the contact. However, it is very important for the investor to know what properties lenders will lend on before he or she spends a lot of time looking in the wrong direction for properties on which lenders will not make favorable loans. When it is time to apply for a loan, the contacts made within the lending side of real estate will be very valuable. Every potential loan should be "shopped" between at least two or three lenders, and an investor who has spent the time to meet with and develop some rapport with loan officers at different lending institutions will have a much easier time getting the loan officer to "go that extra mile" to get the best loan amount and terms possible.

Building and Zoning Departments

Where Can This Source Be Found?

This source is found within both the county and the city where the property is located. These departments have already been discussed in previous chapters.

Every local community has a building department that may or may not be combined with the zoning department. Investors need to become acquainted with both the city and the county offices, as each may have some control over the use of property within their boundaries.

What Data Can Be Obtained?
Building restrictions and codes and zoning ordinances affect or control what can be built and how property can be used. In addition, these sources become primary data banks for future growth and development as virtually every major project (and many minor ones) goes through the process of **site plan approval**, which may occur months before the groundbreaking occurs.

Who Is the Best Source?
The person to contact may depend on how the departments are organized. In general, there are four people with whom the investor would want to establish rapport:

1. Chief building inspector
2. Head of planning department
3. Head of zoning department
4. City clerk

In small communities, all of these responsibilities may be delegated to one or two people.

How Can the Information Be Used?
This is part of this continual building process of getting to know the "who," "what," and "why" of real estate. The obvious advantage is that the investor can learn of future projects that can give advance lead time to tie up properties that are in the path or just beyond the path of progress. Investors should never assume that just because this information is available, the general public would know about it. The truth is that the general public rarely hears about future projects until they actually break ground. Even when a proposed project is reported in a newspaper, several years may pass without further mention, and whatever the public learned is forgotten. Well-informed investors know this and take advantage of it.

Chamber of Commerce

Where Can This Source Be Found?

Virtually every community in the United States has a chamber of commerce that promotes the influx of new commercial development as well as the exploitation of existing businesses. A private but associated organization, the junior chamber of commerce, consists of local businesspeople interested in accomplishing the same goals. Each of these organizations becomes a good starting place for the investor to build lists of important people and information sources. In addition, the investor can become a member of both the chamber of commerce and the junior chamber of commerce and participate in their frequent functions, which are excellent places to meet the local VIPs on their home turf.

What Data Can Be Obtained?

Statistical data on employment, employers, local government, taxes, investment incentives, future development, and population demographics are just some of the useful information available from the chamber of commerce. Promotional material about the community can be very useful in putting together a brochure or marketing program to sell a property in the investment portfolio.

Who Is the Best Source?

As usual, start at the top and work down to those who actually do the work in the areas of interest. Because the chamber of commerce is a good meeting place of important people, the best sources of information may come from the contacts made there rather than the chamber itself.

How Can the Information Be Used?

The chamber of commerce is a sphere-building organization in addition to being a good source for growth trends. Contacts made within this and other such organizations will provide good references as well as become an excellent source of referrals.

County-Recorded Documents

Where Can This Source Be Found?

Public recording of documents is one facet of the detailed record keeping that is a part of most modern societies. In the United States, as elsewhere, the usual authority for record keeping falls to the local county offices. All transactions required to be recorded that have taken place within that county would be on record at those offices.

What Data Can Be Obtained?

The magnitude of the different kinds of records that must be or are recorded is monumental. A partial list of such documents is shown below:

- **Adverse possession:** A person or other entity claims title to a property by virtue of having taken possession of the property according to the provisions of state law.
- **Affidavits:** Statements legally attested to as being truthful.
- **Deed transfers:** All real estate deed transfers should be recorded to protect the rights of the new owner.
- **Divorce actions:** Generally these are recorded to show change of marital status and legal obligations thereof.
- **Leases:** May be recorded.
- **Liens:** Several different kinds of liens are recorded. The most usual are tax liens, mechanics liens, and legal judgments.
- **Lis pendens:** A form of lien against the property.
- **Mortgages:** Both the note and the mortgage are recorded to ensure proper notice to any subsequent lender that there is already a loan made with the property pledged as security.
- **Satisfactions:** When any lien or mortgage has been paid in full, a satisfaction of lien will show that the property owner has been released from the obligation.

It is easy to see, from the different items mentioned above, that county recorded documents can provide many potential leads for the real estate investor. The most useful data is the deed transaction records, which, along with other property records, are assimilated by the local tax assessor and can be viewed in one composite set of records in the **deed search** mentioned earlier in this chapter. The deed search, however, will not have the full details that would be visible in the copy of the recorded deed or other document that can be found within the county records.

Who Is the Best Source?

Most county records departments have one or more people who assist the public in finding information. Because the information may be spread among different departments, the investor should anticipate spending a few hours to learn where and how the information is retrieved. Most modern records offices have data on microfilm or microfiche, which is updated frequently to ensure that the latest recorded documents are included. Because making microfilm and microfiche takes time, the data available is *never* current. In searching for important documents, it would be helpful to know how many days it usually takes between recording and the microfilm or microfiche being available for that specific system.

How Can the Information Be Used?

The use of the information depends on the data obtained. Deed searches are used most because the information applies directly to the investor's goals. Find out who owns the property, what that owner paid for the property, and what improvements have been made. Discovering details on the property such as size, square footage, tax assessments, and the like are all part of the learning process to become an expert on the comfort zone. Death notices suggest possible properties for sale; birth notices suggest the need for a larger home and the sale or other disposition of the existing one. Mortgage satisfactions indicate that the mortgagor no longer has an obligation to meet and may now be ready to move up and take on more debt, and of great importance, the mortgagee may have received cash ahead of time that could be spent on something else. Divorce data opens up other doors that are both buy and sell possibilities.

Government Planning Offices

Where Can This Source Be Found?

Government is almost everywhere until you try to find the right person to help you with your problem. With real estate investing, several different government planning offices or departments are very helpful. These offices may be duplicated within an investor's comfort zone because of adjoining city, county, or state offices that may have some control or effect within cities. The investor should start with the city offices and departments and expand from that point. The question, "What other office or governmental department has control or affects real estate?" should become a habit whenever dealing with any governmental department. Often, unless this question is asked, the needed information is not volunteered.

Important Government Planning Offices or Departments
- Department of transportation
- Health department

- Department of planning
- Building rules review
- Utilities (water and sewer)
- Parks and public works
- Schools
- Hospitals

The investor should be aware that the titles for these offices or departments may vary, and that each office or department may have several divisions. The department of transportation, for example, may have a bus division, roadway division, metro division, and so on.

What Data Can Be Obtained?

A vast amount of data flows through these offices and departments, and in general, the investor should divide the data into two types: data on control and data on changes to the status quo.

Data on **control** would be any information that shows or indicates where the government exerts control over real estate, whether directly or indirectly. A direct control would be the building codes or city ordinances that limit or restrict what can be done on or to a property. Indirect controls are less obvious and generally occur in administrative procedures that must be met prior to building or obtaining permits. An example would be the requirement for the *community itself* to meet state or county standards before any new building can occur. In this situation, the individual may be prevented from doing something and may have no direct remedy until the city meets the standards set by higher authority.

Data on **changes to the status quo** is very important because the proposed changes may have a major impact on the property values in any area— either positive or negative.

Who Is the Best Source?

Start with the head of any government department.

How Can the Information Be Used?

Investors increase their sphere of reference by building their contacts within the governmental offices that control or affect real estate. The contacts themselves can become more important than any single bit of information, unless that bit leads you directly to the bargain property that is turned into a gold mine. The investor will look for any data that points to a change in the status quo because this is the kind of information that leads to opportunities.

Industrial Development Board

Where Can This Source Be Found?

This organization, when present within a community, functions for the sole purpose of bringing new commercial development to the community. This body often has the power to assist in financing by the issuance of industrial bonds, which are usually a tax-free investment for the purchaser of the bond, guaranteed by the local community. The funds are then lent to companies to pay for new construction, training of employees, plant investment, and other start-up costs for new enterprises coming to the area. These loans are usually issued on a long-term payback at a modest interest rate lower than the usual bank rates available from institutional lenders.

What Data Can Be Obtained?

The usual information that would be helpful to a real estate investor would be growth in the business or industrial sectors. This office or department also may provide lists for new companies interested in locating in the area. These new companies may become tenants for investors who have existing properties to rent or in future buildings to be built. A major employer who comes to the community can have a major impact on real estate values, so land and other property may go up or down in value depending on the nature of the employer (or up in one place and down in another). The sooner the investor knows where that employer is going to locate (even if that investor has nothing to do with the relocation), the better the investment opportunity.

Who Is the Best Source?

The chairperson of the board is usually an appointed member but may be an elected official who has been given this added authority.

READ THE DAILY NEWSPAPER ANNOUNCEMENTS

A good habit for any real estate investor is to read the daily review of local public announcements published in local newspapers. These announcements occur in both the classified section of the newspaper and in normal display format, which may have no specific location in the paper. These announcements may be required by law and may provide information on anything from sheriff sales to foreclosures on properties. Divorces, marriages, deaths, public meetings, zoning changes, proposed public works, and so on are all part of the usual public announcements, courtesy of the local newspaper.

Over the next several days, look for any public announcement such as those described above. Many can be seen as relatively large display advertising, often showing a sketch or drawing of community boundaries; others are in classified form and are frequently found at the beginning of the classified advertising section. Find and read several different ones, but most importantly these three:

1. Foreclosure notice of sale
2. Deed transfer
3. Mortgage satisfaction

If the local newspaper does not carry each of these three legal notices, then find out if there is a "legal newspaper" published in your area. The local library as well as most lawyers' offices would have a copy, and you can always subscribe to it later

Obtain a copy of the plat of a subdivision in your target comfort zone, or any area of the local community where you reside or work. Pick one block of residential property and ask a realtor contact to run a deed search (in the detailed long form of data it will contain) for that entire block, from which you would get the names and addresses of present and past owners, legal descriptions, property assessments, taxes, prices paid in the past, and much more data. Or, better, go to the local tax assessor's office and tell the clerk you want to do a deed search for the entire subdivision where you live (or work, or want to live or work). Make sure you have a subdivision in mind prior to asking this question. Once you have the computer printout, ask the clerk to go over a sample listing to explain each of the codes and abbreviations in the search.

The information that you now have in front of you will show you the magnitude of the data that is available. If this subdivision becomes part of your comfort zone, you are well on your way to learning about the market for those properties. You have a history of sales, what buyers paid, tax data, assessed values, and the names and addresses of the property owners. Use this as a building block

16

HOW TO EVALUATE A PROPERTY BEFORE YOU BUY IT

The best way to ensure future profit is to make sure that the purchase price paid does not exceed the current value and that the potential as an income-producing or speculative investment for appreciation is within your financial reach. By this I mean, will you be able to sustain a sufficient period where you may be required to carry the property from your present pre-investment income and/or your savings? Even if there were no debt to worry about, maintenance, taxes, and insurance costs will exist. Most prospective investors tend to buy with as little capital invested as necessary, and many over-leverage the investment with excessive debt service. Living on the edge might be exciting if you are an athlete, but it can bring you to financial ruin in the investment world. This is magnified a thousandfold when 70 percent of the purchase price (or more) is borrowed.

After introducing some key terms, this chapter list some issues to consider when choosing an evaluator, then describes three basic methods of property evaluation: the income approach, market value approach, and replacement value approach. All income properties should be valued using the first two methods, and it is not critical which of the two is completed first. Normally the market value approach will show a greater value than the income value approach once the prospective buyer has adjusted the data supplied by the seller. The replacement value approach has merit only when the replacement cost is considerable and the use in the present condition can substantiate a value close to the income approach. Generally, an investor looks for a property that generates income and can be substantiated with a matching market value. Many older properties would not be replaced as they were originally built, so concentrate on the first two methods.

KEY TERMS

In this section, the following terms related to property evaluation are defined and explained:

- Cash flow
- Desired return
- Net operating income calculations

Knowing and understanding these terms and issues related to them will help you to learn and apply the concepts presented in this chapter.

Cash Flow

Cash flow is the actual cash, or money in the bank, that is left at the end of any period after all expenses and debt service (except depreciation and income taxes) are deducted from the income from the property.

For example, Paula owns a building with eight one-bedroom apartments that are rented at an average of $500 per month. She has a first mortgage on the property of $210,000, with monthly payments for the next 24 years of $1,583.34 per month (principal and interest). Paula feels this property is worth $362,000. After subtracting the amount of the first mortgage from this price, Paula has an equity of $152,000.

Presumed value:	$362,000
Less mortgage amount:	−$210,000
Equity:	$152,000

Paula's Eight-Unit Apartment Complex

	Average	Annual
Gross rents	$4,000.00	$48,000.00
Less operating expenses	−$1,150.00	−$13,800.00
Less mortgage payments	−$1,583.00	−$19,000.00
Cash flow	$1,266.66	$15,200.00

Paula rationalizes that if a buyer paid $362,000 for the property there would be a 10 percent cash return on the $152,000 cash to mortgage investment, based on Paula's calculations of income and expense.

This would be true if the income remained at the level shown above. Even then, an investor must take into consideration a reasonable amount for vacancy and replacement as well as costs such as roof replacement, new air-conditioning, and the like.

Desired Return

The yield or return investors hope to make from their invested capital is the **desired return**. For example, if Paula had invested $76,000 in the eight-unit apartment complex along with the money obtained in the first mortgage ($210,000), she would realize a return of 20 percent based on the cash flow shown above of $15,200 per year. Most apartment properties are valued at a return after all expenses and taxes of 6 to 10 percent return on the cash invested. However, this is a relative issue, and many investors hope for far more than they will realize. In reality, as you will see shortly, it is possible to reap larger yields even if there is zero cash flow.

Net Operating Income Calculations

Arriving at the NOI is important because this is much the same as cash flow, except that the debt service is not deducted from the income. In the case of Paula's eight units, the net operating income would be as follows:

Annual gross income:	$48,000
Less operating expenses:	−$13,800
Net operating income:	$34,200

Because this is an eight-unit apartment building, a prospective buyer would see that this property is producing $4,275 of NOI per apartment ($34,200 ÷ 8

= \$4,275). If the prospective buyer is comparing another property with more or fewer apartments, a comparison of the price per unit and the NOI per unit may indicate which of the two properties is a better buy. This concept will be examined in more detail later in this chapter.

FACTORS IN CHOOSING AN EVALUATOR

The best evaluation is one that is made by a person who:

1. Has personally inspected the property
2. Is familiar with the area and comparable properties in the same general market category
3. Has no emotional connection to the property at the time of the evaluation
4. Does not receive compensation that is based on the results of the evaluation

Any of these four items can mitigate the results of an evaluation. Be careful with the fourth item because the fact that the evaluator is being compensated for the report does not in itself diminish the value of the evaluation. However, all buyers should be cautious of comparative evaluations that lean toward a property if the evaluator has a connection to the property, the owners or sellers of the property, or another person (such as a friend, relative, or associate) who will receive compensation if this property is selected for purchase.

INCOME APPROACH

Prior to attempting any evaluation, the investor or appraiser would require certain information to enable the evaluation to be as accurate as possible. The following pre-evaluation checklist can be used to gather the required information for rental apartment buildings; similar checklists can be made up by the investor for other types of properties following the same pattern.

Pre-Evaluation Checklist for Rental Apartment
Nave of apartment: _____
Address: _____
Owner/broker: _____
Phone number of owner/broker: _____

Number of units: _____

Studios: _____ 1 Bedroom: _____ 2 Bedroom: _____ 3

    Bedroom: _____

Asking price: _____ Evaluation: _____

Mortgage: _____

Monthly debt service: _____

Item on Checklist	Standard to the Market	As Presented by Owner	As Adjusted
Average rent per apartment	❏	❏	❏
Price per unit	❏	❏	❏
RE tax per unit	❏	❏	❏
RE tax per % gross rent	❏	❏	❏
Operating expenses per % gross	❏	❏	❏
Operating expenses per unit	❏	❏	❏
Vacancy per % gross rent	❏	❏	❏
Amount of repairs per unit	❏	❏	❏
Management expense	❏	❏	❏
NOI per unit	❏	❏	❏
Total NOI	❏	❏	❏
Less debt service	❏	❏	❏
Cash flow (NOI − debt service)	❏	❏	❏
Desired return or return available	❏	❏	❏
Evolution based on NOI	❏	❏	❏
Evolution based on cash flow	❏	❏	❏

Given the data on Paula's eight-unit apartment complex, a prospective investor, Frank, would analyze the property as in this manner.

Pre-Evaluation Checklist for Rental Apartments

Name of apartments: Paula's 8-unit apartment complex

Address: 1807 W. Marine Drive, Chicago, IL

Phone number of owner/broker: 312-555-5555

Number of units: 8

Studios: n/a   1 Bedroom: 8   2 Bedroom: n/a   3 Bedroom: n/a

Asking price: $362,000   Evaluation: _____

Mortgage: (1st) $210,000/with potential second from Paula

Monthly debt service: (1st) $1,583.34 per month (P&I)

Item on Checklist	Standard to the Market	As Presented by Owner	As Adjusted
Average rent per apartment	$500–525	$500	$500
Price per unit	$38,000	$45,250	
RE tax per unit	$760	$750	$750
RE tax per % gross rent	12.66%	12.5%	12.66%
Operating expenses per % gross rent	26%–35%	28.75%	30%
Operating expenses per unit (after vacancy)	$1,560 to $1,725	$1,995	$2,205
Vacancy per % gross rent	5%	0	5%
Amount of repairs per unit	$265	$100	$265
Management expenses	4%	0	4%
Estimate reserve for replacements per unit	$147.55		$147.55
NOI per unit		$4,275	$3,842.45
Total NOI		**$34,200**	**$30,739.60**
Less debt service		$19,000	$19,000
Cash flow (NOI−debt service)	$15,200	$11,739.60	
Desired return or return available	9%–12%	10%	12%
Evolution based on NOI		$342,000	$256,163
Evolution based on cash flow		$362,000	$307,830

Frank's Income Evaluation Approach of Paula's Eight-Unit Apartments

Based on the information provided by Paula, and prior to any review or adjustment to Paula's figures, Frank's initial evaluation of this property would be $285,000. Frank determined this by dividing the NOI by the desired return of 12 percent ($34,200 ÷ 0.12 = $285,000; remember when you divide or multiply by a percentage the decimal must be moved two places to the left). In essence, Frank has determined that $34,200 is 12 percent of $285,000. If Frank wants to earn a minimum of 12 percent on his investment, then the maximum he could pay (under the stated income and expenses) would be $285,000. Note carefully that the 12 percent figure is what Frank wants and is not an amount *fixed in stone*. Another investor may be very happy with a 9 percent return. At a 9 percent return the acceptable purchase price would be \$380,000 (\$34,200 ÷ 0.09 = \$380,000). A slight change in the desired return rate has a major impact on the purchase price a buyer would be willing to pay.

At this point the debt service is not considered, even though the actual debt service may have either a positive or a negative effect on the desired yield. The reason for this is that Frank is attempting to find a value for the property based solely on the income and operating expenses. Once that value has been found, additional study of the property and the terms of purchase will be pertinent.

Review of Income and Expenses

Any analysis of an income property should be reviewed in comparison to the local "standards" of operating expenses. Often the local tax assessor's office publishes these norms. It is important to follow the local standards of operating expenses because textbook rules of thumb are not accurate and can lead an investor into economic disaster. In addition, most sellers view their property optimistically and often show lower expenses than really exist.

This standard may show, in the case of Paula's eight apartment units, that the operating expenses for a rental with a rent of \$450 to \$550 per one-bedroom unit per month would be between 26 and 35 percent of the actual collected income. If the income actually collected was \$48,000, this would mean that the expenses could run between \$12,480 and \$16,800 per year for the unit. In his review of Paula's figures, Frank feels Paula has understated the **repairs** by failing to take into account future nonrecurring expenses by not showing actual capital expenses for major replacements or repairs. Frank decides that 30 percent of collected income for operating expenses would be sufficient as an estimate.

Adjusted Income and Expenses of Paula's Apartment Units

Gross	\$48,000.00	
Less vacancy factor (5%)	−2,400.00	
Collectable rents less operating expenses and sinking fund	\$45,600.00	
30% of collectable rents	\$13,680.00	\$1,710 per unit
Reserves	−\$1,180.40	\$147.55 per unit
Net operating income	\$30,739.60	\$3,842.45 per unit
Less debt service	−\$19,000.00	
Cash flow	\$11,739.60	

If Frank invests $97,830.00 and assumes the existing debt, he gets a real $11,739.60 return that will equal 12 percent on his invested capital. This is found by dividing the cash flow of $11,739.60 by 0.12, which equals $97,830.00. Adding the principal amount of the mortgage to this equity, per Frank's calculations to earn his desired rate, would place an evaluation on the property of $307,830 (the mortgage principal owed of $210,000 plus the equity of $97,830 equals $307,830).

In hopes of buying the property at this amount, Frank may offer Paula less to give himself a safety factor in case the calculations are optimistic and to leave some room for negotiations with Paula.

If Frank decides to reduce his desired return to 10 percent, the equity picture would change dramatically and he would be able to pay more for the property. For example, at a 10 percent return, the cash flow of $11,739.60 would reflect an equity of $117,396 or an overall price of $327,396 ($210,000 + $117,396 = $327,396).

Positive leverage is present in this situation, as is evident from the increase of evaluation between the NOI and cash flow calculations. In this example, the annual mortgage debt payments are at a lower *constant rate* than the desired return. The constant rate is the combination of interest and principal paid on the loan and is found by dividing the annual payment by the total amount of principal due at the start of that specific period. In the case of Paula's mortgage of $210,000 with a total annual payment of $19,000, the constant rate is 9.0476 percent ($19,000 ÷ $210,000 = 0.090476, which is then converted to a percentage by moving the decimal two places to the right: 9.0476 percent). The effect of the positive leverage increases the amount an investor could pay for the property and still earn the desired return over the NOI-based evaluation.

In this example, Frank has examined all the pertinent details and has taken a conservative approach to the evaluation of the property. In view of this it would be reasonable to expect that he would also look to a more realistic return, which according to the current marketplace could well be in the area of 9 to 10 percent.

Whatever Frank's final determination based on the income and expense approach, Frank would still want to follow up with the second evaluation process: the market value approach.

MARKET VALUE APPROACH

The market value approach to property evaluation does not consider current income and expenses in the evaluation process. Instead, this approach is a comparative analysis of one property against all others that have recently been sold and that are still on the market.

In many respects, this approach to value becomes the *fine-tuning* of the income and expense approach when the property in question is being valued for its income production. However, when the property has a value above that which is substantiated by its current income, the market approach may be the only realistic method of determining the relative value of the property.

The best way to determine the market value is to have a real estate broker review the **current listings** and **sold listings** from the local board of Realtors or, when available, the **deed transfer** information from the local courthouse property records. This kind of data is very valuable to real estate investors because it enables the investor to view entire subdivisions at a glance and see every real estate transfer that has taken place. By breaking down these transactions, real estate investors can find out the exact price other investors paid for similar properties.

The key to obtaining accurate information from a market approach is to look at data of *similar properties*. The investor should not look at broad-based data for this purpose. It is important to draw a conclusion from the specific market area only. This narrows the amount of data necessary and will produce a more accurate result. The question arises, how narrow an area determines the **market area**? The answer is found by asking several Realtors how broad an area *they* review when making a **listing presentation** to arrive at a market value. The answer generally is a very narrow approach into three or four subdivisions or areas of town where similar property attributes are found.

In some communities it is possible that a property is in a truly unique setting and that very few similar properties can be found. This type of property presents a major difficulty in obtaining a market value and thus is not for the novice investor.

The price per unit, average rent per unit, and NOI per unit are the three criteria that will help the investor narrow comparisons to similar properties.

In general, unless there has been a dramatic drop in property values, sold properties will indicate a lower per-unit price than the unsold property information. The investor must look at all available information about the geographic area to determine if property values are going down or if a poor seller's market has reached its bottom and therefore property values are about to rise. The market approach may not disclose this fact until the turn has already happened. A far better guide to such trends is when there is a sudden decrease of property on the market. This phenomenon occurs whenever there is a shift of the market in favor of the seller because casual sellers (sellers who say anything is for sale at a price) are the first to withdraw their property from the market when activity heats up.

Comparisons to market conditions should be made on the smallest increment of a property. Income per unit, price per unit, NOI per unit, and so on enable the investor to accurately compare different sized apartment complexes, different square footage shopping centers, and so on.

REPLACEMENT VALUE APPROACH

The cost to replace the land and buildings is often the method that the seller or seller's agent uses to establish property value. This method of evaluation is subject to unknown factors such as the following:

- The land value
- The cost to construct, furnish, and equip the property
- The value of any present tenants or income
- The cost associated with the time it would take to build the property new

Because of these more esoteric quantities, I discourage anyone from relying too much on a replacement cost, except when the price that can be obtained for the existing property is substantially less than the replacement value. The principal reason is this: If you were going to build a new building, would you do it at that location? Usually the only time that would be a yes is because that is exactly your plan, to tear down the existing structure and build new.

SEVEN KEY STEPS IN ACCURATE PROPERTY EVALUATIONS

The following steps will help you to ensure accurate property evaluations.

1. Inspect property weekly.
2. Keep good inspection records.
3. Track property history.
4. Maintain good property and investment files.
5. Review records before and after inspections.
6. Inspect other rental properties in the area.
7. Compare rent of competitive properties.

Each of these is explained in detail in this section.

Inspect Property Weekly

Personal inspection and then a review of those inspections are essential to building knowledge about what is going on in the market. Every investor should set up a series of files designed to aid in making future evaluations.

Keep Good Inspection Records

The basic file would be called the **inspected property** file. Along with listing brochures and other sales material available on the property, the investor should have a property inspection checklist like the one on the next page with personal notes indicating the investor's opinion of the property at the time of inspection. The property should be filed by address or legal description, with a note made in an **inspection log** that would show the exact date the inspection was made along with phone numbers of owners or agents for fast reference.

Track Property History

A **property sold** file would allow the investor to know where the comfort zone is moving and at what price. This information can include or be cross-referenced to the inspection file so that the investor begins to get a feel for values. When several properties have been inspected that later sell for different prices than expected, the total picture of value and why a buyer will pay more for one property over another begins to take firm shape.

Maintain Good Property and Investment Files

Three other files are very valuable to the real estate investor. These are **property listed**, **offers made**, and **property acquired**. The property listed file would contain a list of every property on the market in the comfort zone. Ultimately all of these properties should be inspected or reviewed (some may be vacant land or rental properties). When one of these properties is sold, the data would simply be moved over to the property sold file.

Records of an investor's offers to acquire property should be kept regardless of what happens to the offer. I know many investors who discard their old and unsuccessful offers. This is a mistake. When working in a comfort zone, there may be a future opportunity to acquire that same property.

Review Records Before and After Inspections

This might sound obvious, but it should be stressed. Having a constant reminder of what is going on is never a bad habit when it comes to real estate investing.

Property Inspection Checklist for Homes
Date of inspection: _____
Property address: _____
Legal address: _____
Description of property: _____
Owner: _____
Owner's address: _____
Owner's phone: _____
Reason for selling: _____
Broker: _____ Phone: _____
Property size: _____
Year building was constructed: _____
Bedrooms: _____; Bathrooms: _____
Family room: _____ Den: _____;
    Basement: _____
Eat-in kitchen: _____; Living room: _____
Dining room: _____;
    Dining area: _____; Pool: _____
Other features: _____

Inspect Other Rental Properties in the Area

Before making an offer on an income-producing property, inspect all rental properties in the immediate area (up to five blocks distant).

Once you are down to the wire as to what amount to offer and what terms you should present to the seller, you should make your offer as one-sided as you can by looking at the worst-case scenario as to data you have been given and the condition of the property. Make sure your offer has an out clause and is subject to further, more in-depth inspections. Once you have a lock on the property, you can fine-tune your evaluation. Do not hesitate to reopen negotiations if you are not satisfied.

Compare Rent of Competitive Properties

Make aesthetic and benefit judgments between the properties you are considering purchasing, and compare these to the amount of rent they produce.

This is often the final balancing act as to which property to purchase (you might have two or more offers out there and be trying to decide which is the best one to go with). Aesthetics and benefits to the tenants are critical, as one complex might have a pool, or even tennis courts, which might attract tenants but will also increase operating and replacement costs.

If you are planning to upgrade the property you are buying, which is always a good idea, then look for elements in the properties under consideration that you will be able to upgrade without much cost.

4

HOW YOU BUY ESTABLISHES HOW YOU PROFIT IN REAL ESTATE INVESTING

17

FOUR CREATIVE BUYING TECHNIQUES

E very real estate investor should become familiar with this chapter, as it introduces four creative real estate investment techniques that can help the reader begin a real estate investment career without large sums of capital. These techniques are basic and simple to use and understand, and they are often a part of major real estate transactions. Simplicity often works best. The four techniques are the option, sweat equity, lease/purchase, and secondary seller-held financing. First some key terms will be defined, and then each of these techniques will be explained in detail.

KEY TERMS

In this section, the following terms related to creative buying techniques are defined and explained:

- The "G" syndrome
- The "greener grass" phenomenon

Knowing and understanding these terms and issues related to them will help you to learn and apply the concepts presented in this chapter.

The "G" Syndrome

There is a bit of **greed** in most people, and smart real estate investors know how to use this in negotiations to acquire or sell property. Through the subtle use of purchase terms and conditions or other techniques, the seller can get exactly what he or she wants, while at the same time the buyer gives exactly what he or she wants to pay. There is a phrase that most real estate investors are acquainted with: "I'll pay your price if you accept my terms." This summarizes exactly the way the "G" syndrome functions. After all, most real estate sellers want to get the most they can when they sell their property. The fact that there may be more important motivations than the large sum of money can often be overlooked in the heat of negotiations.

The key is to look for a focal point of each acquisition.

The "Greener Grass" Phenomenon

When it comes to greener grass on the other side of the fence, people are no different than the horse that sticks its neck through the fence to eat what is on the other side. The problem is that the property we are closest to is often more valuable than that "grass," which only seems greener.

Mistakes often are made when an investor travels out of his or her comfort zone. A new set of rules and regulations may not be remotely similar to those the investor has mastered back home. The new surroundings may appear to be bargains that just cannot be overlooked. Differences in pricing may give the appearance that the property is half the price of what is available back home.

The reader will find several examples of the greener grass phenomenon in the balance of this book.

THE OPTION

The option is a highly flexible buying technique that almost always gives the buyer an edge in the transaction, but when properly used, the option works on the seller's "G" syndrome and produces signed transactions that may ultimately work for both parties. The following examples illustrate how to use an option.

In the first example, suppose Frank has looked at Paula's eight apartment units. Frank is almost convinced that if he could convert the eight apartments into executive offices, he could increase the rent from $700 per month per apartment to over $1,000 per month. However, to do this conversion Frank must request and be granted a change in zoning from the city in which the property is located. Frank enters into a contract with Paula to buy the property only if Frank is successful in obtaining the rezoning. Paula will get her full price (enter the "G" syndrome), and in turn Frank is given a period of five months to attempt to get the zoning and to be satisfied with the conditions the city may impose on him. Of course, Frank can elect to proceed to close on the purchase regardless of the outcome of the zoning procedures.

Frank puts up a $5,000 deposit that would be applied toward the purchase price at closing or be refunded to Frank if the zoning matter is not acceptable to Frank. The deposit is to be held in an interest-earning account with interest credited to Frank.

In the above example the term *option* is never used. Even in the contract there would be no need to use the term, yet this is a classic use of the option. Frank is in the driver's seat in this transaction, and if he ultimately buys the property, the deposit of $5,000 is applied against the purchase price. He has obtained five months of time at no appreciable cost.

Often an option is part of another transaction. For this second example, suppose Alex has purchased an apartment complex from Gary, and as a part of the deal Alex asks for a 12-month option to buy the adjoining property, also owned by Gary. The price and terms for this second deal are included in the terms of the option, but Alex does not pay anything more for the option other than the acquisition of the first apartment complex. Gary, not knowing if Alex will take the first complex without granting him the option, agrees.

Why do sellers agree to grant an option to buy (or any other aspect of the transaction)? Again, look to what is on the table. The offer Alex made can be compared to whatever other offers exist for the property. But *never* trust the seller when he or she says, "I've already turned down more than that." Even if the seller did turn down another offer, the seller most likely wishes he or she had not done so. Your offer and how that offer helps the seller move closer to his or her goals is the key.

Some sellers try to compare what is offered with what they want, which can often be a very unrealistic approach. The reason this can be unrealistic is that *there may never be a buyer who will offer what the seller wants.*

When it is a buyer's market, some properties are very difficult to sell. Vacant tracts of land may require rezoning before they are usable. Improved properties may need to be remodeled to attract a tenant. All of these factors take *time* to resolve, and time is on the side of the buyer.

There are five ideal times to use options:

1. **When the investor has no immediate use for the property.** The option can "buy" time. This time may be **investment maturity**, which is the time needed to let the value go up or to let other events the investor knows about to occur will ensure future profit or make the property usable.

2. **When the investor is not sure about the investment and wants to tie up the property to allow for more investigation.** For example, a rezoning may be necessary, soil tests may be required, or a building permit must be granted; otherwise the investor has no use for the property.

3. **As a negotiating tool when buying other property.** The investor asks for an option as part of a contract on some other property, either to give the seller something to negotiate out of the offer or to tie up the property in the event of a property value increase due to some future event (caused by the investor or others).

4. **As part of a lease that would give the investor time to get to know the property or time to hold on to the property at a reduced cost prior to buying it.** Many leases contain some type of option as a part of the transaction. It might be an option to continue the lease for a longer period of time, or to actually purchase the property. In the case of an option to purchase, this puts the lessee in the position of being able to fix up the property, perhaps even improve the value to the point where financing the purchase price would be relatively easy.

5. **As a negotiating tool to give the seller something he or she can insist on removing.** Most sellers like to get their way, so buyers often put in terms and conditions that really don't mean that much to them. A particular term or condition might be nice to have, but if the seller wants to take it out, and that makes him or her feel better, then okay, take it out.

SWEAT EQUITY

Sweat equity transactions enable a buyer to enter into a transaction to acquire a property that can be a "win-win" situation for both the buyer and the seller. This is a form of option in which the buyer gives the value of his or her *sweat* as equity to "buy" the option, as in the following examples.

In the first example, Frank goes to Paula and convinces her that if her eight apartment units were painted inside and out and the yard given a major upgrade with new plants, brick walkways, wood decks, and flower arrangements, the rents could be increased to a minimum of $600 per month. Frank says that if Paula will give him a 12-month option to buy the property, Frank will, on his own time and effort, do all these things.

Paula agrees, and Frank also promises to add extra remodeling and fix-up if Paula pays for the material. These items include new kitchen countertops, sinks, door hardware, a partial fence, a gas grill for the backyard, new mailboxes, and some other minor repairs Paula knows need to be done. Paula agrees to this as well, the price is set, and Frank starts the work.

Paula has little to lose except time, but as no one has been knocking her door down to buy the apartments, the chance to get a lot of the required work done appeals to her "G" syndrome. The real clincher in this deal, however, is that Frank has agreed to pay her cash to the mortgage, which means he will take over or pay off the mortgage (perhaps by refinancing it) and give her cash for the balance of the purchase price. Frank believes that at the end of a year, after all the work and fix-up is completed, he will be able to refinance the existing mortgage and generate enough cash that he will end up financing 100 percent of the price. He anticipates he will be able to do this because the property will have increased rents reflecting a higher value. The incentive is very strong for Frank to do good work because he is improving what he hopes will become his own property.

In a second example, Ted has found a beautiful home he wants to buy, but he doesn't have a down payment of $25,000 to close the deal. In doing his homework, Ted discovers the owner of the home also owns a 30,000-square-foot strip store. Ted offers to repaint the commercial property as his down payment if the seller pays for the paint. The seller agrees to the deal on the condition that Ted must complete the work before the closing on the home.

In each of these situations the outcome is that the prospective buyer ends up building equity to be used as a down payment on the desired property. While sweat equity is best when the work improves the value of the property being acquired, which occurred when Frank agreed to do the work at Paula's apartment complex, it is not essential, as in Ted's case.

Sweat Equity Pitfalls

The prospective buyer in any kind of future closing should have some control over the property for any situation that may extend past the closing date. For example, Frank would want to have the right to approve any leases that Paula might execute that would lock in a tenant past the closing date when Frank would become the owner. This would ensure that Paula would not rent the apartments for less than the amount Frank feels would be warranted. As Frank wants to show a greater income potential to refinance the debt, leases that were less than the needed rent would be counterproductive. Without firm and written protection in the contract between Frank and Paula, Paula might "fall in love" with the newly remodeled eight-unit apartment complex and start looking for ways to keep Frank from being able to close on the deal.

LEASE/PURCHASE

The long-term **lease** with an option to purchase is a good way to tie up a property for a longer period during which major improvements can be made to the property that will greatly increase the value and ensure a profit for the tenant/buyer. The advantage to the tenant/buyer is that the amount of cash or equity needed to initiate this transaction is often much less than the amount required for a straight purchase. Because the landlord/seller retains title to the property and all the benefits of ownership during the lease, there is often greater incentive for the landlord to enter into a lease with an option if an ultimate sale is what the landlord wants. If the immediate benefits are strong enough, the landlord may agree to the option to buy with the ideal that the prospective buyer may not actually *be in a position to buy when the option period ends*. This is the "G" syndrome appearing again.

Here's an example of a lease/purchase agreement. Alice offers to lease one side of David's two-unit duplex. At the moment David's parents live in the other side, but he expects that within a few years they will be moving out of state to live with David's sister. So when Alice first agrees to do some needed repairs to the building as her *sweat equity* for the first and last two months security on the lease, David agrees. But Alice also asks for an option to buy the duplex within 90 days following the date David's parents vacate the property.

David does not want to be tied down quite that much, but he does agree to give her the *first right of refusal*. This is spelled out in the agreement they sign to indicate that anytime David wants to sell the property and there is a valid offer (an offer in writing with deposit and no contingencies other than mortgage assumption), Alice has a period of 60 days to match the offer. Alice accepts this because she knows it is better than no option at all, and often the 60-day tie-up scares away other prospective buyers.

SECONDARY SELLER-HELD FINANCING

Any mortgage included in a real estate transaction that is not a first mortgage on the property being acquired is called **secondary financing**. The best secondary financing is when the seller holds paper for part of the deal—for example, an investor buys property and the seller holds a second mortgage as a part of the transaction. This second mortgage is called a **purchase money second mortgage**. The term *purchase money* is used whenever the seller is holding a mortgage that is secured by the property being sold. If, as part of the purchase price, the buyer gives the seller a mortgage from another property, then this is not a purchase money mortgage and is referred to simply as a second mortgage.

The greener grass phenomenon works well with several secondary financing techniques that involve debt secured by other property. In fact, when the circumstances are right, it is possible for an investor to acquire two different properties using secondary financing from each to acquire the other.

The Advantages of Using Secondary Financing

Possible buyers look to seller-held financing because they can avoid the problems and cost of obtaining an institutional loan. Sellers are often far more motivated to make a deal, whereas banks and other lenders are less motivated to part with their money unless they can be convinced they are in a very secure position. In today's difficult times, the rules and regulations that lenders impose on their borrowers can make the investment less attractive.

Most lenders shy away from commercial ventures or at least ask for (and generally get) terms of payback that can be very hard on the investor if conditions falter and high vacancy factors result. Short-term loans, nonassumable loans, and adjustable interest rates can make long-term projections impossible or dangerous. Therefore most sellers of commercial or investment properties are open to some form of secondary financing.

What to Look for When Using Seller-Held Financing

When the seller is asked to hold a purchase money second (or first or third) mortgage, the contract should be very specific as to the exact terms of the mortgage, and it should contain details as to the form of note and mortgage to be used, the property that will be security to the mortgage, and other data that the investor may feel is essential or that the seller insists on including.

Important Questions About Seller-Held Mortgages

- What is the interest rate?
- How is the interest rate charged?
- What is the method of determining amortization or principal payments?
- What are the dates of payments?
- What are the terms of payback?
- What is the date the final payment is due?
- What is the amount of final payment (assuming no prepayments)?
- What is the balloon payment date and amount (if any)?
- Is there a grace period for late payments?
- What is the penalty for late payments (if any)?
- What is the penalty for prepayment of principal (if any)?
- What is the form of note and mortgage?
- Who prepares the note and mortgage?
- Can the mortgagor (buyer) substitute other property as security on the note and mortgage? If so, how?
- Is there any subordination (present or future) of the mortgage to what would normally be a lesser position mortgage?

One way to ensure that there is no misunderstanding between the buyer and the seller who is going to hold a purchase money mortgage is for the purchase contract to include a copy of the note and mortgage that will be used, properly drawn to show all the terms and conditions of the loan.

18

DISCOVER THE TAX-FREE BENEFIT OF A 1031 EXCHANGE

When the money market dries up, and mortgages are difficult and even impossible to obtain, the concept of "barter" enters the playing field. The goal of this chapter is to present to the reader one of the best tools the real estate investor has at his or her disposal.

This tool is exchanging. This chapter is designed to explore the fundamentals of exchanging ranging from the tax-free exchange as provided by Internal Revenue Service Section 1031 to the most basic of all exchanges, barter.

KEY TERMS

The following key terms are important in the use of tax-free exchanges under the IRS Section 1031 code. These terms distinguish whether or not the exchange would qualify as a tax-free exchange. Keep in mind that although many exchanges do not totally qualify under the 1031 rules, they may still be partially beneficial in avoiding all the capital gains tax that may be due. Even exchanges that totally fail as a tax-free exchange are still worth doing if they take one or both parties closer to their goals.

- Boot
- Equity balance
- "Havers" and "takers"
- Legs
- Like-kind property
- Property basis

Knowing and understanding these terms and issues related to them will help you to learn and apply the concepts presented in this chapter.

Boot

The term *boot* refers to any cash or other items of the exchange that would not qualify as a part of the tax-free characteristics of the Internal Revenue Service Sec. 1031 exchange. There are many benefits of using an IRS Section 1031 tax-free exchange, but the reader should be aware that the vast majority of real estate exchanges are not made with tax savings in mind. Nonetheless, the following is an example of a tax-free exchange that demonstrates the use of boot.

Suppose I want to own a vacant lot you purchased 10 years ago in a North Carolina mountain area. You value it at $50,000. I offer you a diamond ring that has a jeweler's appraisal of $50,000. By the IRS rules the diamond ring is considered boot, as it is not a direct like-for-like exchange. (Like-kind property is explained in more detail later in this chapter.) Therefore this exchange will not qualify as a tax-free exchange for you. However, if instead of offering you the diamond ring, I offered either of the following properties, it would qualify as a tax-free exchange because either would be a like-for-like exchange.

- A home worth $150,000 that has a $100,000 mortgage on it
- An office building worth $55,000 that has a $5,000 mortgage outstanding

Equity Balance

The equity balance procedure balances the equity between the two or more parties entering into an exchange. The equity balance of a simple two-party exchange is shown in Table 18-1.

Table 18-1   A two-party exchange balance board.

Two-Party Balance	First Party	Second Party
Owner's value of real property		
Less existing mortgage		
Real property equity		
Balance mortgage		
Real property equity to transfer		
• Gives boot		
• Gives boot		
• Gives boot		
• Gives other real property		
Total to transfer		
• Gets boot		
• Gets boot		
• Gets boot		
• Gets other real property		
Balance of real property equity		

To illustrate the use of this balance board, consider the following exchange. Mike wants to acquire Anna's four-unit apartment building. The apartments are on the market for $160,000, and there is an assumable first mortgage for $100,000.

Mike has a vacant lot in Naples, Florida, which he has priced at $42,000 and is free and clear of any debt. He wants to offer this lot to Anna and can balance the equity with a purchase money second mortgage of $18,000 to be held by Anna. Review the balance board in Table 18-2 (notice that unnecessary items have been removed from the board).

Table 18-2   Mike and Anna's equity balance board.

Two-Party Balance	Mike	Anna
Owner's value of real property	$42,000	$160,000
Less existing mortgage	0	−$100,000
Real property equity	$42,000	$60,000
Less balance mortgage (new second mortgage)		−$18,000
Real property equity transfer	$42,000	$42,000

In using the balance board, the reader must distinguish between the balance mortgage and the "gives" and "gets" items. When the balance mortgage is used to balance the equity, this mortgage is secured by one of the properties in the exchange. In the two-party balance board, the mortgage becomes a purchase money mortgage and is held by the party giving up that property.

Paper, in real estate language, refers to a promise to pay. This might be evidenced by a promissory note or a letter of credit. It is treated as boot in an exchange transaction so does not qualify within the tax-free part of the deal. However, it does not disqualify the transaction for tax-free treatment. This promise to pay is never secured by one of the properties of the exchange and need not even be a mortgage.

The introduction of an additional mortgage on Anna's property (which Mike wants her to hold) reduces her equity in the real estate by the amount of the mortgage and brings it down to $42,000, which matches the equity in his property offered to Anna.

Assume that Anna rejects this exchange because she does not want to hold a second mortgage on her own property. She does agree, however, to accept $5,500 cash at closing, take a car from Mike worth $6,000, and balance off with a first mortgage of $6,500 on another property Mike owns. The adjustments to the balance board are shown in Table 18-3.

Remember that the balance should be zero at the bottom of the board and that everything each party gets becomes a deduction from the total to transfer.

Havers and Takers

Havers and **takers** are important terms that are used by real estate exchangers when putting together a multiple exchange. *Havers* refers to property owners who *have* what another investor or broker is looking for. A *taker* is anyone who would *take* a property being offered. It is not unusual for several parties to work together to effect an exchange. Party A gives his property to party B, who gives her property to party C, who gives his property to party A. To start the exchange process, the parties are interested in learning who has what each needs, regardless of what this person wants in exchange, and who will take what each party has, regardless of what this person has to offer in the exchange. Often a taker has other properties that may appeal to a second haver who has what the first haver wants, and a three-way deal is possible.

Table 18-3 Mike and Anna's equity balance board, adjusted.

Two-Party Balance	Mike	Anna
Owner's value of real property	$42,000	$160,000
Less existing mortgage	0	−$100,000
Real property equity	$42,000	$60,000
Less balance mortgage		0
Real property equity to transfer	$42,000 (A)	$60,000 (B)
• Pays cash	$5,500	
• Gives boot (paper)	$6,500	
• Gives boot		
• Gives boot (car)	6,000	
Total to transfer	$60,000	$60,000
• Gets boot (cash)		($5,500)
• Gets boot (paper)		($6,500)
• Gets boot (car)		($6,000)
• Gets other real property		
• Real property equity transfer	($60,000)	($42,000)
Balance of equity	0	0

The reader should make an attempt to become associated with a real estate exchange club, either by joining (if possible) or by getting to know several active members in a local club.

Legs

A **leg** is the term for the stages in multiple transactions. Sometimes a deal that starts out as a two-party exchange develops beyond the ability of the two parties to match up acceptable equity. When this occurs, one side may accept the exchange provided another property can be found within a reasonable time. An example of this may have occurred in the exchange shown between Mike and Anna (see Table 18-3 balance board). Anna might have told Mike that everything was fine, except that instead of the $6,000 car that Mike offered in the second go-round, she would accept a time-share week in an Orlando resort of the same value. Mike would now need to acquire such as week (or make another proposal to Anna). If Mike attempts to find a haver that owns one or more of the needed time-share weeks, then Mike is attempting to bring a **leg** into his transaction with Anna. If Mike found a haver who would take the $6,000 car for the time-share week, the three-way exchange has been *perfected*, and the deal can proceed to close.

Like-Kind Property

This term describes the kind of property that qualifies for the IRS Section 1031 tax-free exchange. This exchange is also called the **like-kind** exchange. The definition seems to confuse many people, and it is not unusual to find accountants and lawyers who will tell you that *like kind* means an office building in exchange for an office building or a farm for a farm. *This is not what like kind means. Like kind* is directed to the *category of property* and not the specific nature of the property. For the purpose of this discussion and its use relative to real estate, there are two categories of property: the legal residence of the investor and investment property owned by the investor. The provisions of IRS Section 1031 exclude the exchange of the legal residence for another legal residence (provisions for this kind of exchange are found in IRS Section 1034, which leaves investment property as the real estate that is covered under IRS Section 1031).

It is important to note, however, that the intent of ownership is what establishes investment property. This can be any kind of real estate as long as it is intended to be an investment. This can include a property that was once the legal residence of the owner. If a property is owned as an investment, is not "inventory" (as would be vacant lots a land developer is selling), is not the investor's personal residence (which qualifies under Section 1034 and not Section 1031), and is not located in a foreign country, then the property can qualify for the full tax-free benefits of the IRS Section 1031 provisions.

Property Basis

Every asset purchased, including real estate, has a book value, or basis, that can change over the time during which the property is owned. **Basis** is an important figure as it establishes two possible tax consequences. The first is the income tax on the **capital gain** at the time of a sale or nonqualified tax-deferred transaction. The second is a sale or exchange with a **mortgage over basis**, which occurs when a mortgage is placed on a property and the amount of money borrowed exceeds the basis of the property. Because money borrowed is not taxed as income, any amount of a mortgage that is in excess of the property basis at the time of a transfer will be treated as though the seller received *cash* as a part of the transaction.

Basis is a function of the price paid for the real estate plus any additions to it during the time it is owned, less any depreciation taken or improvements removed. Not included in the calculation is any personal property, inventory, or other items that are leased and not owned unless there is a value to those items (lease purchase agreement).

Most property owners do not properly maintain their basis records, and it is recommended that every property owner use the following Property Basis Adjustment Checklist to do an annual update of the basis of their real estate. The best time to accomplish this is during preparation for the year-end IRS reporting.

Property Basis Adjustment Checklist
1. Basis at beginning of year $_____
2. Plus improvements made $_____

   _____

   _____

   _____

   _____

   _____

   Subtotal $_____
3. Less depreciation taken $ −_____
4. Less improvements removed $ −_____
5. New basis at the end of the year $_____

FIVE REASONS REAL ESTATE EXCHANGES WORK

Real estate exchanges work for the following reasons.

1. They provide tax-free benefits.
2. They move the parties closer to their goals.
3. They offer a "face-saving" prospect.
4. They can be an accommodation move.
5. They allow a seller to be proactive in a buyer's market.

Each of these reasons will be discussed in this section.

Tax-Free Benefits

In a tax-free exchange under IRS Section 1031, the IRS provisions permit parties to move their basis from the property owned to the property they will acquire, with several adjustments to be taken into account. Review the following example.

Charlie has a large vacant tract of land that he purchased 20 years earlier for $50,000. No buildings are on the property, and it has a small mortgage of $15,000 that Charlie took out two years ago. The current value of the land is $700,000. Charlie wants to offer this tract to Don as a down payment on a hotel Don owns. The hotel is valued at $3,000,000 and has a first mortgage of $1,800,000. Charlie offers to balance the equity with a purchase money second mortgage that Don will hold.

The first step is to ascertain whether Charlie will have a tax savings in this exchange, and if so, how much. To accomplish this, Charlie would anticipate the tax on the capital gains he would pay in the event of a sale. To be realistic he assumes he will have a commission to pay. His tax calculations are shown in Table 18-4.

Table 18-4   Charlie and Don's equity balance board.

Two-Party Balance	Charlie	Don
Owner's value of real property	$700,000	$3,000,000
Less existing mortgage	−$15,000	−$1,800,000
Equity	$685,000	$1,200,000
Less balance mortgage (new second mortgage)		−$515,000
Real property equity to transfer	$685,000	$685,000
Charlie's Tax Calculations		
Sales price	$700,000	
Less commission and cost of sale	−$80,000	
Subtotal	$620,000	
Less his basis (no mortgage over basis)	−$50,000	
Capital gain	$570,000	

Calculate Charlie's tax
   at 28% of the capital gain: $570,000 × 0.28 = $159,000 tax
Balance of sale to reinvest:
   $620,000 less the tax of $159,000 = $461,000 balance

By creating an IRS Section 1031 qualified exchange, Charlie is able to save on tax, as calculated above, and will get full reinvestment potential from the increased value of his vacant land.

A Move Closer to Your Goals

This is the second most important aspect of exchanges. When everything else fails, a transaction that involves an exchange may solve problems and help you move closer to your goals. This kind of strategy is best suited to investors who have gotten themselves into a problem. The problem may be complicated further due to a poor seller's market, the impossibility of refinancing, and balloon mortgages coming due. When things turn against the investor, the whole market can dry up. Money is not available, buyers are not interested in what you have to offer at any reasonable price, and investment confidence disappears. Until that situation turns around, sellers should become aggressive buyers if they want to sell or exchange their own real estate. It is a logical step because when it is a poor seller's market, it is a very strong buyer's market.

Any exchange that moves you closer to your goal is a good exchange.

This approach may require a reassessment of investment goals. The question to ask is, "Do I need to change my direction in light of the current economic circumstances?" Take a hard look at what is going on around you. Are there opportunities that can open up new directions to follow? Are you hanging onto bad investments that are getting worse? The best time to do real estate exchanges is when the real estate market shifts in favor of the buyer. Why? Motivated sellers will often do anything to solve their problem—even take a property they would not buy otherwise. Review the following example to see how Sylvia adjusted her plan to achieve her original goals.

Solve someone else's problem and you may solve your own.

Sylvia has a town home she has been trying to sell for nearly two years. She has dropped the price several times and is now asking $125,000. She has a first mortgage in the amount of $70,000. She plans on moving to Atlanta as soon as she can sell her property.

She has recently learned about real estate exchanges and suggests to the listing broker that they encourage a prospective buyer to offer something in partial exchange as part or all of the down payment. Sylvia is going to make it easy for someone to buy her townhome by holding a purchase money second mortgage for the balance of the price.

Armed with this information, her broker attends one of the local exchange clubs and presents the townhome. The broker explains that Sylvia wants to move to Atlanta. Several mini-offers are given to the broker by members of the club. These mini-offers are informal proposals discussed among members that often result in a more formalized offer. One member suggests the broker call an exchange club in Atlanta. After a few calls, an offer is formalized. Sylvia is offered $15,000 of prepaid rent in an apartment complex in Atlanta as a down payment on the townhome. A friend of Sylvia's in Atlanta inspects the complex, and based on what she is told Sylvia accepts the contract based on her holding an additional second mortgage for the balance of $40,000 payable over six years at 9 percent per annum interest. Sylvia conditions the contract on her own personal inspection of the apartments available in Atlanta and the terms and conditions of the lease. She wisely has the agreement fully executed prior to spending the time and money to make the trip to Atlanta.

A "Face-Saving" Prospect

For many sellers the need to maintain "face" is very important. After all, no one likes the prospect of buying high and selling low. Worse, no one wants to be in a position where he or she has to sell property at a loss. One way around this humiliating experience is to agree to accept something in exchange for all or part of the deal.

There are many different reasons why sellers will accept something in exchange for part of a deal. The more motivated the seller is, and the closer he or she can be moved toward his or her goals through the exchange, the better the chance of making the transaction work for all parties. Review the following exchange.

Bobby has a five-acre tract of land in a rural area of Maine. He has had it for more than 15 years and always thought he would build a summer home there. He paid $2,500 for the tract and knows of similar property that has sold recently for $30,000. This land is free and clear of any debt.

Phyllis has a summer home about 20 miles away, worth $80,000 with a first mortgage of $50,000. Phyllis needs to sell because the taxes and mortgage payments, which total $7,000 per year, are more than she can handle. She has not even had time to use the home more than a couple of weeks in the past three years. Phyllis has the home on the market but has had no offers over $65,000.

An exchange between Bobby and Phyllis could be very attractive for both parties. Under the right circumstances, Bobby would qualify for the IRS Section 1031 tax-free provisions and have no capital gains tax to pay, and taking a free and clear tract of land solves Phyllis's problem. Both parties can reach their ultimate goals in one exchange. Best of all, Phyllis "saves face" by getting her price.

An Accommodation Move

The **accommodation move** is the most common of all real estate exchanges. In this situation, one party will accept something in exchange solely because it is a part of the offer even though the property or item taken in exchange does not have any real or apparent benefit to him or her. Often the item taken in exchange amounts to less than 20 percent of the total value of the property given up, and it may be something other than real estate, as shown in the following example.

Donna has a marina that she has not been able to sell. Its current price is $7,500,000, lower than the original $10,000,000 price two years earlier. The existing mortgage totals $5,000,000, and Donna is very motivated.

Bill has been looking for a boat repair yard. He sees Donna's marina and instantly realizes that in addition to the existing marina business, Bill can add his boat repair facilities, taking over one of the two dry storage buildings that are not even being used by Donna. Instead of operating at 50 percent (as Donna is now) Bill will have 100 percent use for the facility. However, Bill doesn't want to come up with all the cash Donna is asking for.

Instead, Bill offers Donna $800,000 equity in a $1,000,000 waterfront site in Miami. This site was an old boat repair yard that Bill's family owned and operated for many years. Rising values of waterfront land in Miami have made the site triple in value as a future condominium site. To balance the equity Bill will give Donna a purchase money third mortgage secured by Donna's marina for $1,700,000.

Review the balance board in Table 18-5.

Table 18-5 Bill and Donna's equity balance board.

Two-Party Balance	Bill	Donna
Owner's value of real property	$1,000,000	$7,500,000
Less existing mortgage	−$200,000	−$5,000,000
Real property equity	$800,000	$2,500,000
Balance mortgage		−$1,700,000
Real property equity to transfer	$800,000	$800,000

While the site in Miami does not have any obvious benefit to Donna, it becomes a way out of the marina she has been trying to sell. Bill would have a possible tax-free exchange. The key to getting Donna to accept this exchange is by showing her that her problem has been solved.

Virtually every large transaction can absorb some small portion of exchange. If investors have dividable items in their inventories, those parcels can be "moved out" as investors become buyers of other property. The reader should remember that these items need not be real estate and can include services or personal property. The maximum use of any investor's assets is realized every time one acquisition can convert an idle asset into a new investment.

Allowing a Seller to Be Proactive in a Buyer's Market

Roy unsuccessfully tried to sell his $650,000 condominium located in Boca Raton, Florida, for two years. It was a difficult task to do living in San Francisco, where his work had taken him. The condo rules would not allow rentals, so he was forced to bite the bullet for carrying costs, which when the condo maintenance, insurance, taxes, and mortgage payments were added up, was running close to $55,000 a year. Added to that, even though the market in San Francisco was the softest it had been for decades, he needed to recover as much of his $300,000 equity in his apartment as possible.

I suggested that he become a proactive exchanger and attempt to use that $300,000 equity as a value in an exchange. His first attempt was to see if he could acquire a home or apartment in the San Francisco area so he could stop paying rent. But no one was interested in taking a property in Boca Raton, Florida. He went onto the Internet and sent a professionally prepared offering that included a video of the apartment, the stunning views it had of the Boca beach and Intracoastal Waterway, and the two golf courses nearby that could be seen from his 25th floor apartment. There was a list of comparable sales, names and phone numbers of Realtors in the area should an interested party want to double-check his values, and his "want list" that itemized things and property that he would consider.

His goals were as follows:

1. Get rid of the Boca apartment.
2. Recover as much of the equity as possible.
3. Reduce as much as possible of the annual drain to his bank account.
4. Acquire a property in the San Francisco area.
5. Acquire a property anywhere that would take him closer to his goals.

It didn't take long for offers to start coming in. You see, he discovered that there were other people who were in the same predicament. These other people had the same or similar goals as did Roy. Here is a sample of five offers with the owner's value (OV), mortgage (M), and resulting equity (E). In each case Roy would need to assume some debt and possibly, if necessary, take back additional second financing on his Boca condo.

1. A log cabin in Hawks Nest resort area in North Carolina Mountains:
   Owner's value: $450,000
   Mortgage: $150,000
   Equity: $300,000
2. A townhouse in Thousand Oaks, California:
   Owner's value: $700,000
   Mortgage: $500,000
   Equity: $200,000
3. A home in Tampa, Florida:
   Owner's value: $550,000
   Mortgage: $380,000
   Equity: $170,000
4. A smaller apartment in the same building in Boca Raton:
   Owner's value: $300,000
   Mortgage: $100,000
   Equity: $200,000

5. A 42-foot sailboat:
   Owner's value: $200,000
   Mortgage: 0
   Equity: $200,000

Would any of these offers take Roy closer to his goals? Under the right circumstances, they all would.

MAKING THE OFFER TO EXCHANGE

Printed forms for real estate exchange offers may be available at local business supply stores or from the local board of Realtors. If no forms are available, investors can ask their lawyer or local title insurance company to draft one. Following is the author's standard two-party exchange agreement. This agreement is stored on a computer disk and can be filled in and modified for each of the author's offers. The following offer form should not be used as presented, but it may help a lawyer draw one appropriate for the specific state in which the investor resides.

TWO-PARTY EXCHANGE OFFER

Date of offer: _____ Date closed: _____

Agreement to Exchange
First Party: The undersigned, _____ and/
or his assigns and hereinafter called First Party, does agree to exchange
to the Second Party the following property:

Description of Property Given by the First Party:
_____
_____
_____

**Said property is subject to the following debt, which will be assumed
by the Second Party:**
_____
_____

In addition to the above property, the First Party agrees to pay to the Second Party, at the closing, the following:

_____

_____

Second Party: The undersigned, _____ and/or his or her assigns and hereinafter called Second Party, does agree to exchange to the First Party the following property:

Description of Property Given by the Second Party:

_____

_____

Said property is subject to the following debt, which will be assumed by the First Party:

_____

In addition to the above property, the Second Party agrees to pay to the First Party, at the closing, the following:

_____

Terms and Conditions of This Exchange
1. **IRS Section 1031 Exchange:** It is the intention of the First Party that this agreement meet the requirements of the United States Internal Revenue Service Section 1031 exchange and both parties agree to cooperate with any documentation required at or prior to the closing to substantiate this intent.
2. **Standards of real estate transactions:** Attached to this agreement are Standards that are common to real estate closings in this area. In that these standards refer to "buyer" and "seller," these terms shall apply in that each party shall be treated as a "buyer" of that property received and as a "seller" of that property given up. These terms do not alter the provisions shown in Paragraph 1 of these terms and conditions with respect to the fact that as an exchange, this agreement is not to be considered a buy and sell contract.

3. **Inspections of the property to be received:** The First Party has a period of _____ calendar days following the acceptance of this agreement by the Second Party to review and inspect the property and the following documentation: Recent land survey showing all improvements and possible encroachments, all leases, tenant agreements, advance rents and rent rolls, copies of service agreements, employment contracts, mortgage notes and mortgages to which the property is security, copies of any liens or unpaid assessments against the property, and to make any other inspection provided for in the Standards attached, which may include but not be limited to structural, electrical, plumbing, roof, termite, and mechanical and to *approve said reviews and inspections without qualification, no later than noon of the deadline stated herein, unless extended by mutual agreement or as a function of Paragraph 4 below.* In the event the First Party fails to approve in writing said reviews and inspections for any reason, this agreement shall be considered null and void, and each party is hereinafter released from further obligation to the other. The Second Party may likewise inspect that property to be received in this exchange *prior* to execution of this agreement to exchange and the First Party agrees to cooperate fully with said inspection. According to the number of days provided for the inspection, the deadline for the notice in writing from the First Party is (date) _____.

4. **Delay of inspections or reviews:** If at no cause of the First Party the inspections by that party cannot be made due to inability of the Second Party to provide access to the property or to deliver the required documents as mentioned above, then the time period called for in Paragraph 3 above for the First Party to make said inspections and reviews shall automatically be extended by the delay, providing that both parties make reasonable attempt to reschedule inspections. In the event some or all requested documentation cannot be made available to the First Party, the Second Party shall give notice of this fact, and the First Party shall have an additional period equal to the calendar days indicated in Paragraph 3 from the date the Second Party has given notice that certain documents are not available as requested, to give notice to approval or disapproval of the subject property without the requested documentation.

5. **Closing:** The closing of title for this exchange shall take place at the offices of a closing agent to be selected by the First Party. Said offices are to be within the same county as that property given up by the First Party or any other location mutually agreeable between the parties. Said location to be given to the Second Party at the same time written notice of approval of the inspections and reviews is made. The closing shall occur on or before the _____ day following delivery of the approval of the inspections and reviews.

6. **Brokers and broker commissions:** Each party has listed his or her properties with his or her own real estate broker, and will solely be responsible for the fee paid by him or her to that broker. Neither party shall owe to any other person, broker, principal, or agent a fee or commission as a result of this exchange except where evidenced by a signed agreement, or _____ as per separate agreement not made a part of this contract.

7. **Recording of this agreement:** Both parties agree that this agreement shall not be recorded.

8. **Valid contract:** Unless this agreement is fully executed by both parties on or before noon of _____, then the agreement is withdrawn and shall become null and void and all deposits, if any, shall be promptly returned to the First Party.

Other Terms and Conditions

1. Standards as attached consist of _____ pages and are initialed by the First Party in the lower right-hand corner.

2. Exhibits attached to this agreement are:

   _____

   _____

   _____

3. Other terms and conditions are shown below:

   _____

   _____

   _____

   _____

   _____

AS TO FIRST PARTY
Date Signed: _____
Witness hereto

_____

_____

First Party

AS TO SECOND PARTY
Date Signed: _____
Witness hereto

_____

_____

Second Party

To illustrate how this standard form could be used and modified, review its use in the following exchange. John Parker offers on March 5, 2010, to exchange a four-unit apartment building for a small office building owned by Sid Goldman. The details of the exchange are shown in the following agreement. Each of the two parties has his respective property listed with a real estate agent and is bound by a commission agreement as shown in the offer. Following is the "Agreement to Exchange" portion of the Two-Party Exchange Offer for this exchange, which has the "Terms and Conditions" shown in the sample offer form above.

TWO-PARTY EXCHANGE OFFER

Date of offer: July 5, 2010 Date closed: _____

Agreement to Exchange
First Party: The undersigned, John Parker and/or his assigns and here-inafter called First Party, does agree to exchange to the Second Party the following property:

Description of Property Given by the First Party:
A 4-unit apartment complex located at 2134 West Hillmont Avenue, Savannah, Georgia. Also known as Lot 7 of Block D of West Hill Mont

Subdivision Unit A of Savannah, Georgia. Together with all furniture and fixtures as is shown on the attached inventory list.

Said property is subject to the following debt, which will be assumed by the Second Party:

A first mortgage held by First Union of Savannah, in the amount of $75,000. Payable over a remaining 5 years at 7 percent per annum.

In addition to the above property, the First Party agrees to pay to the Second Party, at the closing, the following:

A cash payment of $20,000.

Second Party: The undersigned, Sid Goldman and/or his assigns and hereinafter called Second Party, does agree to exchange to the First Party the following property:

Description of Property Given by the Second Party:

An office building located at 91 South River Drive, Savannah, Georgia. Also known as Lot 20 of Block 8 of Savannah Commercial Park, Savannah, Georgia.

Said property is subject to the following debt, which will be assumed by the First Party:

A first mortgage held by North Carolina National Bank of Savannah, in the amount of $310,000 payable over a remaining 11 years at 7.5 percent interest per annum. And a purchase money second mortgage to be held by Sid Goldman in the amount of $55,000. Said mortgage to be payable interest only at 6 percent per annum, annual installments, with a balloon of remaining principal due at the end of the 10th anniversary of the closing of this exchange. Said note and mortgage to be as is standard to Savannah real estate closings and a blank copy of the note and mortgage are attached. Said mortgage will provide for a 5 day grace period on all payments and no penalty for prepayments of principal. The sole security to be the office building at 91 South River Drive as described above.

All real estate investors know that in most deals there is some give-and-take between the two parties. If the market is a very strong seller's market, then outright exchange may not be possible since buyers would be numerous. But sellers with a tax problem and the opportunity to qualify for an IRS Section 1031 exchange are well advised to revise a buyer's offer and to turn the sale into a delayed exchange so they can reinvest the proceeds from the sale without having to pay any capital gains tax. This procedure must be accomplished with all the IRS rules carefully followed. Any seller of an investment property (if it isn't the house or apartment where you live, and it is not inventory that you buy and sell, it is *investment real estate*) may qualify. If there is a large capital gain and you are not sure if you will qualify, ask an accountant or tax lawyer *who is knowledgeable about the IRS Code 1031 provisions.*

19

MAKING OFFERS AND COUNTEROFFERS

This chapter dissects what can become the most critical stage in the buying and selling process: the **offer** and the **counteroffer**. This chapter's primary goal, after defining some key terms, is to describe the three stages of the offer process: doing homework before the offer, structuring the offer, and negotiating the offer and counteroffers. Each of these stages has its own unique problems that the successful investor must deal with and overcome, and this chapter also explains how to deal with some common pitfalls in offer and counteroffer negotiations. This chapter is designed to help the investor negotiate to attain satisfactory results whenever possible.

KEY TERMS

In this section, the following terms related to offers and counteroffers are defined and explained:

- Assumable mortgages
- Buyer's broker
- Earnest money deposit
- Letter of intent

Knowing and understanding these terms and issues related to them will help you to learn and apply the concepts presented in this chapter.

Assumable Mortgages

Not all lenders will allow an existing mortgage to be assumed by a buyer. The lender would rather start the process over and force the buyer to make a new application and obtain a new mortgage (often at a higher rate and shorter term) to repay the old loan. When the existing loan is at a lower rate than current lending would provide, the buyer would rather take over the existing loan.

However, even with a "not assumable" provision in the loan documents (note and mortgage) the buyer can sometimes circumvent this situation by entering into a lease option where the buyer is initially a tenant of the property and will take title (and pay off the existing loan) at a future date. The lessee/buyer may still pay extra funds to the lessor/seller in the form of an option to purchase, which can mitigate risk to the lessor/seller, and as the lessor/seller retains title to the property, no sale has actually transpired, retaining the mortgage in place.

This end run around the assumption provision may not work in all situations, but it is a creative way to make the transaction attractive to a would-be buyer or during a period of time when new mortgages are hard to get. Generally, when a mortgage is created, the property owner goes to the lender and gives that lender a document (the mortgage) that shows the property being used to secure (collateralize) the loan. In addition to the mortgage is a **promissory note**, which is evidence of the sum of money lent, the terms of the payback, and the person responsible for paying back the money. If there is no **personal liability** on the loan, the property pledged is the only asset at risk in the event of a default. If there is personal liability, then the signing party, as well as any cosigners, is liable for the amount borrowed even if the asset pledged no longer has value to secure the loan. The person who borrows is the mortgagor, and the lender is the mortgagee. When the lender agrees to allow another person to step into the shoes of the original mortgagor, the lender allows the mortgage to be assumed.

Because most institutional lenders structure their loans so that they can be packaged and sold to other investors (insurance companies, mortgage-backed funds, and others), a standard set of rules and regulations has been developed to provide certain limitations on the flexibility of the mortgagee in relationship to the mortgagor. The most critical regulation for the borrower concerns the assumability of the mortgages. The lender inserts wording in the mortgage document that states that in the event of a sale, exchange, and in some instances, if there is a long-term lease, the mortgagee is under no obligation to allow the mortgage to be assumed by the new owner. This provision means that if the lender does not agree to such assumption the loan must be repaid. Many private loans do not have these provisions, and when an investor is able to negotiate a loan that can be assumed, the investor has won a major point that could mean the difference between a future sale and a property that cannot be sold. A pitfall in such mortgages is that a mortgage may appear to be assumable but in reality it may not be. This occurs when some lenders put a positive statement in their mortgage such as "This mortgage may be assumed without penalty. (See procedure for Loan Assumption Application on page 16 of the master mortgage document)." On page 16 (if you are lucky enough to find page 16), the explanation of the loan assumption process gives the lender the right to reject an applicant for a wide range of criteria, such as poor or inadequate credit, bad past loan history, and poor net worth. In addition, the lender can collect a fee for loan application, change the terms of the loan, and require the borrower to do all that would be necessary to obtain a new loan: in short, pay off the old loan by getting a new one. This kind of mortgage is not actually an assumable mortgage.

Buyer's Broker

Unless the broker or agent has entered into an agreement with the *buyer* to act for that buyer as a **buyer's broker**, both the real estate salespeople and the broker actually represent the *seller*. That means that they owe their loyalty to the seller and not the buyer. Most buyers get the impression that the agent represents them, but without specific understanding to the contrary, this is not the case. This simple fact limits the service that the buyer can receive. As a buyer's broker, on the other hand, the agent can use all his or her tools and information available to help the buyer obtain the lowest purchase price with the best terms. The buyer's broker must in turn notify any prospective seller or seller's agent that the agent is acting as a buyer's broker. The buyer's broker is paid by the buyer, and the fee is taken into account when the buyer makes his offer to buy.

Earnest Money Deposit

All real estate salespeople are taught to make sure that the offer they draw up has an earnest money deposit, which generally is equal to or greater than the commission that would be due. There is no law that says every buyer must make an earnest money deposit, nor should every seller expect one.

However, as a seller, you would want to make sure that if a long time will pass between signing the contract and closing, the prospective buyer has something at risk to compensate you for taking your property off the market pending the closing.

Some sellers feel the buyer should have some money placed in deposit to show his or her "good intentions." While it is true that money does talk, money isn't the only thing that can be put up as a deposit. Creative investors and real estate exchangers know that the following option provisions can work for them.

- **The promissory note:** This is an unsecured note or promise to pay in the event certain conditions or circumstances are met. A prospective buyer could use such a note as an earnest money deposit. A standard note could not be used, however, as the note must detail the exact terms and conditions to those terms for payment.
- **Collateral:** This is a very simple way to secure any contract. The buyer gives an item of value to a third party to hold as an indication of the buyer's serious intent to follow through with the contract. The item of value can be anything: a ring, a watch, a title to a car, a third-party promissory note (one made payable to the buyer from another party), gemstones, and so on. The contract would simply give reference to the item as the deposit, and it would be treated as though it were cash. This item could be applied to the purchase price, or simply held until the closing and the payoff of the transaction, then returned to the buyer. As with any deposit, it could be subject to forfeiture if the buyer does not meet the conditions of the contract.
- **Promise to exchange other property or services:** This occurs in most exchange agreements. The first party agrees to give to the second party one item in exchange for the other. By execution of this kind of agreement, each party has created an obligation to deliver what he or she has for something else.

Letter of Intent

A **letter of intent** is a form of agreement that may not be legally binding depending on the wording of the letter but can be used to start negotiations. Because the letter of intent may not be a valid contract, it often has less impact than a formal agreement that details property at risk. However, since some formal contracts are cumbersome and expensive to draft, the more informal letter of intent is frequently used. Sometimes the very fact that the letter of intent is not legally binding allows the parties to come to terms on the basics without having to deal with all the legal language that the formal contract will contain. In complicated agreements that require a lot of "good faith acts" between the parties, the letter of intent can be a very good starting point. Another name for this kind of preliminary negotiation is the **agreement in principle**.

Great care needs to be taken to keep the letter of intent or the agreement in principle from becoming a legal contract. This is necessary because this initial probe rarely has all the details and fine-tuning that would be necessary in a formal purchase or exchange agreement. Below is an example of how the author would use a letter of intent. The sample letter is not meant to be a pattern you should follow. As with any potential legal contracts, seek legal advice.

As you can see, the letter of intent is meant to be a simple, straightforward expression of the buyer's interest and intent to enter into an agreement with the seller. If the situation is best served by a formal offer right from the very start, then the buyer should have no objection to making a formal offer provided there is no excessive legal cost to do so.

To: Harvey Winninghold
From: Jack Cummings
Hand delivered by Alex Bresnan, Realtor

Dear Mr. Winninghold,

The purpose of this letter is to express my intent to enter into an agreement with you to acquire an office building you own that is located at the corner of Broadway and East 22nd Street, in New York City, commonly known as Broadway Towers.

If the terms and conditions of this acquisition as will be outlined in this letter are acceptable to you, or if you care to make some refinements to these terms and they are acceptable to me, I will need a period of 10 working days from the date we have a meeting of the minds as to mutually acceptable terms for my legal staff to draft the formal agreement for your review. It is fully understood that neither this letter nor any other correspondence we have between us in this letter of intent format shall constitute a legally binding agreement, but serves simply to bring us together to a meeting of the minds. Only the signing of a formal contract presented to both parties for review and approval would constitute a legal and binding agreement between us. The following are the terms that the formal contract would contain:

Price—$1,450,000.

Subject to buyer's assumption of an existing first mortgage in the amount of $850,000 at terms that must be renegotiated with the mortgagee to reflect the total remaining years following the closing of title, at an interest rate that can be adjustable but not to exceed 6 percent and will begin 1 percent above prime rate or 4.5 percent, whichever is the lower, said mortgage to self-amortize.

Seller to hold a $150,000 purchase money second mortgage, for a term of 15 years payable interest only for the first 5 years at 6 percent per annum, and then interest at 7 percent on unpaid balance plus annual reductions of $15,000 until amortized. No penalty for prepayment in all or part for either the first or second mortgages.

Seller to take in exchange a vacant tract of land in San Francisco, California, known as Cummings Tract A, of which there is a copy of the legal description attached. Said land is free and clear of debt and is valued at $250,000. The balance will be paid in cash at the closing of title.

The purchase agreement would provide that the buyer would have a period of 120 days to make and approve of inspections of the building, rental records, leases, contracts of employment, service records on mechanical and electrical apparatuses within or that serve the building, and other such inspections that may be required of the building as is normal in this kind of transaction. Naturally, your cooperation would be required to gain access within reasonable hours with reasonable notice.

The closing of title will occur no more than 60 days following confirmation that the mortgagee of the first mortgage has agreed to the required changes in the terms of that mortgage.

Unless there is a reply from you no later than noon of the last day of this month, I will presume that none of these terms is of interest and that you do not care to respond further.

However, I hope that we can move ahead on this matter as soon as possible. Please communicate directly with my broker, who will be delivering this letter to you.

Sincerely,

DOING HOMEWORK BEFORE THE OFFER

When the buyer has a good idea of the seller's motivation, it is much easier to draft an initial offer that will be directed toward the most important problem the seller wants to solve. All buyers should embrace the concept that *if you can help solve the other party's problem, you can help solve your own.*

Both parties to an agreement may purposely mislead the brokers or other parties to the transaction. In addition, agents often create reasons or motivations for their clients that the other agents think "sound good" but have little or no connection to reality.

Often the best way to learn about the other party is to meet the person in his or her home (the person's workplace might have to do if you cannot get access to the home). The key to the learning process is not to attempt to negotiate anything at that time but simply be interested in anything the person has to say. Getting people to talk about themselves is relatively easy and only requires that you ask simple questions such as, "How did you get started in real estate?" and then be a good listener. Observing the "home turf" surroundings can be an important, unbiased source of 100 percent accurate information, too. Look around and ask questions that are not offensive and seem innocent. Many people open up nicely to that approach. If things are going well in such a meeting, there is one really effective question that can be asked: What can you do to help me to acquire your property?

STRUCTURING THE OFFER

There are five key factors when structuring the offer:

1. Do not burden the investment with excess debt.
2. When new debt is created, attempt to make it assumable.
3. Introduce a provision that would allow the borrower or future buyer to slide the mortgage to another property of equal or greater equity.
4. Future profit or loss can be a direct result of the terms and conditions of the acquisition.
5. Remember that all parties to a transaction want to come away feeling that they have won something. Some buyers and some sellers tend to leave a sour note at the closing table by making disparaging remarks about the deal, the parties, or agents involved. There is no benefit in this kind of action. You never know where your next deal is going to be, so don't burn bridges no matter what.

How Much Do You Offer?

All buyers should determine the maximum values that can be paid for the subject property for each of the following: price, down payment, monthly payment on debt, and minimum term of debt.

Once investors have a clear understanding of the highest values they can pay in certain circumstances, then the initial offer can be presented, reflecting a reduction from these maximum values to provide room to negotiate and to allow the buyer to see how good a "buy" can be obtained.

How Little Should the Buyer Offer?

There is no set rule. The practical approach is to find out how low an offer can be made with some rational justification. If the listing agent or the investor himself or herself has some solid facts to back up the reason or rationale for the offer, then obtaining a counteroffer is easier. It may be that the low offer made is far more realistic than the asking price, but the difference may be a sudden shock to the seller. Buyers must be very careful that the "sudden shock" is not interpreted as an insult.

As a seller you should never be "insulted" when someone makes an offer—just think of all those people who don't even like the property enough to make an offer.

The real estate agent can be helpful in providing information on other similar property in the same area that has sold recently. This will give statistics to substantiate the "low" offer. However, a good listing agent should have already made this kind of data available to the seller (in an attempt to adjust the price to the market value).

If the market is in favor of the seller, a buyer will ultimately pay the seller's price or very close to it. A highly motivated seller may have already reduced the price sufficiently to attract a buyer.

NEGOTIATING THE OFFER AND THE COUNTEROFFER

For most real estate investors the offer and counteroffer procedure is similar to the following scenario.

First, the buyer and the buyer's broker meet with the listing agent to review the property. The buyer's broker has done his or her homework well, as the property shown is exactly what the buyer wanted. Thus the buyer and the buyer's broker draw up an offer.

The buyer's broker later phones the listing agent and says, "I am expecting an offer on the listing we just saw. Can we get an appointment with the seller for later this afternoon?"

Keep in mind that even if the buyer's broker is looking at the offer, he or she will not tell the listing agent that the offer was already completed, nor would he or she give any details as to what the "pending" offer would be.

The buyer's broker then meets with the seller to discuss the offer and any changes the seller requests to it. These proposed changes to the offer are called the counteroffer. The broker then writes in the seller's proposed changes to the offer (if this is possible) in pen and ink to put the counteroffer in writing. The buyer's broker would then ask the seller to initial each point of change and to sign the counteroffer.

The buyer's broker then takes the counteroffer to the buyer, where the process is much the same. The listing agent (if present) would in both meetings look for points of agreement and places where the gaps of differences could be changed.

PITFALLS IN OFFER AND COUNTEROFFER NEGOTIATIONS

When the process fails to produce conditions and terms that both parties can agree to, the proposed contract becomes a dead issue. Experienced investors know that once this happens it may be very hard to bring a deal back to life, so it is important for both the buyer and seller to work hard to keep the door open and the flow of negotiations moving back and forth.

A number of common problems can be anticipated, and sometimes these problems can be dealt with easily. Following are the three most common problems in offer and counteroffer negotiations:

- **Insulted sellers:** It may not matter why the seller is insulted. What is important is to keep things in their proper perspective. After all, if a seller is insulted when a buyer makes an offer, how are investors going to feel about people who *don't even think enough of the property to make an offer?*
- **Sellers who will not counter:** It should be obvious that if the seller will not counter at all, the buyer who is reviewing several other properties may simply move on to another to see if a more cooperative seller can be found. All investors look for two things in an investment: a property that will serve to move them closer to their goals, and a seller who will cooper-

ate to help that happen. Sellers should help buyers acquire the property that will help them achieve their goals. It is worth repeating that *to solve your problems and attain your goals, help others do the same.*

• **Objections to seller-held mortgages:** To overcome these objections, the person presenting the offer should be aware of the tax advantages to an installment sale. It could be that the seller would profit by spreading some of the gain from a sale over a few years, and the interest rate in the second mortgage would likely be higher than the interest the seller could earn at a savings bank, which is another plus for the seller.

20

HOW TO FIND THE BEST SOURCE OF FINANCING FOR YOUR INVESTMENT

The primary goal of this chapter is to increase the investor's knowledge of how to use these techniques. Financing is an important factor in real estate investing. The material and terms covered here should help the investor in making these key financial decisions.

KEY TERMS

In this section, the following terms related to financing are defined and explained:

- Adjustable rate mortgage
- Amortization
- Balloon payment
- Blanket mortgage
- Wraparound mortgage

Knowing and understanding these terms and issues related to them will help you to learn and apply the concepts presented in this chapter.

Adjustable Rate Mortgage

The adjustable rate mortgage is a very common mortgage, offered by many lending institutions. Often referred to as an ARM, this mortgage allows the lender to have periodic adjustments of the interest rate. This rate can go up as well as down and is usually several interest points above a standard rate. This standard rate may be the interest earned on Treasury bonds, an average prime rate from the major commercial banks, or any other rate the lender wants to use as a benchmark for its loans.

The advantage of these loans is that they usually offer the lowest initial rate when compared to a fixed rate for long-term loans. The reason for this is that the lender is not locked into a low rate if market conditions cause interest rates to rise. These rates can be good for investors when the standard goes down or at least remains fairly stable. The provisions of any ARM can be used by any lender, or even for private loans between individuals. Most institutional loans have a cap, or a maximum rate to which the ARM could adjust over amortization.

Amortization

The term **amortization** simply means to reduce periodically. In finance terms a mortgage amortizes over the life of the loan.

There are five basic types of payment schedules for mortgages, which can be used separately or in combination with one another. Each has an impact on the payment schedule and the principal owed. The five types are as follows:

1. Equal installments of combined principal and interest
2. Equal principal payments plus interest
3. Equal installments or equal principal payments with a balloon payment
4. Interest-only payments
5. Deficit payments

Equal Installments of Combined Principal and Interest
This is the most common form of amortization. For example, a $100,000 mortgage payable over 240 months (20 years) at 8 percent interest repaid with equal installments of $836.42 per month would have the following monthly amortization for the first four months.

Month	Payment	Interest	Principal	Principal Remaining
0				$100,000,00
1	$836.42	$666.67	$179.75	99,830.25
2	836.42	665.53	170.89	99,659.36
3	836.42	664.39	172.03	99,487.33
4	836.42	663.24	173.18	99,314.15

The monthly payment remains the same for the entire 240 months. As small portions of the principal are paid against the principal owed, the interest, which is calculated each month on the remaining balance owed, grows slightly smaller each month. As the total payment does not change, the principal paid each month grows and the amortization, or the reduction of the principal, accelerates slowly. By the end of the 15th year, the principal still owed will be $44,541.76 and the monthly payments will still be $836.42.

Equal Principal Payments Plus Interest

The second type, equal principal payments plus interest, might seem similar to the first method, but this type of amortization provides an equal principal payment that is found by dividing the principal owed by the total number of payments. A $100,000 loan payable over 20 years would have a principal payment each month of $416.66 ($100,000 ÷ 240 months = $416.66). To this amount would be added interest on the principal owed at the start of each month. The schedule below shows several months of this type of schedule at 8 percent interest.

Month	Payment	Interest	Principal	Principal Remaining
0				$100,000.00
1	$1,083.32	$666.66	$416.66	$99,583.34
2	1,080.48	663.82	416.66	99,166.68
3	1,077.76	661.10	416.66	98,750.02
4	1,074.99	658.33	416.66	98,333.36

The change in the wording in a contract can dramatically change the monthly payment. In the equal installment example, the monthly installment was $836.42, while in this mortgage the payment begins at $1,083.32 and declines. An investor who may need every penny of cash flow a property is producing may find that this mortgage will make the venture impossible. On the other hand, an investor who has other income coming in now and wants to channel that extra cash into debt reduction may be inclined to take the equal principal payment plus interest form of amortization.

While this is an interesting form of mortgage, the better choice would be the equal installment example but with the provision that the borrower can make *prepayment in all or part anytime without penalty* to allow principal reduction along the way if extra cash is available. Borrowers should recognize that paying more principal than the payment schedule calls for will speed up the repayment of the loan. If the interest on the loan is more than interest that can be earned in a savings account, it might be wise to put some of your savings to work for you by reducing your debt. Always start with paying down debt that is at the highest interest—which will likely be your credit card balance due.

Either of the Above with a Balloon Payment

The amortization process for either equal installment or equal principal payment mortgages can be established for a longer term than the balance due term. For example, in the first mortgage of $100,000 at 8 percent interest for 240 months (20 years) the lender could set that term solely to reduce the payment, but have a balloon provision under which the mortgage would come due at an earlier date. If that earlier date was 10 years from the start of the repayment schedule, for example, the total outstanding balance and any interest due would have to be repaid on that date. The balance is quickly found by dividing by the constant annual payment (refer to Constant Annual Rate table found at 36hourbooks.com) 20 years at 8 percent is a constant percent of 10.0037. This number times the $100,000 loan amount gives a total annual payment of $10,037.04.

If the balloon is at the start of the second 10 years at that same payment, find the constant rate in the table for 10 years at 8 percent, which is 14.559 percent. Dividing $10,037.04 by .14559 gives the balance due at that time, $68,983.09.

In the second type of payment schedule, of equal principal payments plus interest, the balance due at the start of any selected year will simply be the amount of the monthly principal payment times the number of payments remaining. In this case, a balloon at the end of 10 years would be the balance of 120 payments times $416.66, or $49,999.20. You can see that this is a substantial difference from the balance due in the first mortgage example.

Interest-Only Payments

Interest-only payments are technically not a form of amortization, as no principal is paid off. However, this form of payment is included here because many mortgages incorporate this provision as a part of an amortization schedule. The terms of the mortgage may read as follows:

> Principal owed of $100,000 shall be paid interest only at 8 percent per annum in 24 monthly installments and then beginning on the 25th month and continuing through to the 240th month change to equal installments of interest and principal combined.

Month	Payment	Interest	Principal	Principal Remaining
0				$100,000.00
1	$666.66	$666.67	0	100,000.00
24	666.66	666.67	0	100,000.00

The payment schedule changes on the 25th month

Month	Payment	Interest	Principal	Principal Remaining
25	875.00	666.67	$208.33	99,791.67
26	875.00	665.27	209.73	99,581.94

The interest-only payment for the first 24 months keeps the payment at the break-even point to carry the debt. Then amortization begins on the 25th month, which gives that mortgage 18 years of more normal amortization.

Deficit Payments

Some mortgages use a schedule that reduces the early payments to a point lower than the actual interest charged. Deficit payment mortgages are examples of a mortgage in which the principal owed actually *grows* each month because the payment is less than interest-only payments. With this mortgage the unpaid interest is added to the principal owed. This type of mortgage may be used in combination with an adjustable rate, which means that as the interest charged on the mortgage changes, so does the level of deficit. Review the wording of this mortgage and a portion of the payment schedule.

> Principal of $100,000 with an ARM, which will begin at 8 percent and adjust annually to 2 points above prime, the annual payment shall not exceed $7,500, with any unpaid interest adding to the principal. All adjusted principal shall be due and payable in a balloon payment on the 8th installment.

For the following sample payment schedule, assume the ARM adjusts as follows: years 1, 2, and 3 remain at 8 percent; years 4, 5, and 6 are 10 percent; and years 7 and 8 are at 7 percent.

Month	Payment	Interest	Principal	Principal Remaining
	$7,500.00	$8,000.00	$500.00	100,500.00
2	7,500.00	8,040.00	540.00	101,040.00
3	7,500.00	8,083.20	583.00	101,623.00
4	7,500.00	10,162.30	2,662.30	104,285.00
5	7,500.00	10,428.50	2,928.50	107,213.50
6	7,500.00	10,721.35	3,221.35	110,434.85
7	7,500.00	7,730.44	230.44	110,665.29
8	118,411.86	7,746.57	0	0

During the life of this mortgage, unless the interest rate went considerably below 7.5 percent, the principal would grow until the mortgage was finally paid off.

Balloon Payment

This is a prescheduled payment that can be all or part of the principal owed plus interest due, often a partial payment made during a term of a mortgage or a sudden payoff of the mortgage that has been set up on a longer amortization schedule than the actual repayment of principal. For example, in the first mortgage shown of equal installments of a 20-year mortgage at 8 percent interest, with the provisions of the mortgage calling for a *payment in full* at the end of the 10th year, this payment is called a balloon payment. This payment is the principal that the amortization schedule would indicate is due. If interest is calculated for a period of time following the previous payment made, interest for that period would also be added to the balance outstanding. Balloon payments are used quite often but have the disadvantage of sneaking up on the investor who fails to keep track of the due date.

Blanket Mortgage

A blanket mortgage occurs when a single loan is secured by more than one property. Blanket mortgages are quite common in real estate developments in which many residential lots or tract homes may be used as the security.

Most blanket mortgages allow the mortgagor to release the security as the loan is paid. This enables the developer to sell individual lots or homes and to separate them from the blanket mortgage. Any mortgage can be a blanket mortgage.

Wraparound Mortgage

The wraparound mortgage is one of the best tools to consolidate a payment schedule for a buyer or to give the seller positive leverage when taking back a purchase money mortgage. Actually, the wraparound mortgage was used extensively in the late 1960s and early 1970s until institutional lenders started the practice of requiring existing loans to be renegotiated or paid off in the event of a sale. The lenders realized that the sellers, taking back a purchase money second wraparound mortgage, were leaving the original lower interest rate first mortgage in place and leveraging their own return on the purchase money second mortgage at the same time.

While this practice made for very good real estate investing and was good for both buyers and sellers, the lenders argued that they were being hurt because they were forced to stay with the deal (which they originally agreed to) at the low rate. There is no real logic in that argument, because if the seller could not or would not sell, then the lenders would also have been "forced" to do exactly what they contracted for when they made the loan.

Wraparound mortgages have their place in the investor's toolbox because they can be and still are useful when the underlying loans do not require loan renegotiation or repayment.

When a seller holds a wraparound mortgage, the buyer makes *one* payment to the seller to cover *all the underlying debt*, including any seller-held purchase money mortgages. In a situation in which there are several mortgages in place plus a third mortgage position the seller is to hold, there is increased risk that the buyer may not be able to meet a heavy debt payment. The seller is not as secure as he or she would want to be because the buyer could let the mortgages go into default and actually get many months behind payments before the seller would ever know about it. Even though the underlying mortgagees "say" they will notify the holder of any inferior debt, because of the magnitude of business that the larger lenders do each day, with main offices handling debt collection often a thousand miles away, no investor can count on being notified of a late payment. The wraparound mortgage eliminates this problem and at the same time can give the buyer a steady debt service.

The seller and buyer agree to an independent collection agent or management firm that collects the single payment and then makes the corresponding payments to the previous and still-existing debt. The seller gets the remainder, and when existing debt is paid off sooner than the terms of the wraparound mortgage, the seller receives more. Because the wraparound mortgage often has an interest rate slightly higher than either of the underlying mortgages (but this is not a requirement), the seller leverages over that sum.

For example, if the wraparound mortgage was for $250,000 at 8.5 percent and the total existing debt was $200,000 at 7.5 percent, then the seller gets 8.5 percent on the seller's equity of the wraparound of $50,000, as well as *an additional* 1 percent on the existing $200,000. This can be very attractive because 1 percent of the additional $200,000 is the same as an additional 4 percent on the equity of $50,000. This would approximate a net return of 12.5 percent (the 8.5 percent plus the extra 4 percent); however, because other factors are taken into account (the most important is the time at which the seller gets paid off), the actual yield is not so easily calculated. A moderately priced handheld financial calculator can perform the exact calculations if the investor finds it critical to know those exact details.

21

TIPS ON SURVIVING REAL ESTATE PROBLEM AREAS

T he goal of this chapter is to show you a comprehensive list of items and documents, many of which have already appeared in this book. However, this chapter is dedicated to looking at these items from a worst-case scenario so that you will already know some of the problems that can come with them. The purpose of this chapter then is to let you know up front that there is a light at the end of every problem, even if that light is for you to decide not to purchase the property. In fact, that is the best light of all because it can save you from making a mistake.

When entering into a purchase contract, it is prudent that the agreement contain all essential documents. It is a good idea to list as many of the important aspects that you can that may be hidden time bombs (as well as potential gems) to alert the seller that you may request certain documentation to support your findings. Remember, however, it will be impossible or improbable that you will specifically be able to list everything that you ultimately should inspect. The initial inspection may lead into different directions of things and documents that will need to be reviewed.

The following is an alphabetical list of subjects and elements that you will want to inspect or at least be aware of. Some of these elements can create road blocks, cause problems, add unnecessary cost to property management or operations, and in general become a headache unless you anticipate the problem. I recommend that you review this chapter from time to time, and add some of your own newly found items that you encounter.

AC AND HEATING

When the property you are purchasing has air conditioning equipment, it is important that you have a thorough inspection made. Critical elements to make note of would be the age of the compressor, fan motor, and fuel containers (for heating oil or propane). The actual age of the system is usually visible on the information plate that indicates its serial number, model, manufacturer, and other information. However, repairs or replacements made after it was installed may not show the age of new parts. The inspection would have to look at the parts to ascertain the actual age of the critical elements in the operation of the system. Compressors and motors may still have several years or more of warranty even though the system itself is out of warranty.

ACCOUNTING AND FEES

Unless you are comfortable with your understanding of accounting procedures, you should include accounting fees as a normal part of any income property expenses. The fact that the previous owner did not show accounting fees may have been an oversight, much the same as many property owners attempt to enhance the "bottom line" of their income and expense statement by omitting many "service" fees. These service fees may also include items such as property management, night clerk, yard maintenance, and a host of other "I do it myself" kinds of chores to properly maintain the investment.

AIR-CONDITIONING AND HEATING EXPENSES

A careful review of all operating expenses of any property you are considering purchasing may sound like obvious advice; however, few buyers do a thorough job at that task. Actual bills should be reviewed with a monthly check to see if there are spikes in the bills that may indicate problems with various systems. If the tenants are paying their own bills, it still is important to check to see what costs are involved. Most prospective tenants will want to know what those cost are, and the only way to give that information is to do a periodic check of their bills. Of all utility bills, water consumption is the most important because that bill triggers other charges that are based on the amount of water that is going through the meter. In a multitenant building it may be difficult to track down which unit may be wasting water by having a leaky toilet or dripping tap.

ANSWERS

Answers you didn't understand or didn't listen to. Okay, you asked the right question, but you did not understand the answer or perhaps didn't even listen to the answer. This is a problem that you do not want to have. It is a good idea to write down the questions you need to have answered. Leave a blank space after the question so you can make note of the answers you are given. This chapter is a great place to start to build that list. If your entire list is covered in one session, put the date of that session at the top of the first page along with the name of the individual or individuals answering the questions. If the question list is staggered over more than one date, then put the dates you get the answers and the appropriate source for each question.

APPROVED USES

Every zoning generally has more than one use allotted to it. You might be surprised at how flexible that list can be, and there may be a use that will produce an instant profit to you that the seller did not anticipate. This is one of the hidden gems that many properties keep secret because buyers and sellers alike tend to assign a use to a property based on what they see. If you see a single-family home on a large lot, double-check the zoning codes. It might be that the lot itself is large enough to support more than one legal residence, or even allow commercial use so the extra land space can be used for the needed parking. If a multifamily building can be constructed, you may have found that gold mine you have been dreaming of. One important word of warning: Just because the zoning might indicate that you can use the site for several or many different uses does not automatically mean the city will approve these uses due to other rules that might affect the specific use you have in mind. Also, impact fees and the need to bring the building up to a new code level might be cost prohibitive even if zoning gives the green light.

ASSESSMENTS

When buying a property there may be unpaid assessments that have gone unnoticed by everyone except the seller. Some assessment that could be past due are condominium or homeowners' association assessments or impact fees from local city government authorities. These are particularly important for condominium or homeowner association properties as they generally have the power to lien the property. Other "assessments" may not use this word, but are called "fees" that are levied by various government authorities. An impact fee, which may occur whenever a new building is contemplated or as a part of some local infrastructure expansion, is really a tax, but it will be payable by whoever presently owns the property. If you are the new owner you may have the right to go after the seller to recover the cost, but it may be futile and expensive.

AUTHORITY TO MAKE CONTRACT

Did you check to see that the seller was the owner of the property you just closed on? Or if not the seller, did he or she have the authority to enter into a contract? No doubt you have heard of the cliché of the person who bought the Brooklyn Bridge. But how about the home you are living in? One day the real owner may come back from his or her trip around the world. Checking the name alone is not good enough. Make sure your closing agent follows a strict review of the title to ascertain the right individuals who can pass on good title. This is important when you are selling as well. The person who gives you a mortgage on the property you just sold to him or her may not be the person who writes his or her name on the note and mortgage. This could be a sticky matter if you had to foreclose because the person didn't make any payments to you.

BANKS

Holds, transfers, postdated checks, and other banking procedures can create problems you never expected could or would happen. Some banks are very quick to put a hold on a deposit, which may cause checks you write to bounce because the bank is waiting for the funds to be transferred into their hands before allowing any funds to flow out of your account. Some banks do this even if there were already sufficient funds cleared in advance (from prior deposits). Postdated checks create other problems because if you take one from someone and it bounces, you may not have a legal position to collect those funds. Also, many banks will cash a postdated check or at least allow it to be deposited into an account. If the maker of the check postdated the check thinking that by the time it was used (or cashed) the funds will be in the bank will surely be surprised to find that the bank has already cashed the check and is now charging the maker for making an overdraft. Payday lenders that advance loans to people based on the fact that their payday is still two weeks away may ask that the borrower give them a postdated check that the lender can use to recover the loan. If there are insufficient funds on the check date, this can cause another surprise when the lender deposits the check, which is then reported back to you as an overdraft.

In many countries the banking system is used to the postdated form of repayment of loans. Called notes or letters of credit, or simply *lettras*, the person writing these notes may create a series of future payments that cover the entire repayment of the loan. A five-year payback, for example, would require 60 such documents, each looking much like a postdated check. These would not be cashable under normal circumstances, as they would not be "good" until the date shown on the date line. If your intention is to comply with the lender's request for such a series of advance date repayments, make sure your lawyer has drafted the right kind of document to avoid the sudden withdrawal of the entire amount.

CLEAR CONTRACTUAL UNDERSTANDING

Every document that pertains to the transfer of use or title of a property should have a clearly defined purpose, and all the terms and obligations surrounding that transfer should be completely understood by all parties. This means that the person who drafts the document should also know and understand exactly what the intentions are and how they are to be followed. Omission of a single word can make a world of a difference, so it is critical that you read the document slowly and best aloud. This also goes for the elements to the contract, such as legal description, sizes, and survey data.

CODE VIOLATIONS

This book has covered this subject from many different points of view. You can take a look at the index to see the page numbers where the words "code violations" occur to verify that statement. Enough said on this subject.

COMFORT ZONE VISITS

Having a comfort zone of investing is important because it defines the area where you are going to concentrate your investment efforts. But as with any part of town, you need to make sure you are a frequent visitor to the area. Failing to drive around the area on a regular basis may cause you to be unaware of some unpleasant things taking place. Your ability to quickly recognize opportunities long before the general public can recognize them demands that you keep your eye on what is happening. This means more than a fast drive around, it means being aware of future plans in the works. A sign posted on a property might be a rezoning notice or a foreclosure notice— each a different event, and each important to you. A sudden increase in "for sale" or "for rent" signs is a sure clue that something is happening.

CONTROL OVER THE PROPERTY

Not tying up a property before spending a lot of time investigating it is a mistake that most investors make. To be thorough in your investigations is important, but it is wrong to waste your time only to discover that the seller is really not very motivated, or that another investor has jumped ahead of you and has tied up the property. A completely thorough investigation of any property will require you to ask questions. But asking too many questions to too many people may spark more competition from those same people.

CRACKED OR LEAKING POOL

Just because you don't see the crack doesn't mean the pool is structurally fine. Check the water level and the water bill at the property. Those two elements in combination may suggest a constant input of water to hide the fact that the pool is leaking.

CREDIT CHECK

If you are taking any kind of future promise of payment (rent or mortgage) you may want to do a credit check on the person responsible to make the future payment. You can contact credit bureaus through the Internet or by phone: Equifax.com (1-888-202-4025), Experian.com (1-714-830-7000 or 1-224-689-5600), or TransUnion.com (1-800-493-2392).

CRIME

The level of crime in a neighborhood may not be as obvious as you think. Nonetheless, begin with the obvious by checking with the police department that is responsible for responding to crime in your comfort zone. If this zone is close to other cities or unincorporated areas, find out which police department covers those areas. Get in contact with the public safety officer or other individual who is responsible to maintain statistics of the crime within your designated area. The police report can dictate which of the following next steps you can take. A drive through the area during various times of day and night may turn up a level of crime that may not be reported to the police. This is crime that is so rampart that the people of the neighborhood are actually frightened to even call the police. Drugs and prostitution can be part of an even bigger problem. Keep in mind that checking on the level of crime is one of the very first things you will want to do before settling on that area for your comfort zone. If you detect crime you may want to look to another area.

DELIVERY PROMISE

Any promise to do something in the future in a contract is subject to a future default. By this I mean that a future payment, service, labor, or any other thing to be accomplished should have a corresponding penalty if it is not fulfilled. The penalty should be clearly defined as well as the remedy to the default to ensure compliance.

DRIVE-THROUGH

Inspections of a property should include physical visits to the area where the property is located during various times of day and night. Weekend visits are also important because that may be the only reasonable time to ascertain the presence of children.

DUE DILIGENCE

There are many companies in most areas of the United States and some other countries as well that conduct property inspections. A careful review of the service agreement will outline the items that are covered in the inspection. The agreement may also indicate certain aspects of the real estate that are *not* covered. Most property inspections are limited in scope and may not uncover building and zoning code violations. A buyer of a commercial property is advised to seek a company that is experienced in conducting an inspection of a commercial building. If any inspection uncovers evidence of the presence of a potential environmental hazard, special companies that will test soil and groundwater may be required.

ELECTRICAL SERVICE

The most common code violations will have some connection to the electrical service within a building. This is generally the case with older buildings that have outdated and no longer permitted wiring or electrical panels. As these present a fire danger, these kinds of problems must be promptly dealt with. A review of the electric bill may also give a clue to excessive electrical use, which may lead to a tenant operating equipment that is in violation to the lease. Electrical systems, as with plumbing, bring problems that are not obvious to the novice, mainly because they are hidden and out of sight. Trust professionals to advise you on how to fix a problem before you close on the property.

ELEVATOR SERVICE

There are two factors to the inspection of elevators of a building that must be attended to. The first is the service agreement, if there is one in place. This agreement is important because it may be an old agreement that needs to be updated to more modern techniques. If there is a service agreement, the history of repairs should be inspected as well, and what recommendations for prevention or reduction of service calls the inspectors have made. If costly repairs or replacement have continued to go untreated, the next call could be the one you, as the new owner, must face. The second factor to check is whether the elevator meets the current building codes. If not, you will need to ascertain the cost to remedy that problem and pass that cost on to the seller.

EMPLOYEES

If you purchase an investment where you inherit employees and service contracts, you need to discover what, if any, employment or service contracts exist and how you can terminate them. I have seen service contracts where there were family members of the seller that had long-term contracts of employment. Settle up with the seller on these issues before they become a legal issue after the closing of the transaction.

ENVIRONMENTAL HISTORY AND TESTS

Environmental problems are generally not visible, although the source of the problems is generally easy to ascertain. These usually come from the use or storage of certain chemicals on or near the property. It can be the asbestos in the building materials used, or lead in the paint that once was used and is now below several layers of newer paint. Vacant property that was once used for farming may have had an irrigation pump run by a gas or oil internal combustion engine with a large tank of fuel next to it that remains on the property. Auto service and repair areas are known to spoil the land where the chemicals inside their various parts leaked into the earth. This list could continue for several pages, but each of these sources is easily traced to a former tenant or use. Some of these problems are not worth the cost to find a remedy. Some are allowed to continue to exist providing there is no continuation of a contamination. If inspections find any environmental problem, take it seriously.

ESTOPPEL LETTER

When there are tenants in the property you are purchasing, the seller or his or her agent delivers a separate estoppel letter executed by each tenant which verifies that the data provided in the letter as to the terms and history of the lease is correct. If there are outstanding penalties, those will also be mentioned in the letter, as will the amount of any deposit, and often a copy of the actual lease and any amendments will be referenced and attached to the estoppel letter. An estoppel letter can also be used to verify the terms and conditions of any accessory contract or debt instrument between the seller and a third party.

EXCHANGE PROGRAM VALIDITY

If part of a transaction pertains to a future use of some other property or service, it is important to have a copy of the documentation that spells out the details of that use or service. A timeshare, for example, may have exchange rights through a master company that provides a network of other timeshare operations and facilities. Your ownership of a timeshare connected to that service may be the real benefit to its ownership, and the sudden loss of that benefit may reduce the value to you to the extent that you would not want to own the property at all.

EXCHANGING FOR A FUTURE ANYTHING

Hotels, airlines, rental car services, and other services and businesses may provide points for initial purchases that can be exchanged into other products or services. Because this is a value in exchange, it may be used as part of a real estate transaction. For example, Judy offered Macken the use of any RCI timeshare in their timeshare network for one week a year for eight years as a part of her purchase of Macken's home. Judy showed Macken the RCI catalog, which was impressive, and the value of $8,000 for eight weeks of use seemed reasonable to Macken. But what if Judy drops out of the RCI network, or does not "deposit" the needed the weeks in the system so that Macken would be able to draw down on a week a year for the full eight years? You can see how this could become a future problem for Macken. The remedy could be an offset to some other aspect of the transaction. Macken could hold a note and mortgage on the house with eight corresponding payments each totaling the supposed value of the use of an RCI week. Now what Judy has is the right to pay the eight payments by delivering Macken an RCI week. In fact, Macken may want to change the method so that every other year he could take two back-to-back weeks in the resort of his choice (based on occupancy, of course).

EXPENSES

When acquiring any real estate that comes with continuing expenses, you need to verify that the seller has properly and fully disclosed all expenses pertinent to the property. You must recognize the motivation for a seller to fail to disclose some of the real expenses in his or her attempt to show a greater cash flow than truly exists. This is not totally criminal in nature, as many owners really do not have the expenses that you might have if you own the property because of the definition of an expense. If the seller does the work or task in question himself or herself, he or she is not spending money to have that work accomplished. So the seller can argue he or she does not have to report the expense. However, unless you intend also to do the work yourself, it will be an expense if you purchase the property. In my many years as a real estate broker selling hotels and motels (and other income properties), I have seen this occur time and time again. The owner and his or her family members are working their fingers to the bone to manage and take care of the property while serving their customers day and night. But you? Well, you are not looking for such a low-paying job, are you?

FLOOD HAZARD

There are places in this world that are prone to floods. In fact, some of these places flood every spring, summer, or even fall. You come along and find the place a paradise (oh so green and fertile), but you don't understand that it is that way because of the annual floods. It is a good idea to question the history of the seasons for any area of the country that is new to you. Even if the closest river is 10 miles away, question why it has high flood banks along its path. Ask the local emergency services if there is a flood problem here, and if so, how often has this property experienced its venture into scuba time.

FLOOR AND WALL TILES

This tip will save you or a prospective buyer a lot of headache. If you build a building that has floor or wall tiles, keep an extra box of the tiles in a safe place. In the future of this building there will likely be a tile or two or more that need to be replaced. Or a remodeling job that opens walls that suddenly show concrete between 10-foot strips of tiles on either side. At the same time, make note of where the tiles were purchased and the manufacturer of the tile and its model name. Some tiles are so well liked they stay in production for many years.

FORECLOSURE

The worst thing that can happen to you and your real estate is not foreclosure. The real estate generally survives, and so will you. There are, however, certain steps you can take both before and during the process that may help you avoid the circumstances. If not, you surely can lessen the impact to you and your family.

Look at the following four things to consider:

- **Be proactive.** You need to pay close attention to your financial situation. If things at work are looking bad, consider what will happen if you get laid off or cut back to part-time work. How long can you keep making your mortgage payment along with all your other expenses? Take action immediately to discuss your impending financial problem with the loan officer at the lending institution that processed your loan. No lender wants to trigger a foreclosure situation if they can avoid it, so both you and they are looking for a solution. Discuss unemployment compensation benefits with the local officials. Do not wait until you are already a month behind in paying bills.

• **Look for programs that can help you.** Your loan officer can usually direct you to one or more programs that are designed to help people in your situation. Be careful of the "pay up front for help" kind of program.

• **Seek legal help.** There are public forums that provide free legal help, and even your own lawyer will give you advice at little or no charge. There are remedies that you can take, such as bankruptcy or giving the lender a deed in lieu of the institution filing foreclosure (you lose the home but are free of the obligation). Which avenue you take may depend on whether or not the property is worth the amount owed. If you are upside down (you owe more than the value), then the deed in lieu may be a simple approach. But get legal advice because there might be other circumstances that should be considered, such as secondary financing that may still go after you, or improper lending practices where someone took advantage of you.

• **Maintain honesty.** Maintain your dealings with the lender in an open and honest manner. This does not mean you have to disclose every detail about your problem. What it means is that you do not attempt to use lies to cover your sincere attempt to solve the problem in a fair and prudent way.

HEALTH CODES

Many commercial uses require approval from the local health department, or even from the state health department. These deal with codes that govern the building rules and restrictions that require the operator of the business, often a restaurant, bar, food production facility, and the like, to meet high sanitary standards. If you are purchasing a property that has such a business as a tenant, question the rules and regulations that the tenant should meet. It is possible that due to a slip in protocol that tenant obtained approval to operate without having told the truth or by some other devious method. By allowing this to continue to slide through the system, you might be the owner who gets caught with a violation. The results can be multiple. You can lose a tenant, get a fine, and have a vacancy that may not be allowed to continue as its present and highly profitable business operation.

HIDDEN GEMS

Hidden gems are the good news side of an inspection of the property. These gems come in many different packages, the best of which might be that hardwood oak floor or barn wood flooring that is worth its weight in gold, which you find under 45-year-old linoleum flooring. Or the gem could be as simple as a perfect terrazzo floor with no cracks under glued-down carpet. Other gems might include copper plumbing, a copper roof, double studded walls that improve soundproofing, large bedrooms and bathrooms, and other construction elements that were done with such precision and expertise and superior material that they just cannot be reproduced in this modern mass-produced world.

HOMEOWNERS' ASSOCIATION

Be careful with this term. You need to understand that not all "HOAs" are equal. A lot depends on the local or state rules in this direction. So, if you are purchasing a property that is disclosed as part of an HOA, find out exactly what the association's rules and regulations consist of. Is there a fee? Can the association lien your property if you do not comply with its rules? What restrictions does it impose? Your future sale may depend on this, as HOAs can become more restrictive over the years.

IMPACT FEES

This is a relatively new term in real estate ownership. It is a way for a community to generate additional revenue, and in this modern world of topsy-turvy, up-and-down revenue collection, most cities look for any way they can generate revenue. In general, an impact fee is something like a tax that is imposed on a developer who wants to build on a vacant property or add to an existing building. The addition might be a major structure, something rather simple such as an added turn lane into the property, or some extra paving for additional parking spaces. Whatever it is, you might be able to fight the imposition of an impact fee by taking the issue up the ladder of the building department. However, prior to doing that, talk to a lawyer who is an expert on these kinds of matters. You might be making things worse by contesting some minor expense. You do not want to willingly make enemies of the local authorities.

IMPACT WINDOWS

The modern laminated glass used in residential and commercial construction is made much like the windshield of your car or truck. Depending on where your real estate is located, it may be required to meet certain standards, of which the hurricane-prone South Florida codes are considered the more restrictive and stringent. Do not believe, however, that this kind of glass is storm proof. If you have the choice between going to impact glass or hurricane shutters, you might consider the shutters over the glass. Discuss this with a specialist in each product and make your decision.

IMPROPER INSTALLATIONS

Every year many homeowners or real estate investors are suckered into hiring unqualified weekend workers to accomplish repairs or improvements to their real estate. Some weekend workers are skillful professionals that deliver the same level of work that they do during the week when they work for a reputable construction company. However, there are those weekend workers who are novices or worse. Some are even shysters who are out to take their customers for the deposit or advance payment then after a short while disappear. The key for you to avoid this problem is to ask for references and then to follow up on those references. Ask questions like the following: How did you make initial contact with this person? Did you get references? Could you share those references with me? What work did they actually do? Are you satisfied with their work? You get the idea.

INCOMPATIBLE TENANT

Would you put a known drug dealer into a strip store you own? Not willingly, I would hope. But how much attention do you give to the nature of your tenants when you are sitting there with a strip mall that is half empty? Many property owners faced with continuing cash drain through operational expenses and debt service may be drawn into the trap of accepting a tenant who turns out to be a nightmare tenant. If prospective tenants have been in business elsewhere, make an effort to find out if they were successful, and if not, why not. Get some references from them of landlords that were happy with them as a tenant.

INSURANCE

If you do not shop around for insurance annually, you may pay too much for the insurance you are getting. But worse, you may not be getting the level of insurance you need. This goes for property you acquire as well. If you have a good insurance agent, he or she will suggest an annual review of your coverage. You have seen countless advertisements from insurance companies that all seem to tout that if you switch to them you can save up to $350 a year. What works for auto insurance works for other kinds as well. Follow these tips to keep your insurance at the best for the least:

- Consider bundling your insurance with the same carrier for even greater savings.
- Keep your insurance documentation in a safe place that you remember where it is.
- Be careful about having more than one agent because you may accidently end up with two policies covering the same building.
- Go over your needs with your agent and ask what additional insurance you can get for just a few pennies more. You might be surprised at what added insurance you can get that way.
- Business interruption insurance is something you should consider because even minor damage can shut a business down for months.

There is another kind of insurance you should have as well as the usual casualty or liability insurance. This is called "title insurance" and will insure you against problems that might arise if there is a cloud in the title (problem of an outstanding lien or faulty conveyance in the past that puts your ownership in jeopardy). Take note that there are loopholes in most of these policies that may allow the insurer to slip out of responsibility. Be sure to discuss these potential problems that can occur.

INTERNET SERVICE

Most businesses and most businesspeople cannot function effectively without ability to connect to the Internet. No matter what kind of income property you plan to acquire, you might find that if the building is wired for wireless Internet connection it improves your chances to attract tenants. As with any modern technology, there are many advances in Internet everything. Companies that offer bundled service of Internet, phone, and TV are in competition with each other, and prices may continue to fall while service continues to improve. Internet phone, called simply IP, is available anywhere you can connect to the Internet, so consider having this service available for not only your own use, but your tenants' as well. With IP you pay for the Internet connection and aside from that a low monthly connection charge, and you can call virtually anywhere in the world without added cost.

LAND LEASES

There are two sides to this issue: the land lease you hold as landlord and the land lease you pay as lessee. The critical element to each side is whether or not there is subordination involved. If you are the landlord and you allow subordination, the tenant can borrow money using the property as security. This places your interest at risk in the event of a default. So why do it? You may subordinate with a relatively low risk, but you had best know exactly what you are doing and have strict limitations to the amount of money to be borrowed, how it will be used (generally to improve the property, which offsets the risk factor to a degree), the interest rate allowed, the term of the payback of the loan, and that the lender is an institutional lender and not the borrower's brother. As a lessee you take control over the property to an even greater degree than owning a leasehold interest in the property. By being able to give a lender a security in the form of a first mortgage, for example, you can borrow at a better rate with softer terms than if you are pledging your leasehold interest. Both landlord and lessee should use a lawyer (not the same one) who is knowledgeable of land leases.

LAWYERS

Never attempt to save money by using the same lawyer in a real estate transaction as the person or entity on the other side of the deal. And remember, not all lawyers graduated at the top of their class, and not all lawyers are pillars of the community. This means you should use some due diligence in selecting your own lawyer, or lawyers, as the case should be. I say this because if you are diverse in your acquisitions you may need more than one lawyer so you can contact whichever is best qualified for your present need. Remember, for example, some lawyers are absolute shining knights litigating before a judge and jury but would not be any good drafting a complicated trust agreement.

LEGAL DESCRIPTION, SURVEY, AND EYEBALL

As with much that is in this list, I have touched on this issue earlier in this book. It is a good idea to make a direct personal comparison between the legal description, the survey, and your eyeball walk around the property. Some years ago I went shopping for a waterfront lot on which to build a new home. I found a vacant lot in an older subdivision in Fort Lauderdale that appealed to me, except for one aspect. While the lot was much larger than most of the other lots in the area, it was sandwiched between two homes where it came down to the deep-water canal (there were no fixed bridges between the lot and the Atlantic Ocean, and I was seeking ocean access). Fences on either side indicated that the seawall, and therefore the docking area, was only around 20 feet—not enough for my 42-foot sport fishing boat. So I continued looking, but did not find anything.

I went to the city to research the area to see if there was something I had overlooked. What I found was the home that adjoined this waterfront lot on the north side had been sold five times over the last nine years. I went back to the lot and walked down to the seawall and noticed what looked like a survey marker nailed into the top of the concrete seawall. On closer inspection, however, it turned out to be a Doctor Pepper bottle cap with a nail through it. So, back to the city records, which showed clearly that the seawall that was the waterfront boundary was 50 feet in length.

I purchased the lot with a 30-day due diligence to allow extra time to double-check my findings. Sure enough, the original owner of the home to the north had owned both lots and built on the northerly one but landscaped most of the vacant lot as part of her yard—so much so that a fence and hedge that incorporated a nice patio, with brick barbecue and beautiful fruit trees plus around 30 feet of the dock area, turned out to be on the lot I had purchased.

My find was one of those hidden gems.

LEGAL FEES

As with all fees, there is no etched-in-stone price on the legal service you will get. This is another reason you should know several different lawyers that you might use for different services. It is one thing to hire a lawyer to handle a tough battle with the building department or a rezoning issue and another to have a lawyer fill out the forms to file a small claims court action. The difference in hourly rate can be substantial. Remember, most lawyers will grant you an appointment to discuss what you need and what they will charge, and they generally will not charge you for that first hour. (If they do, make sure you take advantage and use up the whole hour.)

LIEN STATUS ON PROPERTY OR BORROWER

When your closing agent or lawyer checks the title of a property, liens that are still outstanding should show up. Errors are possible in the recording of liens, which is one reason you are advised to have title insurance. However, it is also a good idea to check the lien history of the buyer or seller because if you discover that there is a long history of liens being filed against the person, that may lead to a lien that should have appeared against the property but due to an error or improper filing did not show up.

LOCKS

When you buy a building, it will undoubtedly come with locks and keys. Make sure you get a key for every lock prior to the closing, or you may never get them. As a seller or landlord I encourage the buyer or tenant to change the locks and to give me a set of the new keys. If this occurs, I double-check to make sure that the keys work as assigned. Storage of keys can be a problem, so make sure that each key is coded in such a way that you can clearly identify which key opens which lock.

MAINTENANCE AND RESERVES

The maintenance of any building and the amount of reserves that are set aside for replacements is an issue that is critically important when purchasing a condominium (residence or office). Repairs to a large building can be very expensive, and to replace just one of the massive air-conditioning units can run into many thousands of dollars. Many such properties have a monthly maintenance fee charged to the owners, and often a portion of the fee goes toward a savings account to cover planned replacements and major repairs. These would include things such as all mechanical apparatuses, such as AC and heat, elevators, pumps, exterior painting, interior furniture replacement, pool maintenance and interior resurfacing, and so on. When you purchase one of these types of property make sure you know how these fees are charged and what the present status of the reserve account is. You might discover that it is zero. This happens because the entire reserve was spent already without time to build up again, or the building does not have a reserve account at all. When no reserve account exists, any sudden repairs or replacements are generally made by borrowing funds (yes, the building management can do that if it is allowed in the condo docs), then assessing the owners to recover the amount to pay back the loan. If the building has a poor maintenance history, and the elevators, AC, and other items are getting close to their replacement age, then you should factor into your purchase price some pending assessments. They are pending only historically, but legally they may not be pending because they have yet to be assessed. As a buyer you get nailed in that instance.

MANAGEMENT

This word covers a host of potential problems. First of all, purchasing a "business investment," which I call any real estate that you plan to operate rather than to simply lease out, will come with a management situation. Yet sellers of these business investments rarely take into account the management expense because they do it themselves. You must take into account what your time is worth if you plan on doing the management, or figure in the real cost to hire someone in the case of a condo or any property that has any outside management. Or it could be the Hilton hotel you purchased in a limited partnership with other investors, which is being operated by Hilton. Pay close attention to the expense in these situations. Make sure that you have the right to change management companies; some hotel companies balk at allowing this, for what they call "quality control" is to be in their hands. You may find yourself at their mercy if that is the case. Other management agreements may have a penalty or an override due the management firm if you cancel the agreement. Be careful of these types of agreements.

MOLD OR OTHER ENVIRONMENTAL PROBLEMS

Mold is often a major problem and should be included in any inspection of the property. Make sure that the person or firm you select to inspect your intended purchase is qualified to test for mold and the more common environmental problems. One common failure is underground oil storage tanks.

The heating system may have been changed years ago, so there may be no evidence aboveground that a rusting tank is still under the dirt somewhere. A review of the original building plans may show that a permit was issued at the time the tank was installed, and it may still be there. If so, you may have to take this into consideration, and if it turns out to have leaked, it may become a major expense to clean up.

MORTGAGE

Mortgages are either a first mortgage or fall into a secondary position. It might be that you are the mortgagor, who is the person who gives the lender the mortgage document that evidences the security on the loan. Or you could be the mortgagee, who is the lender. Mortgages have been given the rap for causing the financial chaos that began around 2007. The reality is it was the "easy credit" that drove the lending industry to make loans in a grand rush to let people buy, refinance, and then flip properties one right after the other . . . until the bubble burst. This never would have happened if the lenders had held back on the ease with which people had access to these loans. In any event, the lesson is a simple one. Never borrow more than you can easily repay. Have a safety net in the bank to cover potential financial problems, and balance your outside debt by not letting your credit card debt go beyond one month's interest. The most expensive debt the average person will ever carry is that 24 percent or higher interest on their credit card balance.

NATURAL DISASTER AREAS

There are places in this world, and plenty of them are in the United States, where it seems that natural disasters happen time and time again. Hurricanes, tornados, floods, mudslides, angry oceans, sinkholes, earthquakes, volcano eruptions, forest fires, avalanches, drought, and this sort of thing is Mother Nature at her most distressed state. If you are purchasing a property anywhere where you don't have a personal history of experience as to the potential disaster waiting to happen, check it out. One of the best places to do this is with your property insurance agency and with the fire department's emergency response department. Weigh the risk, and find out how much insurance you might need (but might not be able to afford) before you close on the deal. Some insurance companies simply will not insure a property at all in some circumstances or will insist on such a high deductible that it would be like buying the property again every three or four years.

NOISY NEIGHBORS

You don't have control over a neighbor who moves in after you did, but you can at least choose between those who are already there. This is more reason to visit a property during various times of the day and evening and weekends. Most communities have laws that control certain activities such as workmen, loud parties, and so on. Condominiums and rental properties generally have strict rules that abate such circumstances. Make sure you discover what they are and how to bring them into effect if and when a noisy neighbor surfaces.

PAINT

Have you ever needed to touch up a wall or door and not known what color to buy? It is rare to buy a building that has records that will lead you directly to the right color chart, but you can at least make sure that anytime a building you own gets painted the location of the painted surface is identified in your records along with the type, brand, and color name of the paint used. It is also a good idea to keep the color chart or at least cut the color sample out of one. When selling a property, records like this demonstrate that you are over the top in maintaining your property. The efficiency of this kind of record could also extend to tiles and other types of flooring.

PERSONAL PROPERTY THAT REMAINS

If you are a landlord, there will be times when a tenant moves out but leaves behind a ton of personal property. Worse is a fully stocked refrigerator (that belongs to you), and worse still is the fact that he or she moved out two weeks ago because the electric company shut off the power due to nonpayment of the electric bill. You may never get the smell out of that apartment, just as you will never find out how all those cockroaches were able to get inside the refrigerator. You can have all the provisions in your lease that you want, and none of them will ensure you that this will not happen. When the decision to leave comes, tenants will leave in the middle of the night, sometimes taking the refrigerator, stove, AC units, and more with them. The junk they leave behind is yours to deal with. So, what can you do? First of all, make sure you have a sufficient security deposit to cover part of your cost to return the unit to full rental capacity. Second, be on the lookout the moment a tenant is late in the rent. Tenants sometimes take the position that the security deposit can be used as the last month's rent. Even though the lease says this is not the case, they will take that position. Either you or your property management team should pay a visit to the property, make an inspection of the property, and continue vigilance. This may stop the theft, but likely not the junk left behind.

PEST CONTROL

The most prudent pest control is to keep trash from building up in or around a building. Periodic spraying for insects can be effective, but it is rarely fool-proof. In residential buildings, a combination of yard and interior control is the best when tied to tenant observance of certain rules. One good rule is to make sure that garbage inside the apartment is in a container that has a top to keep the insects from having access to their food source. Another way to cut down on cockroaches is to purchase a box of roach tablets and put one in the drip pan under the refrigerator to remove their source of drinkable water. Prior to buying a property, you should question the current tenants to ascertain if there any problems—one of the problems might turn out to be a pest infestation. Call this to the seller's attention and seek remedy prior to closing.

PLUMBING

Plumbing, like electrical service, is often out of sight. Original drain lines might be made of inferior products that might not even be allowed in your area today. It might be necessary to find a set of the original building plans to ascertain how the building was constructed, what path the drain line takes, what material was used, and whether a building permit was issued and later inspection made for all the plumbing work.

POOL SERVICE

A commercial pool must have the right kind of filtration and sanitation equipment to meet most local codes. Have a professional pool contractor check it out, and seek remedy prior to closing if it does not. Other pool problems can be costly to repair even for smaller single-family pools. Pools in small multifamily properties should have strict rules as to use to ensure that 3 A.M. skinny-dip parties do not occur (at least you should be invited).

POSTDATED CHECKS

See *Banks*.

QUESTIONS

This is the single item in this list that can save you from making a tragic mistake. Simply asking questions, and of course listening to the answers. Most answers will prompt another question until you finally have exhausted the knowledge of the person or persons you are asking. Basically there are no wrong questions, and never too many questions. To educate yourself to be able to make a judgment about the property and the area, continue to ask questions. You must be careful of asking too few questions because you believe you have all the information available or all that you need. If the element is a critical one, be sure to verify the answers you get by asking another source, and if there is conflict then seek a third or even fourth source. Most people who go to a government department tend to be intimidated to a certain degree. It might not be the fault of the individual who works there; it is just natural to assume that because a person stands behind the counter he or she is an expert in the subject at hand. I always prompt my question sessions like this: "I am looking at certain properties in this county and need to make sure I do not make any mistakes. I have been directed to this emergency response department (or whatever) to find out what natural forces may affect this county over a reasonable period of years, such as fires, floods, storms, and the like. Can you direct me to someone who has been in this department for a number of years who would be able to talk to me about this?" What you never want do is to embarrass people by directly asking them your main question without finding out if they have any knowledge on the subject. Give them a reasonable out by simply asking for them to refer you to the more experienced person without saying that they may not be experienced.

RECREATION LEASES

Some properties, such as residential subdivisions, condominium complexes, trailers, mobile homes, manufactured home subdivisions, and rental projects, may have a separate recreation area for which there is a use fee or lease for users. For ownership properties, there may be a provision in the lease that will allow the owners of the properties given access to the area to purchase the property, thereby ending the lease. This sounds good, but what are the mechanics of this purchase, and who will look after the maintenance, repair, and management of the recreation area? These are all potential problems. Ask questions until you are satisfied with the answers.

RESIDENCY

Every state wants to claim you as a resident. Where this becomes a problem is the fact that as a resident of one state you cannot legally be a resident of another. You can be a resident of New York and spend much of your time, even most of your time, away from New York. But as a resident of New York you cannot, for example, claim homestead exemption in the state of Florida. You should learn the rules of your state, and if you own or rent a residence in more than one state you should ask your lawyer what options you have to change your residency from one state to another. You could possibly save a lot of money that way. By the way, if you are unsure about your actual residency, it will be the state where you vote in local and other elections.

RESTRICTIONS

We live in a world of restrictions, and they can control use, occupancy, pets, common areas, rental potential, workers, movers, parking, security force, utilities, and more. Prior to purchase or rental of any property you should ascertain what restrictions are imposed. They will be imposed by local codes, subdivision deed restrictions or rules, homeowner rules, condo documents, rental agreements, and rules and restrictions of the building or complex.

ROOF

The roof of any building is generally one of the more expensive items to replace. Because of this, good maintenance of the roof is essential and should be done on a regular basis. If there are pending problems with the roof's surface, they should be treated or repaired before the problem escalates into a major disaster. The minimum effort would be an annual inspection, or even more often a simple walk around to see if anything looks different than it should. Do this once with a roofer and make sure it is a learning session so you or your management team will know what to look for. With simple repairs the integrity of a roof can be made to last much longer than its guarantee.

ROTTED DOCK OR DECK TIMBERS

Rotted wood may be hiding below a coat of paint. However, if rotted wood is tapped with a small hammer, it will sound hollow or at least not return a sharp sound of solid wood. Periodically check all such wood, and at the first hollow sound, replace the rotting wood right away. A dock or deck that collapses due to rotted timbers can result in personal injury as well as damage other parts of the structure.

SEAWALLS

These are structures that protect a waterfront property from being washed away. Heavy flooding may overwhelm these structures, which are different from dikes that may parallel a river or surround a lake. Seawalls are widely used in Florida and California as well as other states that have residential developments that have dockage in their backyards. If you are purchasing waterfront property and it has seawalls, make sure they are properly inspected. They can be very expensive to repair, and if one is greatly damaged, new regulations may prohibit it being replaced at all. Some oceanfront communities have had to bite that bullet, and once a seawall is breached and there is nothing structural or solid between the house and Lisbon, Mother Nature is going to eventually take its course. Don't purchase a property that can be in this predicament unless you can stand (economically and emotionally) to watch it slip into the waves.

SOIL TEST

There are several reasons why you should, as a buyer, condition your purchase agreement on your approval of a subsoil test. Many parts of the world have nasty subsoil conditions. They may consist of layers of muck, or quicksand-like soil, or substantial other unstable conditions that can make the property you are about to purchase worthless, or at least less valuable than the seller is trying to make it appear to be. If there is any local history of such conditions or even neighboring property tests that you can get your hands on would suggest a subsoil problem, then insist on your contract having a subsoil test to your satisfaction.

STAFF

Whenever you are purchasing a property (condominium, residential, office, or other commercial structure) that comes with a staff about which you only have a very minor vote to approve, take a careful look at the nature of that staff and the management that hired it. I have seen many buildings that were so overstaffed that the cost to the owners was a good 30 percent higher than it should be. My approach in looking at any residential building is to consider it as a hotel. Why? Because the hotel industry is one of the oldest and most documented (accounting-wise) of all businesses. If the expenses shown for this complex exceed hotel standards, then something is wrong, or at least needs to be reviewed and questioned further.

TAX PAYMENTS

A multitude of taxes come with real estate and any income that is produced on the property. Not all states share the same laws in this respect, so you have to examine what is going on in your community. Even within a state there may be extra taxes that are tied to very local expenses or needs. The largest of the taxes is likely to be the property tax, which is usually levied by the county tax assessor and collected by the county revenue department (note, these names may vary). The county assessor pegs all the property with as close to market value as possible (by legislative order or custom) and collects for all the municipalities within the country. Added to the bill is virtually every department that is financed by property taxes within the county. Usually there is a discount if the bill is paid early, and the payment may not be due until March (this also varies from location to location). In states with homestead exemption rules, a senior, blind or handicapped person, or widow or widower may receive varying levels of discounts in the form of an exemption of part of the value of the property from being taxed. Some states also have a state law that prohibits the state from increasing tax more than a certain amount per year (this also varies from state to state). Usually the set amount is around 3.5 percent. Some states, of which Florida is one, allow a transfer of the value of a property that has been owned and benefited from not having the assessment value increased more than that set percent to be transferred to a newly purchased property. The result can save many thousands of dollars in future tax on the price of the new home.

One of the best and often least known aspects about property tax is that the property owner can appeal the assessment. There are companies, often law firms, that will take the appeal to the proper authorities and charge you a percentage (often 30 percent) of what they save you. All of this is subject to negotiation of course, and it is worth the effort to appeal the assessment because you can't lose.

TIMESHARES

You may own a timeshare, or even wish you didn't. This is a big industry with potentially big problems to owners of this product. First, though, look at some of the different types of timeshare properties. There are those where you can buy as little as one week every two years (perhaps even every three years), or several weeks back-to-back or spread out around the year. There is what is called fractional ownership, which is a block of time that generally consists of a total of 12 weeks or more. Then there is leasehold ownership, where you don't get a deed but a "paid-up leasehold." Then there is the point system, where you buy a given number of points, which gives you access to the system based on so many points per location per day (or week). Some of the networks allow you to convert your week (or some other amount of time) into points. The one thing all these forms of timeshares have in common is that you pay an annual fee for the time you have control over. This fee can be expensive, and may or may not include your share of real estate tax assessed to the property. Problems to look for are these: How well is the property being maintained? Brand-new properties may not stay that way, so you might rather buy into a well-maintained older property. What exchange networks are available to you? There are several, but the two biggest that maintain exchange banks are RCI (RCI.com) and Interval International (Intervalworld.com). Others will be within the developer's own system, such as Fairfield Properties (which also owns RCI).

   If you want to sell your unit, you might have some difficulty getting back what you paid. Generally the best way though is to place an advertisement in the newsletter that your resort may have. You will find brokerage firms that deal in timeshares by searching the Internet for "sell my timeshare."

   The best way to get value from your timeshare is to use it, or barter the use for something (like dental work, or credit at a local restaurant in exchange for a holiday week at Vail). Learn how to make the most of the exchange systems and enjoy your vacation time. It is also a good idea to look into the conversion to points, as this may give you a great deal more flexibility.

TITLE INSURANCE

See *Insurance*

TRASH

When you purchase a property that the seller is occupying (home or office) you can be sure there will be a trash problem that needs to be attended to. Take this into consideration when you make the offer, as it is easier to simply anticipate an expense and not include it in the transaction. By this I mean that if you anticipate three days' work for your trash company to pack up and haul out trash, then set aside that money. The alternative is to simply put into the contract a provision that the property will be delivered to you with floors taken down to the base flooring (wood, concrete, terrazzo, or other), walls stripped of wallpaper, and all trash, furniture, and fixtures (except those listed in the contract) removed.

VACANCY FACTOR

Even the best occupancy history will not be 100 percent all the time. Working up a pro forma balance sheet of income and expenses for any multiple tenant property should include a vacancy factor, which is a reduction of potential income. Many local tax assessors' offices have some local history of occupancy and the corresponding vacancy factor for properties in your area. Check them out, and increase them by a margin of 2 percent to be conservative. If they are using 6 percent vacancy, for example, increase yours to 8 percent.

VEGETATION REMOVAL

That beautiful lot you purchased on which you plan to build a small medical building has a dozen live oak trees and several other exotic hardwood trees. You check with the local authorities, and they say you need a tree removal permit. You didn't check that out and have already closed on the lot. Now you discover you will have a battle with the city just to remove enough trees to provide room for the building and parking. Before purchasing any property with trees, check to see what the rules are that govern this process. Keep in mind that there may be subdivision rules that exceed those of the community. Some communities have strict rules that if you remove a tree you must replant it or a replacement elsewhere on the property. This can be very expensive, but even when that rule is in place look for an exception.

In one situation I had a 60-acre tract of land that was zoned for commercial use; however, the previous owner had applied for agricultural use, which while it did not change the zoning greatly reduced the real estate tax for 10 years as the owner kept cattle on the former bell pepper farm. I had an offer to purchase the property at a very attractive profit, but I had to remove the trees that had been planted some 20 years earlier as windbreaks for the pepper plants. These trees were now 30 to 40 feet high, and we counted over 4,000 of them planted in rows around 100 feet from each other that ran nearly half a mile in length. Word from the city was that we had to replant similar trees in the same exact number as were removed. I knew there had to be a way around that, and I discovered that on agricultural land farmers were allowed to clear the land of all trees. I leased the property to a You-Pick-It farmer I knew for one dollar for the year it would take for the developer to get the approvals he needed to build a private hospital and a shopping center next to it. Two days later, every tree was part of a dozen piles of trees, limbs, and stumps that were, one at a time, set ablaze. The resulting strawberries plus a crop of bell peppers were the finest that had ever come from South Florida. Between the years of cattle on the site, plus the highly nutritious ash from the burned trees, not an ounce of fertilizer needed to be used. As it turned out, it was nearly three years before the developer was ready to start construction, so everyone benefited. The project was completed some years ago and is a fine example of a well-landscaped hospital campus with a matching shopping center alongside.

VERIFYING TITLE

Title will be verified by a qualified closing agent (who can also be your lawyer), and basically there are several critical elements. Has the chain of title been properly handled from day one until the present seller is going to pass it on to you? Are there any outstanding debts, liens, or clouds of title that must be cleared before you can get good title? If there is any doubt about that, insist that it must be done prior to your paying for the property.

WALLPAPER

Wallpaper looks nice, but it is expensive, and to replace it first requires the removal of the old wallpaper. Don't be led to believe you can paint over old wallpaper. While this might be the case with some types of wallpaper, you may discover that the wallpaper you are dealing with is the wrong kind. There are many unique looks that can be applied using paint that will save you money in the long run. My advice is to avoid the use of wallpaper.

YARD MAINTENANCE

Landscaping and yard maintenance is important to demonstrate pride of ownership. This ensures you attract the right tenants for your rental properties, and a good landscaping plan is one that allows the vegetation to mature and increase in value. If you are purchasing an income property with extensive landscaping, pay close attention to the cost shown by the seller of the present maintenance. If it seems low, you may discover the owner is (or says he or she is) doing the work. In any event, get a price from a local lawn maintenance company or two. Be sure you explain the extent of work they are to do.

ZONING

For the many reasons mentioned in this book, you should be fully aware of the zoning of a property you anticipate purchasing. To do this, go to the community zoning office and first verify that the property is within that city's boundaries. Then check the zoning map and check the classification of the zoning. Review the zoning code book and read the use allowed and all restrictions pertaining to that zoning. If that seems reasonable and you understood everything that you read, ask if there are any other codes that also govern, modify, or restrict what can be built on this property. There will be some such as parking, setbacks, deed restrictions, height and density rules, and distance from a school or church (which may prohibit an allowed use). Read those rules and restrictions. If you plan to move forward, purchase the zoning book, or at least pay to have the pertinent pages copied for your files.

THE REAL ESTATE INVESTOR'S VIP LIST

I recommend that readers fill this list out as they go along in the book. Naturally if you have a laptop or desk top computer, be sure to transfer the information to a folder entitled VIP LIST. Once inside that folder you can form individual folders by each category, which are shown at the beginning of each section that follows. Remember that people will change more often than the phone numbers, so you will need to update your information from time to time. The more of these VIPs that you get to know, the quicker you will become a true real estate insider.

GOVERNMENT

City

1. City Hall

   Phone number: _____

   Address: _____

   Business hours: _____

2. City manager

   Name: _____

   Secretary's name: _____

   Phone number: _____

3. Mayor

   Name: _____

   Secretary's name: _____

   Phone number: _____

4. City council member

   Name: _____

   Secretary's name: _____

   Phone number: _____

5. City council member

   Name: _____

   Secretary's name: _____

   Phone number: _____

6. City council member

   Name: _____

   Phone number: _____

7. City council member

    Name: _____

    Phone number: _____

8. City council member

    Name: _____

    Phone number: _____

9. City council member

    Name: _____

    Phone number: _____

10. Head of the city building department

    Name: _____

    Secretary's name: _____

    Phone number: _____

    Address: _____

11. Head of city zoning department

    Name: _____

    Secretary's name: _____

    Phone number: _____

    Address: _____

12. Head of city planning department

   Name: _____

   Secretary's name: _____

   Phone number: _____

   Address: _____

13. City clerk

   Name: _____

   Secretary's name: _____

   Phone number: _____

   Address: _____

14. Head of the city department of transportation

   Name: _____

   Secretary's name: _____

   Phone number: _____

   Address: _____

15. City fire chief

   Name: _____

   Secretary's name: _____

   Phone number: _____

   Address: _____

16. City police chief

    Name: _____

    Secretary's name: _____

    Phone number: _____

    Address: _____

17. Head of the city water department

    Name: _____

    Secretary's name: _____

    Phone number: _____

    Address: _____

18. Head of the city sewage department

    Name: _____

    Secretary's name: _____

    Phone number: _____

    Address: _____

19. City council meetings

    Usual day of the month held: _____

    Where held: _____

    Address for agenda: _____

    Phone number of contact: _____

Name of contact: _____

Notes: _____

20. Planning and zoning meetings

Usual day of the month held: _____

Where held: _____

Address for agenda: _____

Phone number of contact: _____

Name of contact: _____

Notes: _____

21. Other meetings

Type of meetings: _____

Usual day of the month held: _____

Where held: _____

Address for agenda: _____

Phone number of contact: _____

Name of contact: _____

Notes: _____

County

22. Courthouse

   Phone number: _____

   Address: _____

23. County commissioner

   Name: _____

   Phone number: _____

24. County commissioner

   Name: _____

   Phone number: _____

25. County commissioner

   Name: _____

   Phone number: _____

26. County commissioner

   Name: _____

   Phone number: _____

27. County commissioner

   Name: _____

   Phone number: _____

28. Director of the county building department

    Name: _____

    Phone number: _____

    Address: _____

29. Head of the county health department

    Name: _____

    Phone number: _____

    Address: _____

30. Head of the county zoning department

    Name: _____

    Phone number: _____

    Address: _____

31. Head of the county planning department

    Name: _____

    Phone number: _____

    Address: _____

32. Head of the county department of transportation

    Name: _____

    Phone number: _____

    Address: _____

33. Fire marshal

   Name: _____

   Phone number: _____

   Address: _____

34. Sheriff/Police chief

   Name: _____

   Phone number: _____

   Address: _____

35. Head of the county water department

   Name: _____

   Phone number: _____

   Address: _____

36. Head of the county sewage department

   Name: _____

   Phone number: _____

   Address: _____

37. County tax assessor

   Name: _____

   Phone number: _____

   Address: _____

38. Head property appraiser

    Name: _____

    Phone number: _____

    Address: _____

39. County commission meetings

    Usual day of the month held: _____

    Where held: _____

    Address for agenda: _____

    Phone number of contact: _____

    Name of contact: _____

    Notes: _____

40. County planning and zoning meetings

    Usual day of the month held: _____

    Where held: _____

    Address for agenda: _____

    Phone number of contact: _____

    Name of contact: _____

    Notes: _____

41. Other county meetings

   Type of meetings: _____

   Usual day of the month held: _____

   Where held: _____

   Address for agenda: _____

   Phone number of contact: _____

   Name of contact: _____

   Notes: _____

State

42. State legislature member from your area

   Name: _____

   Phone number: _____

   Address: _____

43. State legislature member from your area

   Name: _____

   Phone number: _____

   Address: _____

44. State legislature member from your area

   Name: _____

   Phone number: _____

   Address: _____

45. State legislature member from your area

   Name: _____

   Phone number: _____

   Address: _____

46. State legislature member from your area

   Name: _____

   Phone number: _____

   Address: _____

47. State legislature member from your area

   Name: _____

   Phone number: _____

   Address: _____

48. State sales tax collections

   Name: _____

   Phone number: _____

   Address: _____

49. State department of transportation

    Name: _____

    Phone number: _____

    Address: _____

50. Head of the state health department

    Name: _____

    Phone number: _____

    Address: _____

Federal

51. Congress member from your area

    Name: _____

    Phone number: _____

    Address: _____

52. Congress member from your area

    Name: _____

    Phone number: _____

    Address: _____

53. Congress member from your area

   Name: _____

   Phone number: _____

   Address: _____

54. Congress member from your area

   Name: _____

   Phone number: _____

   Address: _____

55. Congress member from your area

   Name: _____

   Phone number: _____

   Address: _____

MONEY SOURCES

56. Commercial bank

   Name of president: _____

   Phone number: _____

   Address: _____

   Head loan officer's name: _____

57. Commercial bank

     Name of president: _____

     Phone number: _____

     Address: _____

     Head loan officer's name: _____

58. Commercial bank

     Name of president: _____

     Phone number: _____

     Address: _____

     Head loan officer's name: _____

59. Savings and loan institution

     Name of president: _____

     Phone number: _____

     Address: _____

     Head loan officer's name: _____

60. Mortgage banker and broker

     Name of company: _____

     Name of president: _____

     Phone number: _____

Address: _____

Head loan officer's name: _____

CONSTRUCTION

61. Appliance repairs

    Name of company: _____

    Name of owner: _____

    Phone number: _____

    Address: _____

    Notes: _____

62. Appliance repairs

    Name of company: _____

    Name of owner: _____

    Phone number: _____

    Address: _____

    Notes: _____

63. Carpets

    Name of company: _____

    Name of owner: _____

    Phone number: _____

Address: _____

Notes: _____

64. Carpets

   Name of company: _____

   Name of owner: _____

   Phone number: _____

   Address: _____

   Notes: _____

65. Surveyor

   Name of company: _____

   Name of owner: _____

   Phone number: _____

   Address: _____

   Notes: _____

66. General contractor

   Name of company: _____

   Name of president: _____

   Phone number: _____

   Address: _____

   Notes: _____

67. General contractor

   Name of company: _____

   Name of president: _____

   Phone number: _____

   Address: _____

   Notes: _____

68. Hardware store

   Name of company: _____

   Name of president: _____

   Phone number: _____

   Address: _____

   Notes: _____

69. Large hardware and housewares store

   Name of company: _____

   Phone number: _____

   Address: _____

   Notes: _____

70. Lumberyard

    Name of company: _____

    Name of manager: _____

    Phone number: _____

    Address: _____

    Notes: _____

71. Painter

    Name of company: _____

    Name of owner: _____

    Phone number: _____

    Address: _____

    Notes: _____

72. Painter

    Name of company: _____

    Name of owner: _____

    Phone number: _____

    Address: _____

    Notes: _____

73. Plumber

   Name of company: _____

   Name of manager: _____

   Phone number: _____

   Address: _____

   Notes: _____

74. Plumber

   Name of company: _____

   Name of manager: _____

   Phone number: _____

   Address: _____

   Notes: _____

75. Roofer

   Name of company: _____

   Name of owner: _____

   Phone number: _____

   Address: _____

   Notes: _____

76. Roofer

   Name of company: _____

   Name of owner: _____

   Phone number: _____

   Address: _____

   Notes: _____

77. Other

   Name of company: _____

   Name of owner: _____

   Secretary's name: _____

   Phone number: _____

78. Plans, renderings, architects

   Name of company: _____

   Name of contact: _____

   Phone number: _____

   Address: _____

   Notes: _____

79. Plans, renderings, architects

   Name of company: _____

   Name of contact: _____

   Phone number: _____

   Address: _____

   Notes: _____

ADVERTISING

80. Local newspaper

   Name of paper: _____

   Phone for classified advertising: _____

   Phone for display advertising: _____

   Address for billing: _____

   Notes: _____

81. Local newspaper

   Name of paper: _____

   Phone for classified advertising: _____

   Phone for display advertising: _____

   Address for billing: _____

   Notes: _____

82. Legal newspaper or local legal review

    Name of paper: _____

    Phone for classified advertising: _____

    Phone for display advertising: _____

    Address for billing: _____

    Notes: _____

83. Printing service

    Name of company: _____

    Name of contact: _____

    Phone number: _____

    Address: _____

    Notes: _____

84. Express shipping service

    Name of company: _____

    Secretary's name: _____

    Phone number: _____

    Address: _____

    Notes: _____

ADVISERS

85. Accountant and CPA

   Name of company: _____

   Secretary's name: _____

   Phone number: _____

   Address: _____

   Notes: _____

86. Accountant and CPA

   Name of company: _____

   Secretary's name: _____

   Phone number: _____

   Address: _____

   Notes: _____

87. Interior decorator

   Name of company: _____

   Name of contact: _____

   Phone number: _____

   Address: _____

   Notes: _____

88. Landscaper

Name of company: _____

Name of contact: _____

Phone number: _____

Address: _____

Notes: _____

89. Lawyer

Name of company: _____

Name of contact: _____

Phone number: _____

Address: _____

Notes: _____

90. Lawyer

Name of company: _____

Name of contact: _____

Phone number: _____

Address: _____

Notes: _____

91. Realtor

   Name of company: _____

   Name of contact: _____

   Phone number: _____

   Address: _____

   Notes: _____

92. Realtor

   Name of company: _____

   Name of contact: _____

   Phone number: _____

   Address: _____

   Notes: _____

INVESTMENT SERVICES

93. Property insurance company

   Name of company: _____

   Name of contact: _____

   Phone number: _____

   Address: _____

   Notes: _____

94. Property insurance company

    Name of company: _____

    Name of contact: _____

    Phone number: _____

    Address: _____

    Notes: _____

95. Title insurance company

    Name of contact: _____

    Phone number: _____

    Address: _____

    Notes: _____

96. Barter company

    Phone number: _____

    Address: _____

    Business hours: _____

97. Real estate exchange clubs

    Phone number: _____

    Address: _____

    Business hours: _____

UTILITIES

98. Local power and light company

    Phone number: _____

    Address: _____

    Business hours: _____

99. Local water and sewer

    Phone number: _____

    Address: _____

    Business hours: _____

100. City garbage pickup

    Phone number: _____

    Address: _____

    Business hours: _____

    Day of normal pickup: _____

    Day of bulk pickup: _____

101. Local telephone company

   Phone number: _____

   Address: _____

   Business hours: _____

   Notes: _____

INDEX

ABOUT THE AUTHOR

Jack Cummings is the author of numerous fiction and non-fiction books and is considered the most published contemporary author in the subject of Real Estate Investing. His works on this subject include: *The Complete Guide to Real Estate Financing, The Complete Handbook of How to Farm Real Estate Listings and Sales, Building Your Wealth Through Creative Real Estate Investing, Cashless Investing in Real Estate, The Business Traveler's Survival Guide, The Real Estate Investor's Answer Book, Investing in Real Estate with Other People's Money, Buying Commercial Real Estate in 12 Easy Steps, Successful Real Estate Investing for the Single Person, The Real Estate Financing Manual, The Guide to Real Estate Exchanges,* and *$1,000 Down Can Make You Rich, The Tax-Free Exchange Loophole, The Real Estate Investor's Guide to Cash Flow and Equity Management, The Real Estate Investment and Finance Handbook, 9th Edition.*

Mr. Cummings is a highly successful real estate investor, broker, and developer with more than forty years of hands-on experience. An international speaker and lecturer, he has conducted programs around the world, has served with the International Executive Service Corp., and has been awarded five honorable commendations for his work in Egypt and Kyrgyzstan. Mr. Cummings has appeared on many television and radio programs nationally. His books are easy to read and filled with money-making tips and checklists that guide the reader around pitfalls that can trap even the most knowledgeable investor. This volume has been completely updated to help the reader to be successful in dealing with the modern problems of the greatest buyers market in the past sixty years.